The Career Manifesto

"Drawing on his experience as a successful business leader and mentor, Mike Steib offers invaluable advice to help find your professional calling. If you dream of a career that is meaningful and rewarding, *The Career Manifesto* is the book that you should read right now."
—David Zaslav, president and CEO, Discovery Communications

"As a participant in and witness to Mike's wonderful evolution, I testify wholeheartedly to both the wisdom and actionability of the lessons in *The Career Manifesto*."
—David Bell, chairman, Gyro, and former CEO, Interpublic Group

"*The Career Manifesto* is an easy to implement, step-by-step guide to help you succeed in business and in life. From handling stress to managing complex projects and potentially confrontational meetings, Mike has practical, simple, revolutionary tips and tricks that work. I've sought advice from him on my own career, so I've seen him action—he's the master!"
—Alina Cho, editor and journalist, and host of
The Atelier with Alina Cho at The Metropolitan Museum of Art

"For years, I have referred friends and colleagues to Mike's Career Manifesto; it's an indispensable road map to identifying your north star, accomplishing more, and finding deep meaning in your career and in life. Mike also offers valuable and practical suggestions for staying productive and focused in an always-on world."
—Chris O'Neill, CEO, Evernote

"As an entrepreneur, time is my most precious resource. *The Career Manifesto*'s recipe for maximizing your energy, productivity, and hours in the day is life changing. Everyone with big goals needs to read this book!"
—Amy Jain, founder and CEO, BaubleBar

"Mike is one of the most effective business leaders I have ever met. He drives phenomenal results because he can attract and inspire teams to do more than they ever thought possible. What makes this book especially brilliant is that he has studied and thought deeply about how to help people realize their full potential and has written not just a theoretical opinion piece but a practical guide to doing this in a way that will enable others to feel what his teams have experienced: a way forward to a more fulfilling life."
—Lexi Reese, COO, Gusto

"Mike never fails to inspire those around him with his passion, humor, and keen insights. This book is a must read for anyone who wants to make an impact on the world." —JOE CARLON, CEO, Pain Doctor, Inc.

"Not only has *The Career Manifesto* helped me dream big about my life and my career, but it also provided a step-by-step guide to help me get there. I find myself turning back to it again and again, and I share it with anyone I know who is working through developing their career and their life." —JOHN SAROFF, CEO, Chartbeat

"How many sleepless nights have you woken up and wished that you had a confidant and friend to help guide you through complex career issues and provide clear step-by-step approaches on your pathway to success? Mike Steib is that guy, and his *Career Manifesto* should be in every executive's briefcase and on his nightstand. *The Career Manifesto*, like common sense, is timeless." —JEFFREY SHARP, CEO, Sharp Independent Pictures, and award-winning producer of *Boys Don't Cry*, *You Can Count on Me*, and *The Yellow Birds*

"Over the years, I've shared Mike's original Career Manifesto with hundreds of employees. The book asks big questions and provides practical examples of how to move forward toward your goals. If you are someone who strives to be at the top of your profession and wish you had a cohesive approach to getting there, this book is written for you." —MATT DERELLA, VP of global revenue and operations, Twitter

"This book is filled with real and useful tools, hacks, and insights to help even the most seasoned executive do more of the things that matter and get more done in less time. Mike's writing is fun and BS-free! His chapters on career and life planning offer simple approaches to making big decisions. And the sections on networking, cooperating in teams, and influencing others are gold. Read this book!" —MICHAEL MASLANSKY, CEO, maslansky + partners, and author of *The Language of Trust*

"Mike has long been a sought after mentor and revered manager, and for obvious reason: his practical, inspirational, no-nonsense advice works. This is the book that I will give to all of the motivated professionals that come through my door with questions about how to achieve their career, *and life*, aspirations." —JESSE HAINES, director of marketing, Google

The
Career Manifesto

Discover Your Calling and
Create an Extraordinary Life

MIKE STEIB

A TarcherPerigee Book

tarcherperigee

An imprint of Penguin Random House LLC
375 Hudson Street
New York, New York 10014

Excerpt from "Photosynthesis" by Frank Turner on p. 41

Tarcher and Perigee are registered trademarks, and the colophon is a trademark of Penguin Random House LLC.

Most TarcherPerigee books are available at special quantity discounts for bulk purchase for sales promotions, premiums, fund-raising, and educational needs. Special books or book excerpts also can be created to fit specific needs. For details, write: SpecialMarkets@penguinrandomhouse.com.

ISBN 9780143129349

Printed in the United States of America
1   3   5   7   9   10   8   6   4   2

The author will donate a portion of the proceeds from *The Career Manifesto* to Literacy Partners, a nonprofit providing family literacy programs to thousands of New Yorkers.

While the author has made every effort to provide accurate telephone numbers, Internet addresses, and other contact information at the time of publication, neither the publisher nor the author assumes any responsibility for errors or for changes that occur after publication. Further, the publisher does not have any control over and does not assume any responsibility for author or third-party Web sites or their content.

This book is dedicated to you.
You are capable of amazing things,
and the world needs you.

CONTENTS

Introduction

Part 1—PURPOSE: What to Do with Your Life

Chapter 1. The Hard Things   3

Chapter 2. Your Purpose   11

Part 2—PLAN: How to Get There

Chapter 3. Decisions   27

Chapter 4. Your Career Roadmap   41

Part 3—PRODUCTIVITY: Get Ten Times as Much Done and Feel Great

Chapter 5. Confessions of a Productivity Psycho   57

Chapter 6. Never Tired Again   71

Chapter 7. Five More Hours to Live   81

Chapter 8. Get Sh*t Done   92

Part 4—PEOPLE: Achieve Impact with Others

Chapter 9. Networking for a Cause   127

Chapter 10. If Someone Asks You If You're a Sales God,
             You Say Yes   148

Chapter 11. Every Meeting = Awesome   176

Chapter 12. Stakeholder Management: Heaven Is Other People   204

Part 5—PRESENCE: Enjoy the Journey

Chapter 13. Don't Worry, Be Happy   229

Notes   249

Acknowledgments   261

Index   263

About the Author   273

INTRODUCTION

Discontent is the first necessity of progress.
—Thomas Edison

I think I know you.

You are talented—and ambitious, willing to work as hard as you need to achieve success. You are in the growth phase of your career, and feel an urgency to continue to advance. You play to win, but don't measure success simply by money or job title; you believe there is something more to life, a calling to become the best you can and have a positive impact on others through your work, family, and community.

You are also frustrated. You are working hard, but your career is not moving as fast as you want. Promotions come a little too slowly, and, when you look around, there is always someone who seems less qualified with more responsibility. Sometimes, reading or hearing about the success of others makes you jealously question your own trajectory. Despite your early career successes, you often question your choice of job, employer, maybe even your profession.

You are sometimes stymied at work by other people who are not working as hard as you or who aren't as invested as you are in creating success. You spend too much of your life in meetings that bore you to death, or trying to clear your email in-box of all the junk that gets in the way of your ability to do your job well. You're stressed. You're tired. You want to exercise and eat well, but you are working so hard that you always seem to run out of time or energy.

I think I know you because, not very long ago, I was you.

Now, though, I am a happy father and husband, CEO of a publicly traded technology and media company, board director at a respected Fortune 500 company, chairman of an important nonprofit, weekend athlete, one-time film actor, patented inventor, occasional motivational speaker, guest on various popular TV shows, quoted expert in leading national publications, and, it would now appear, an author. More importantly, I am actively executing my dream career plan, affecting the lives of others in accordance with my values. I feel connected, invigorated, and purpose driven in every aspect of my life. Most days I wake up energized and I go to sleep fulfilled. And all it took for me to get here was years of soul-searching, constant self-reinvention, hard lessons, ugly mistakes, terrific luck, and a lot of kindness and patience from bosses, mentors, and colleagues who, somewhat inexplicably, gave me chances and second chances.

I wrote this book so that you might struggle less and achieve more in discovering and pursuing your dreams. I have lived a version of your career from where you are now to a decent halfway point, and I have been taking notes along the way. Each time I have hit a wall, I have learned from it, and I have written it down. My own challenges have led me to read nearly one hundred books on leadership, management, productivity, human psychology, sales, marketing, strategy, operations, finance, and human health. As a manager, I have observed, coached, and learned from a wide array of incredible people. I have regularly reflected on what I have learned on the job, summarized my lessons, and shared them with my teams to help others learn from my experiences. One document I sent my team a few years back, a guide to designing a fulfilling professional plan, called "The Career Manifesto," went viral and was eventually downloaded and shared nearly ten thousand times. Years later, I still hear from strangers in places ranging from Silicon Valley to Rio to New Delhi who've read my manifesto and tell me it has changed the way they approach their careers and their lives. It is a multipart series I teach at my own company and have shared with dozens of others.

The Career Manifesto is not about me, it is about the most important and interesting topic in the world: you, what you want to do with your life, and how to achieve it. As we move through each chapter, we are going to lay out a career and life plan for you that will change the way you look at everything—from determining your calling to how you will strategically invest every minute of the day to maximize your impact. The Five Pillars of Your Career—Purpose, Plan, Productivity, People, Presence—articulated here will help you recalibrate your goals, multiply your personal productivity, and remove the external roadblocks to your success. You'll get actionable advice that will help you acquire the skills and experiences you need to achieve your loftiest goals. You will become more effective in working with others. You will no longer be so damn tired. You will wake up excited and go to sleep grateful, knowing that you are on the right path and making the most of every day. And you will know that you're not making a difference just in your own life, you are making a positive impact on the world and lives around you, too.

In picking up this book, you haven't simply opened another superficial career guide. You've accepted a call to action, a manifesto, a field-tested personal roadmap to becoming the person you want to be and living the life you are meant to live. Are you game?

Awesome. Let's get started.

The

Career Manifesto

PART 1

Purpose: What to Do with Your Life

The first step toward attaining an extraordinary life and career is to discover why you want to have them in the first place. A meaningful life requires that you understand what's driving you to commit to your own course. The impact that you can have on the world, the things that bring you true joy, and the way you want to be remembered will shape the path you choose and inform your decisions every day. In this section, we're going to establish your purpose—what gets you out of bed every morning, what motivates you more than anything else—and solidify your commitment to pursue a career and life around that.

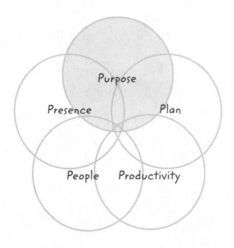

CHAPTER 1

$\longrightarrow$ The Hard Things

*If you do what you've always done, you'll get what
you've always gotten.*

—Tony Robbins

For someone with the advantages you have been given, there is a clearly illuminated "path to success." You work hard in school and get good grades, go to college and graduate, work for a respectable company, complete your assignments on time, and jostle for a promotion every few years. You lust for an important-sounding professional title, seek other people's approval, and never, ever risk failure. Though this track may keep you quite busy, you will rarely struggle. Slowly but surely, you climb to the middle of a ladder specially designed to keep you on it, with small rewards and tokens of prestige adorning each rung. This road is an easy comfort that many people mistake for success.

There is an alternative route, too—one where you make nonconsensus career decisions, eschewing easy jobs for new and harder challenges. On this other path, you choose to do what is important to you rather than what makes you look good. You stretch yourself into areas of personal discomfort, stepping into situations that truly test your abilities. You get to know your own weaknesses the hard way, you fail often, and you grow. For the cost of challenging yourself every day, you get to know a better version of yourself.

Chances are, you are currently on something more closely resembling the first path—almost everyone is. But I think you want something more. You did not buy a book called *Seven Easy Steps for Crawling Your Way to Middle Management and Staying There*; you picked up this book because, deep down, you feel you have the gifts to do something special with your life. You are just not quite sure what or how.

And you are right. You can be truly great.

I know people who have taken the first path and gone on to live perfectly satisfactory, if relatively routine, lives. However, in my career, I have also had the good fortune of knowing people who have had the kind of success that only the second path provides: they are leaders in a wide variety of fields, from business to politics, art to fitness, military leadership to community activism. A few have been the smartest people you'll ever meet, but many were not. Some were privileged Ivy League graduates; others came from nothing. Early in their careers, they were all good, but you could not have pulled them out of the crowd and said, "This one will be one of the most important business leaders in the world," "This one will be a famous filmmaker," or "This one will change outcomes for thousands of underprivileged families." Because what they had was not visible on their faces or on their résumés. They had a vision for their lives and a willingness to push themselves to uncomfortable limits to get there. They chose the second path.

In the next chapter, we will think deeply about what is truly important to you, and throughout this book, we will outline strategies and tactics to obtain it. It is a fundamental principle of this book that you are fully qualified to achieve your most ambitious goals. I have observed enough successful career journeys to tell you: there is no question that you can do it. The only question is whether you will make *the commitment to do the hard things* on that second path.

We are taught early in our lives that the hard things we'll face in our jobs are things like working long hours, paying attention to detail, meeting deadlines, enduring stress. You have probably been doing those things for years, so for you, they may not be hard; they may feel *normal*. And the truth is, none of these are the truly hard things you'll encounter if you commit to the second path.

So what are these hard things that the vast majority of people are too complacent to do? The things that, if you commit to them, will reward you with the best version of your life?

Hard Thing 1: Telling Yourself the Truth

We invest so much energy into trying to get others to be impressed with us that we often start to believe our own marketing. We carefully curate photos of our weekend so that everyone on Facebook, Instagram, and Snapchat believes we live perfect, charmed lives. We find so many ways to describe our current job to make it sound important that we start to forget that, actually, it might not be important. We practice responses to the interview question, "What is your greatest weakness?" and, with a straight face, say things like, "You know, sometimes I just care too much, I'm so passionate about my work."

We lie to ourselves. We reject criticism. We refuse to question our own beliefs. We compartmentalize our goals and dreams that we are not pursuing, convincing ourselves that we will chase them someday, like when we have more money, or when the kids are older.

Change begins with true self-awareness, accepting all the facts, whether or not they are comfortable. Only once you do that can you begin the process of transforming your life. Throughout this book, you are going to be asked to question your values, goals, self-perceptions, and actions. You are going to tear yourself down to the core and rebuild. You will begin by honestly assessing your life and the value of the course you are on, then changing it dramatically to what you want. You will get to know the structural weaknesses of your brain that undermine your self-discipline; then you will adapt to those same structures to unlock massive personal productivity. Later, you will learn to design your interactions with your manager to generate weekly constructive feedback that will open the door to breakthrough personal development in your career. You can be one of the truly successful people in this world who are constantly learning, changing, and reinventing, but only if you are first willing to tell yourself the hard truths about you.

Hard Thing 2: Thinking for Yourself

It sounds easy, and your mother always asked you, rhetorically, "If your friends jumped off a bridge, would you?"* And, yet, our professional paths so quickly fall into the groove of what our peers are doing, and what will appear successful to them. *Everyone is getting an MBA—maybe I should, too . . . My colleague was just promoted to director—how do I get promoted to director? . . . This weekly strategy meeting doesn't seem to accomplish anything, but if I don't go, I am afraid I might miss something . . . Ooh, an industry conference! I guess I should go, too.*

However, when you study people with remarkable careers, you will notice that they rarely mimic the choices their peers are making. This book is going to urge you to make your own life plan and take deliberate steps to execute it. Because you want an extraordinary life, your choices will look strange to your colleagues. For reasons that will become clear in this book, you may sign up for the thankless task, take the job that seems less prestigious, turn down more money, and so on. Everything—from the meetings and events you attend, to the books and articles you read, to the way you use email and run meetings—may seem unusual to others. Good. As the Navy Seals say, "Get comfortable being uncomfortable," because discomfort is the steady state of an exceptional life. Fortunately, it rides along with its close cousins: excitement, success, and fulfillment.

Hard Thing 3: Changing Your Stripes

There are, to oversimplify, two types of personal development: acquiring new skills and changing behaviors. Most people, if they focus

---

* Full disclosure, I did once. Bad idea. More on that later.

on either, focus on the first one, building proficiencies like using Excel, reading a balance sheet, or speaking Mandarin. At the same time, they reject any effort to change behaviors, viewing them as intractable personality traits. They tell themselves stories about the limits of their personality, like, "Well, I'm an introvert, so I can't be expected to have a large personal network" or, "I am a big-picture person, not a details one; you can't blame me for those mistakes" or, "I'm passionate—if that rubs people the wrong way, so be it."

I once worked with a smart, buttoned-up, and diligent manager with a high IQ but a low level of emotional intelligence (EQ): he could not get his team excited or his colleagues to embrace him. He always refused feedback on the topic, saying, "Look, I'm not a rah-rah leader type, I'm an operator," as if he were describing some unchangeable truth, like his height. His core talents had gotten him this far in his career, and he didn't believe it was necessary—or he wasn't willing—to make uncomfortable changes. His career plateaued.

I knew another manager, about the same age, with the same introverted disposition. Unlike our other colleague, this manager was committed to improving the way he engaged with others. He scheduled drinks virtually every week with various teammates or customers, where he forced himself to be vulnerable and engage at a personal level that was unnatural for him. He recorded birthdays in his calendar and would, at first somewhat awkwardly, call and wish you a happy birthday. Even though his natural personality was to expect everyone to be like him and do good work without having to be congratulated for it, he taught himself always to take time to acknowledge the accomplishments of others and thank them for their efforts. Today he is an important C-level executive, well liked, and widely respected.

This book will challenge you to change your mind-set and your behaviors for greater success. It will give you the tools to question your beliefs and values, improve the way you know and connect with other people, and seek out the feedback you need to constantly improve. It will stretch you to change your fundamental behaviors in ways that might scare you. It will provide you with the playbook for being healthier and more energetic, happy, and present. This book is not about acquiring new skills; it is about truly changing your stripes, becoming a better version of yourself.

Hard Thing 4: Forming New Habits

Roughly 40 percent of what we do in life is based on deeply ingrained habits. Changing those habits requires focused and relentless effort. Watching TV too late, snoozing through your alarm in the morning, and not exercising are habits. Spending your whole day toiling around in your email in-box and passively attending whichever meetings you are invited to are habits. So are waking up at five a.m., expressing gratitude, working out, laying out your goals, accomplishing your most important task for the day, eating a healthy breakfast, and arriving at your desk already having done more than your colleagues will do all day.

One goal of this book is to provide you with the techniques to develop successful habits. Acquiring them will take willpower and persistence—but once you have developed them, they will be yours forever. These habits will be the foundation for the achievement of your life's goals.

Hard Thing 5: Doing It

I enjoy seeing friends and colleagues who need advice on work, family, and so on. Last year, two former colleagues, Sam and Joy,* happened to email me the same week, each asking if they could talk to me about their new business ideas. A few days later, I saw Sam, who shared his idea, showed me an analysis of the market, and asked what I thought. I thought it was good, suggested a few next steps, and offered to be his first customer. A few weeks after that, he was still

---

* Unless otherwise noted, colleagues referenced throughout are composites of real-life people and all names have been changed to protect their identities.

thinking about the market size, contemplating different strategies for how to acquire customers, running it by colleagues and his classmates from Harvard Business School. Two more months passed, and he was busy with work, still thinking about the idea, but also questioning whether it was "a big enough market opportunity to pursue aggressively." Sam is still in the same job at the same company; there is no new business, no exciting new life. What happens to a dream deferred? This one died quietly in a PowerPoint deck.

A month or so after I heard from Sam, I saw Joy. Joy had been an assistant at our former company. She had a business idea, too, and it had to do with raw juice for kids. I encouraged her to try it and offered to introduce her to someone in retail who could help. "Oh," she said, "I already lined up some retailers; I just went store to store and got commitments so we could launch something. That part was pretty easy. But selling juice turns out not to be the real opportunity . . ." She went on to tell me about some process that is required to make raw juice, and how there are few factories that do it and she had a six-month wait to get her juice processed. I braced myself for another conversation with a disappointed aspiring entrepreneur, waiting for her to tell me that with the six-month delay, she was losing focus or may give up on the whole thing. But instead she said, "So I asked the retailers to introduce me to some juice makers, and I learned they all had the same problem with this process, and I asked them if they would be interested in having access to another vendor who could do this. I had a few sign letters of intent to pay to have their juice processed and brought them to the bank, which gave me a loan against the LOIs. I'm close—I just need two more LOIs to buy the machine you need to process the juice." Joy had an idea, went out and asked people to work with her on it, kept pressing, and within the year was well on her way to being the proud owner of a gigantic million-dollar juice pasteurizing machine.

The difference between Sam and Joy is that Sam thought about making a change but never took the actions needed to make it real; Joy just did it, and kept doing it, adapting and pushing forward at every roadblock. Which one do you think is going to find success in life?

We all dream about where we want to be in five or ten years. We all have tucked away a secret fantasy to do something we have never done—play an instrument, start a nonprofit, go back to school, write a book. We make New Year's resolutions. We assume something will happen, that someday some unforeseen event will transpire, we will become less busy, less tired, less worried about money, we will make some change, and that secret goal will somehow materialize.

It doesn't work that way.

People convince themselves that they will someday take on a new challenge, tolerate a new risk, pursue a dream, but somehow, someday never comes. This book is committed to a different outcome for you. For you, *someday is today.* Today we are going to take the difficult steps of setting our goals, identifying the new behaviors and habits needed to achieve them, and then immediately committing to the first actions to get started. We are going to perform the quintessential action: *we are going to do it.*

You deserve an extraordinary career, a meaningful life, fulfillment, and true happiness. You have all of the capabilities to achieve it. You just have to be willing to make the commitment to do the Hard Things. Before you turn the page, I want you to say to yourself, "I want an extraordinary life."

Now repeat after me: "So I will do the Hard Things."

Say it again.

All right, let's get started.

CHAPTER 2

→ Your Purpose

The two most important days in your life are the day you're born and the day you find out why.

—Anonymous

When you and I were born, we won the lottery. Not only did we win the one-in-trillions-chance-to-even-exist sweepstakes, we were born into the most technologically advanced society our species has ever known, with life expectancies twice what they were 150 years ago. We are among the most educated people in human history. Being who you are, right now, is the single greatest gift anyone could ever be given. You know it in your bones. Everyone feels it, and the need to make something of these gifts burns inside each of us. *We want our lives to really matter.*

That is why marketers spend hundreds of billions of dollars each year trying to convince us that the meaning we are looking for can be bought: we can be like pro athletes by buying the brand of sneakers they've been paid to endorse; we can become part of the world's "responsible" elite by buying a hybrid car; we can prove how much we care about our family by using certain cleaning products, toilet paper, tissues, or medicines.

The problem is, purpose can't be bought, and it doesn't come easily. The lack of real meaning in our lives leaves a dull ache inside of us that we try, without success, to ignore. It is why we escape quiet moments with our thoughts by checking our social networks, filling our weekends with Netflix binges, and reacting to every push notification—in the absence of true purpose, we can at least score some quick dopamine. Psychologists call this "operant conditioning," a process made famous in the 1930s by B. F. Skinner, who taught a pigeon to push a button every time a light turned on by giving the pigeon small food rewards. Stimulus, response.

Then there are moments of clarity, when we see through the mirage and know we can do more with our lives. We note our admiration for those whose work has affected us or others in some meaningful way: the high school teacher who went well out of his way to point us in the right direction; the boss who took us under her wing when we needed it; the civic leader who would not relent until our laws reflected our values; the entrepreneur who made our jobs possible; the artist who made us feel something special; the physicist who helped us understand our universe. We see people who have given their lives to the pursuit of teaching, building, creating, and inspiring others, and are reminded that someone can really matter to the world.

We burn to do the same. Philosopher John Dewey said it right: "The deepest urge in human nature is the desire to be important." We want a grand purpose, with challenging goals and an ambitious plan to achieve them: a life measured not in the number of likes or retweets we get, but in the things that we have built, the people we have helped or inspired with what we've done.

This chapter is about getting that life for yourself.

In this chapter and the next, we will perform three exercises that will help you establish the values and purpose that can guide your life, a purpose that only you can determine and only you can achieve. Your purpose is what you alone determine to be a meaningful and joyful expenditure of your life's energies—there is no life coach or oracle who can reveal it.

There will be no grade, no trophy, and no one to tell you that you are on the right track. No stimulus, no response. There will be only the personal feeling of fulfillment and the exhilaration of striving for the things that matter to you.

You won't miss the pigeon treats one bit.

Exercise 1: Your Impact

You and I want a life of purpose, and together through this book, we are going to unlock the *why*. Our first step is our first Hard Thing together: we are going to assess, with brutal honesty, how much impact your life actually has today, by drawing your Impact Map.

IMPACT MAP 1: TODAY

Take a blank sheet of paper and write your name in the middle. Draw an arrow from your name to something important in your life—say, for instance, your family. Draw a box around your family. Then draw another arrow from your name to something else in your life, like your job. Put a box around your job. Keep going, creating a sort of hub-and-spoke representation of your life until you have captured all the things that matter to you. Now, under each arrow, jot down a few words about the impact you have on that aspect of your life. Under the arrow to "Family" you might write, "I love and support my family." There may be an arrow to "Church," under which you have written, "I attend and donate a few hours of time each year."

Now, from each of those boxes, draw another arrow and indicate the next-level impact on the world that thing in the box could have because of your contributions. For instance, one of your boxes may have included your job, something like "Sales Analyst," and you may have written under the arrow "Provide sales insights to manager." The new arrow from "Sales Analyst" may connect to a box saying "Customers," and you might annotate the arrow with "My analyses improve sales and help customers."

Now do one more thing: tell yourself the truth. Go back to the chart and draw an X through anything that you don't sincerely believe to be accurate. If the sales insights you provide your manager do not really have a big impact on customers, cross it out. If the annual contribution you make to Unicef is not enough to make an important impact, cross it out.

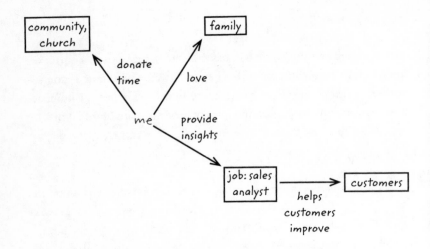

There, in one chart, is your life. What do you notice? When I did mine earlier in my career, I immediately noticed, with great disappointment, how little impact I was having. At roughly the same age, Mark Zuckerberg's chart would have said, "Invented the Facebook; connected hundreds of millions of humans on the internet" and mine basically said, "I draw two-by-two bubble charts for my manager and give a little money to charity." You may have had a similar observation about your own. We have some work to do—but that is okay. At the same age, Henry Ford was working in a lighting factory—he wouldn't invent the Model T for another twenty years. So you've still got plenty of time to get on the right track. And you just did your first Hard Thing: you told yourself the truth. That's progress!

IMPACT MAP 2: SUCCESS ON YOUR CURRENT PATH

We are going to do the exercise again, this time extrapolating out ten to twenty years to the things you could achieve on your current path. Draw your boxes and the arrows describing your impact. In the box that housed "Sales Analyst," you can now claim "Chief Financial Officer." The arrow connecting you to your church may now read "Ensures every family in our church's community has food and shelter." You might replace "Sexy redheaded boyfriend" with "Loving husband; three wonderful ginger kids."

Again, draw another arrow and indicate the next-level impact on the world that the thing in the box could have because of your contributions. Perhaps as "Chief Financial Officer," your impact is "Help lead the company to growth, honorably serving thousands of employees and millions of customers." And so on. For this exercise, do not hold back—presume your own wildest success.

If you continue on your current path, how much impact will you have?

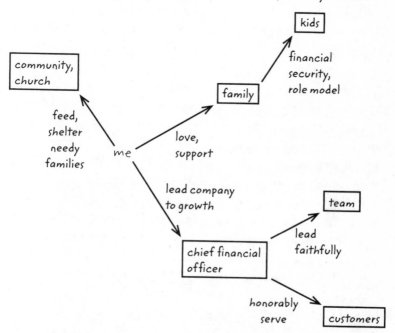

You might now be looking at a personal Impact Map that would make you proud. In which case, as you develop your Career Manifesto, you may already be on the right track, and your focus will shortly turn to how to succeed in your career and life to ensure you achieve this impact.

Or, you might have just looked into the crystal ball and seen yourself as a fifty-five-year-old loser. Don't despair: a lot of people—

in fact, most people—look aghast at this second Impact Map and think, "What am I doing with my life?" Many truly great careers start with this realization. Next, we try a different view.

IMPACT MAP 3: THE ALTERNATIVE

It is now time to liberate yourself from the constraints of your current path. Be as precise or as generic as you like. In this next iteration of the exercise, you can live anywhere, do anything, be anyone you dream. "Sales Analyst" can be "Astronaut" or "Important Political Figure." You can have five kids and ten rescue dogs. You can work for Apple or live in the Amazon. Do it multiple times, taking each possibility that appeals to you for a ride. In each case, again, be sure to capture the impact you have on each.

This will take some time and some iterations. For some people, the answers to this exercise will originate internally—they know in their hearts that they were born to be a scientist, a poet, or a Marine. But many of us will have to look externally, asking, "What does the world need from me?" As I write this book, two billion human beings live in abject poverty; obesity plagues the developed world; the middle class is losing wages and hope; divorce tears apart nearly one in two families; and millions of people die needlessly every year, whether it is from violence, disease, or accident. At the same time, there have never been more opportunities to help. Technology is reshaping the world, scientists are encroaching on a cure for cancer, robots will soon drive our cars, and educators are discovering how to better teach our children for a dramatically different future. There is a need out there in the world to which you can contribute in a big way. Seize this moment. Choose one.

This exercise is not a fantasy—there is virtually nothing you cannot do. With a well-executed plan, English majors have become business leaders, bankers have become community activists, salespeople have become artists, and firefighters have become TV news anchors. Don't hold back in this exercise: draw the Impact Map that would make you truly proud of your life.

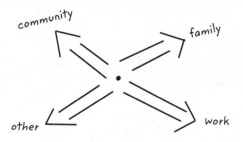

If you did something different, something extraordinary, how much impact could you have?

Now you have a framing for the value your life is creating today, and the value it could be creating in the future. This exercise—while far from a life plan—is a critical first step toward setting your big-picture life goals to have the maximum positive impact on other people. The following exercise will pressure test and hone each of these options to help you narrow in on an enriching career and life path.

(Time out! Did you do the exercise? Your life's goals are not hidden in this book; there is no big reveal in the final chapter that says, "You should get your MBA and pursue a career in biotech." The path to your purposeful career is going to come from your hard thinking and soul-searching. The best way to get your thoughts out of your head and begin to process them is to find a quiet place and write them down or type them out. It helps to organize your thoughts; it forces you to acknowledge and face what you are actually thinking, and it is incredibly cathartic. In a lab experiment, participants who wrote down a commitment were 42 percent more likely to follow through on it. So write it down.)

Once you have your personal Impact Map, you are ready for the next step.

Exercise 2: The Happiness Matrix

In your first Impact Map, you may have found yourself disappointed by the limited scale of your life's work at this moment. In the second, you may have started to see the longer-term possibilities for your current trajectory or realized that the current road is a dead end. The third exercise is the one that many of us find to be the hardest, because without the parameters of our current work and life, the choices are unlimited and overwhelming. It is nice to see that you could do anything and have a broad-ranging impact with your life, but it does not bring much practical clarity. You could be a congressperson or business executive or stay-at-home dad or thought leader or crusader for a good cause—awesome, now what?

Designing a career path has much in common with designing a consumer product—countless possible features could be included in that device. Badly designed products prioritize the wrong functions—like an also-ran smartphone, bloated with software options no one wants, but lacking performance and style. Great devices, on the other hand, focus on just the right features, delivered simply and elegantly.

You may or may not remember the first-generation iPod. Born of the mission to create a fully personal and portable music experience, it had five buttons and a simple interface and was such a joy to use that every other music player was instantly obsolete. The iPod did not launch with the most features—its designers very effectively differentiated between what it *must* have and what it would be *nice* for it to have. They decided that a great music player *must* hold at least a thousand songs, have twelve hours of battery life, be smaller than a deck of cards, be simple to use, and be affordable. It would be *nice* to have more songs, more battery life, less bulk, internet access, and maybe an app that could introduce you to attractive singles nearby. The *must-haves* are a product's "design constraints," which can never be compromised for the *nice-to-haves*.

Within those constraints, and among the list of many nice-to-haves, are thousands of trade-offs. The iPod could have been a little smaller, but that would have required a tinier hard drive, which would deliver fewer songs. It could have had a GPS locator, but the battery life would have suffered unacceptably. A touch screen would have been very cool, but, at the time, that would have made the device unaffordable. Eventually, improving on the ability to deliver the must-haves made it possible to add more features, leading to the indispensable smartphone in your pocket today.

Our lives are similar—we have so many choices, so many life features we could prioritize. We could pursue education, career, wealth, family, hobbies, fitness, popularity, philanthropy, friends, travel, and more. But opening some doors closes others. It would be nice to make millions of dollars. It would also be nice to work with children. It could be hard to do both. Being an excellent parent might be hard to reconcile with an exciting career of global travel. Without clear design constraints, the trade-offs can feel paralyzing.

We are going to design a career path for you, starting with the impact you want to have, then fitting it into the constraints of what you must have versus what would be nice to get out of life. In the previous exercise, you honed your sense of the kind of impact you could achieve. Now you are going to start to see the path more clearly by coming to understand the things that are right for you, with a simple technique: *you are going to maximize the time you spend on the impactful things that you love doing.* Grab your pen again—you are going to create your Happiness Matrix.

Draw three columns. In the left column, write down the kinds of activities you truly enjoy, organized by category (family, community, work, extracurricular, etc.). Set the bar for this column very high: "drinking a pumpkin spice latte" is pleasant, and "watching baseball" is relaxing, but neither is your grand purpose in this life. I want you to write down the kinds of things that make life truly special, from "quality time with my extended family" to "volunteering for Habitat for Humanity" to "helping my customers succeed."

You may find it easier to identify things you enjoy outside of work, but harder to say what you love professionally—if your career were already so obviously joyful, you probably would not be reading a book about how to fix it. Here, focus on the types of activities at work that you find fulfilling or rewarding. For instance, some people's endorphins are really going when they are *being creative*: writing copy for the new ad, brainstorming concepts for the new office space, designing the user experience on the website, or merchandising the in-store display.

Others get deep personal satisfaction from *organizing the world*: implementing customer relationship management tools, designing the system for easily managing and finding creative assets, recommending organizational structures to align sixteen international offices under one regional director, or building the Excel spreadsheet that shows the revenue impact of different product pricing decisions. You might feel most alive when you are *solving problems*: looking at the data to decide which market is right for launching the new product, rationing resources across the department for maximum profit, resolving a dispute between two stakeholders who each have a partially informed view of the right answer, countering a competitor's marketing strategy, and so on. Or you may be at your best when you are successfully *influencing others*: closing a business development partnership, convincing a client to accept a price increase, inspiring a team to do their best work, managing a stakeholder to maintain your project's funding. Pick the kinds of activities you love and put them in the left-hand column, where you are starting to clarify the things you aspire to spend your life doing.

The second column is easy to fill out: here, write down the things you hate doing. Some people are unhappy when they have to travel a lot, work on cross-functional teams, or be on call twenty-four/seven. Others deeply fear public speaking or detest working in spreadsheets. You may have identified fighting malaria in the developing world as a possibility for yourself when you wrote your third Impact Map, but if you really hate hot weather and mosquitoes, this exercise may redirect the way you choose to help the world. Everybody hates something—write yours down in the second column.

In the third column, identify the things it would be hard to live without. Some people cannot be happy without a big family, or a prestigious job title, or a significant amount of time in the outdoors, or frequent travel to Europe, etc. This is the hardest column to populate, because you have to be honest with yourself and acknowledge things that are not popular to admit. For instance, we all know we are not supposed to confuse money and happiness—but if you like big vacations or fancy clothes, you need to acknowledge the cost.

Let's look at an example.

Happiness Matrix (Example)

	Things I Truly Enjoy or Would Truly Enjoy Doing	Things I Hate	Things It Would Be Difficult to Live Without
FAMILY	• Sharing life experiences with my loved ones: travel, city adventuring, culture • Sharing fun quality time with my significant other—dinners, friends, drinking, laughing • Someday: daily, hands-on, teachable-moment-type fun with my kids	N/A	• Great relationship with my spouse, kids, extended family • Good health, fitness • Living by the water • Enough money for comfortable life, travel • Someday: enough money for the best education for my kids
WORK	• Influencing others—meeting partners, learning their business, finding ways to work together • Mentoring—love helping others be their best • Someday: leadership—managing a team, setting goals and strategy • Working on the cutting edge of technology developments and innovation	• Excessive travel • Senseless bureaucracy and hierarchy	• A motivating company mission • Intelligent and committed co-workers

	Things I Truly Enjoy or Would Truly Enjoy Doing	Things I Hate	Things It Would Be Difficult to Live Without
COMMUNITY	• Financial, strategic, and executive-level contributions to non-profit workforce development	• Working with slow, bureaucratic organizations	• Enough income to substantially support causes important to me
EXTRACUR-RICULAR	• I love anything competitive: pickup sports, board games, poker, etc.	• I hate going to parties. I prefer small groups of friends	• Ongoing connection to my good friends through nonwork activities

In this incomplete example, you start to see design constraints coming into focus. This person likes to influence others, to manage or mentor people, and therefore may enjoy something like a sales, marketing, or general management leadership track. She likes technology, which brings some industry focus, and hates bureaucracy, which might direct her to smaller companies and organizations or autonomous divisions within larger companies and organizations. She wants to have a balance in her life—time for family and community (which might rule out some roles that require lots of travel and a high degree of intensity), but enough financial success to contribute meaningfully to the success of her family and community while living a comfortable life (probably guiding her to strive for prominence in a successful for-profit environment). What kind of product or service does she want to help grow, and how senior in her role does she aspire to be? That depends on what she learned constructing her Impact Maps. As the layers of this exercise start to come into view, a more actionable picture of potential career paths takes shape. (Chapter 3, "Decisions," will help you further clarify these choices.)

Now, use the following matrix and do your own. Don't worry if you make a mistake, just buy more copies of my book and try again.*

---

* Just kidding. Use paper. Or go to thecareermanifesto.com.

Your Happiness Matrix

	Things I Truly Enjoy or Would Truly Enjoy Doing	Things I Hate	Things It Would Be Difficult to Live Without
FAMILY			
WORK			
COMMUNITY			
EXTRACUR-RICULAR			

Good! So far, you have compared your current life to what your life could be, thinking broadly and ambitiously about the kind of impact you are capable of having on the world. You clarified the things that you love doing, hate doing, and require to be happy. Establishing the kind of impact that you want to have and the design parameters for what you enjoy doing informs, broadly, what you should do with your life.

The next step is to lay out specific decisions that you need to make on your career path, narrowing down the many options before you to identify the purpose that will bring you the most satisfaction and rewarding experiences. (It doesn't mean you can't also pursue other callings you have, but this will be your primary professional or personal focus.) In the next part of the book, we will make a specific plan to help you have the impact you desire, within your design constraints, for a fulfilling and personally successful career.

PART 2

Plan: How to Get There

The next step to achieving your goals is to chart a course and execute an ambitious plan to reach your intended destination. Here, we hone your career choices and design your Career Roadmap.

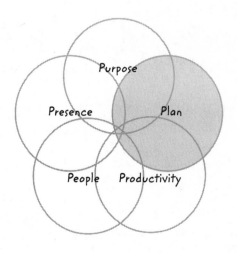

CHAPTER 3

→ Decisions

Your time is limited, so don't waste it living someone else's life.

—STEVE JOBS

Years ago, a rising-star advertising sales rep on my team came to office hours to talk about his career. He seemed generally unhappy in his role, and came to ask for advice: should he switch teams, change functions, maneuver for a certain promotion, etc.? Instead of answering his tactical questions, he and I explored the things that we covered in part 1: How much impact could he have on the world? What made him happy? What did he not like doing? He admitted that he really did not like dealing with advertisers, or sales in general, or working in a big company. It was no wonder he was not enjoying his job in online ad sales at a major corporation. Then I asked if there was anything that he really did like. His face brightened as he said, "Well, I love film; I went to film school, and eventually I am going to produce and direct movies."

I asked why he didn't make movies now, and he rattled off his reasons as if they were rehearsed: "It is a tough industry . . . It just doesn't seem like the right time . . . This is a good job, it would seem irresponsible to leave it now."

All true enough, I acknowledged, but also things that would be true five years in the future, and ten years in the future. "So what you're really saying is you have decided to never make movies?"

"No! I . . . I just need to have success here first, then I can figure out how to get into film . . ." He trailed off.

"Let me ask you, which outcome would you honestly prefer forty years from now: you are a wildly successful executive at this company, wealthy, respected, and important, but you never made a film; or you are a filmmaker who never won an award or topped the box office, but made ten movies that truly touched thousands of people's hearts?"

He was quiet for a minute. "I want to make movies."

One year later, he was making movies.

Many people, early in their careers, land a job for a somewhat arbitrary reason: a personal connection to the company, a LinkedIn advertisement, a call from a recruiter. When I was in college, a number of firms came to campus to recruit undergraduates. I interviewed with anyone who would have me and accepted a position with the company ranked most highly by *Harvard Business Review*, a respectable publication that has no particular insight into my personal goals. A few months later, I was completely absorbed with impressing my new bosses and getting to the next step on the corporate ladder. There was no bigger plan. Some people spend an entire career in this way.

The path to career happiness starts with making choices.

For many people, the dream path may be like our second personal Impact Map exercise, an exciting future not far from the work you are doing today. For instance, you may be a sales rep who would love to run a big sales force, help your clients succeed, and mentor the next generation of sales leaders. You may not (yet) know how to get from here to there, but you have a general sense that you are on the right path. Alternatively, you may be a sad banker who really would rather help run a company, or a depressed lawyer who dreams of opening a yoga studio. Most likely, you don't know: your current job has some pros and cons, the alternatives are interesting but unknown, and the number of choices is overwhelming. You could do the third personal Impact Map exercise for days and still not come to a conclusion.

The following questions can help focus your career path by identifying the characteristics of a career that aligns best with your Impact Map and Happiness Matrix, and eliminating choices that are not right for you.

Which Industry?

An ideal career plan for you starts with an industry that aligns with your Impact Map and your Happiness Matrix.

This is a personal decision and one you should not let others make for you. I live in New York City—if you throw a water balloon here, you will probably hit someone who works in finance or is an aspiring artist. Living here, it would be easy to accept one of those two career paths as your destiny, just as it could be considered the most natural thing for someone from Detroit to work at an automobile company, a Texan to work in the oil industry, or a Silicon Valley resident to apply for a job in software.

But the key to a successful Career Roadmap is to choose the path that fits with your values, not other people's ideas of what you should do. For example, famous industrialist Elon Musk planned his career by asking what problems were most likely to affect the future of humanity, then went on to start successful businesses to address those in fields as varied as digital payments (PayPal), solar energy (SolarCity), electric cars (Tesla), and space travel (SpaceX). Those were not, at the time, obvious career paths for anyone—but because they aligned to one entrepreneur's vision, we now enjoy hundreds of thousands of cars and homes powered by alternative energy.

Start investigating industries and asking yourself: Is the world better for the work these people do? Does the product of this industry make people's lives easier, or more fulfilling? How does it make people feel about themselves? How will I feel for having dedicated tens of thousands of hours to its success? You will spend most of your life contributing to this product or service—make sure it is worthy.

In addition to investing your energies in an industry that has an impact you value, to do your best work, make sure the industry is interesting to you. Here is the Cocktail Party Test: if you can't talk excitedly about a line of work for at least ten minutes over a drink, it's probably the wrong line of work for you.

In addition to importance and interest, you will also want to take into account an industry's growth prospects. The US Bureau of Labor Statistics forecasts economic output by industry, while *Fortune*'s list of the one hundred fastest-growing companies and *Inc.*'s list of the five thousand fastest-growing companies each give you a sense for which segments of the US economy are hot. Your own observations as you read the news and talk to people in your industry are even more valuable—which industries are being disrupted by technology, global competition, or changing consumption patterns? You might conclude, for instance, that brick-and-mortar retail stores will be diminished by online shopping, that traditional health care services will be disrupted by telehealth start-ups, or that traditional media companies will be displaced by social media. As a general rule, you want to be in an industry segment that will be growing for the next couple of decades. The faster an industry is growing, the faster the companies in it are hiring, creating new opportunities, promoting people, and developing new breakthrough ideas and businesses. Conversely, an industry in decline tends to slash investment, halt innovation, and consistently reduce jobs.

Some of the most exciting job tracks were not available just a few years ago. Now is a good moment to push pause and ask whether you are in the right industry, before that premature and uninformed first job choice becomes the determining decision of your entire career.

If you have decided you're in the wrong industry, don't despair; we are going to cover career planning and networking in depth (chapter 4 and chapter 9, respectively). For now, just be clear in your Impact Map and your Happiness Matrix which industry or industries appeal to you. Next, we turn to the job function within the industry that is the best fit for your interests.

What Job Function?

Here is a simple truism that will help you to think through the functional role for you in any organization: ultimately, there are only three jobs—you can make the stuff, sell the stuff, or support the people who make or sell the stuff. This is obviously true in corporations, where one team makes some product, another convinces people to buy it. It is equally true in nonprofits, where one team develops and delivers services, while another works hard to solicit enough donations to pay for the operations. You see the same truism in politics, where one team works on the political platform, another markets the candidate, and others hustle for donations and votes. It applies in art, science, and so on. Here, for example, are those functions in a typical corporation.

People who make the stuff:

- Manufacturing
- Engineering
- Product development
- Design
- Creative direction
- Research and development

People who sell the stuff:

- Direct sales
- Business development
- Inside sales
- Customer service
- Consumer marketing
- Business-to-business marketing
- Channel management (e.g., running the retail outlets)
- Logistics
- Fund-raising
- Lobbying and government relations

People who support the people who make or sell the stuff:

- Finance
- Legal
- Strategy
- Corporate development
- Consultants

Which will you choose? In the Happiness Matrix exercise, you identified things at work that you enjoy, such as "being creative," "organizing the world," "solving problems," or "influencing others." Organizing the world as a logistics supervisor is different from doing it as a financial controller. Influencing others as a high-touch business development executive is distinct from doing it as a paid marketing expert. With your personal preferences in mind, start to explore these roles and get to know people who work in them through reading professional publications (there are trade magazines and blogs for every profession) and meeting people who work in the field.

As you do so, apply the Organizational Chart Test—consider the topmost senior role in any function and ask yourself if you would enjoy it and thrive in the role (assuming, for the moment, that you would want to make the personal trade-offs to achieve that level of success). Next, for whichever function you choose, think of the job of a mid-level role within that same organization. Is that also interesting to you? For example, if chief financial officer is a cool job, is senior financial analyst also something you could enjoy on the way to CFO? If you answer yes to both, bingo, you have identified a potential job function.

(Note: At this point of the exercise, many stop and think, "But I am not good at that function." Disregard your self-doubt. No one is good at his or her dream job at this stage. The purpose of this exercise is to help you pick the thing you would love to do, and then make a plan to become good at it. You are someone who reads books like this on how to achieve your dreams; you are already in the top decile of intellectually curious and ambitious people. I am certain that you can learn finance, computer programming, how to lead a marketing organization, or whatever it is that fascinates you.)

Finally, you will want to determine whether you want to serve in this function as an agent or a principal. Agents are advisers, representatives, consultants, bankers, and lawyers: the people who are hired to solve a specific issue and who bill by the hour. Principals run businesses or business initiatives; they are responsible for the strategy and execution. Agents tend to get a wide variety of experiences—a consultant might have a different client every three months. Principals can spend years in a similar role with a similar area of focus and build deep expertise and experience. Some successful careers start with the more expansive learning experience of agent roles, like consulting, banking, law, or accounting, and move into more focused principal functions after two to three years. It helps focus your career plan to know whether you prefer being on the hook for the advice or for the results.

The Right Company Size and Stage?

Big companies can offer better resources and training, their job roles are well-defined, and their career ladders are regimented. There is more bureaucracy, and more people with whom you will need to cooperate to get things done. Smaller companies, and those at an earlier stage of development, on the other hand, have more work to do than they have people to do them, so your responsibility can expand quickly and you can make more independent decisions. They are also, often, immature organizations with fickle strategic direction and limited resourcing and training. Start-ups often run out of cash and go out of business.

To illustrate, imagine two similar roles: director of digital distribution at a big media company with $10 billion of revenue and ten thousand employees, and director of publisher sales at Mike'sStartup .com. As a part of the Big Media Company distribution team, you will be part of big money initiatives, like licensing content to important distributors like YouTube and Amazon. A meeting will be set up with a relatively high-ranking person at one of those companies with minimal effort, because securing Big Media Company's content is strategically important to them. Over the following months, you will participate in conversations with senior managers at your company about the deal, the company strategy, and the plan for the negotiation. You may be asked to model financial scenarios, draft internal strategy decks, and prepare the meeting materials. Your boss will comment on and request edits to each in preparation for a meeting with her boss, trying her best to anticipate what the more senior person will want, and will most likely have guessed wrongly, so you will be editing again after that meeting. Senior people in your company will be involved because this deal will affect their quotas, and they believe that doing things with cool companies like Amazon carries some kind of prestige (some people at big companies are mentally adding to their résumés on a daily basis). However, if the deal requires extra work by them or their department, they will burden the deal execution with demands for more resources or budget relief, requiring a more senior person to get involved to coordinate a solution to each political crisis.

When the meeting finally occurs, months later, you will be sitting in your office wondering how it went, because the EVP, SVP, and VP decided to go, and it didn't make sense to also bring you, the director. Upon their return you will learn that the company agreed to renew the terms of the current deal with a few changes, and that the Four Seasons Hotel Seattle is very nice. At the end of the year you will receive a performance review and be told if you are on path for promotion. You might be sent off to Big Media Company's well-designed two-day negotiation workshop for up-and-comers, where you will learn the tactics that will be important to you in fifteen years, by which time you hope to be the SVP who is permitted to speak in the meeting with Amazon.

When you look for your next job, most hiring managers will be impressed with your background at such a well-regarded company, value the skills you developed in such a rigorous environment, and likely give you a better title when hiring you.

As director of publisher sales at Mike'sStartup.com, life is quite different. You will enthusiastically contact Amazon and no one will call you back, because they have never heard of your company, and they're getting pitched by people like you at small companies like yours all day long. You will pore through your connections on social media, looking for someone you might know at Amazon, and you finally get introduced, through a friend of your college roommate, to someone who has a role at Audible.com, a distant division of Amazon in Newark, New Jersey. You will set up a meeting with him, you'll prepare and edit the deck yourself, and you will present it alone, because start-ups do not have the luxury of three levels of management for each initiative.

When your new friend at Audible indicates that his boss might be interested in your offering, but that you would need to change it dramatically to fit the unique needs of Audible, you go back to work, whip the company into an excited frenzy because *our company is going to do a deal with Amazon!*, and instantly get an engineer and technical product manager assigned to your initiative by your company's founder. Now you are running a team! Your new team works into the late hours of the night crafting a technical solution to the client's asks. You bond over takeout you've ordered to sustain you through the project.

Two weeks later, just before the follow-up meeting with your new friend's boss, your engineer and technical product manager disappear to a new initiative, because the founder has announced suddenly that Mike'sStartup.com is pivoting to a new strategy, based on feedback from the market (which is founderspeak for "We couldn't raise money with the old strategy"). Your frustration over this disruption is soon assuaged when you are made vice president of customer operations supporting the new strategy and given a sweet new hoodie with the company's updated logo.

These two examples are intentionally exaggerated to give you a sense of the differences between big and small company jobs and the challenges you'll face at each. One of these likely sounds much more attractive to you than the other, and I encourage you to note that in your Happiness Matrix.

Also note that there are many hybrid options in between. Personally, earlier in my career I worked in a new start-up division of a large, century-old company, and it had many of the positive characteristics of both the big and small companies above: we were well resourced, had access to key decision makers at other companies, and could recruit top people to work for us; we also still dealt with some red tape, politics, and big company frustration. I later joined an exciting tech company after its IPO, when it had twenty thousand employees (on its way to over seventy-five thousand today) and still had the culture and urgency of a start-up, but with the benefits of nearly unlimited resources and access to customers. Today I run a twenty-year-old company with roughly one thousand employees that is large enough to commit to and resource big ambitions, but small enough that any employee can bring an opportunity to the CEO. So, of course, there are many options in between, but knowing which of the choices at the extremes feels like a better match for you will help you to recognize the company characteristics that align to your values and personality.

How Much Money?

For the vast majority of people, money is one of the most important professional considerations, if not the most important. It's not because they're greedy, but because earning money makes many fundamental needs or goals possible, such as escaping poverty, getting out of credit card debt, affording health care and food, or giving their children access to higher education. However, a fortunate minority of people have the professional security of a college degree and high-demand transferrable skills, which often gives them access to higher-income jobs and careers over the long run. For this lucky cohort, more money is often something they *want*, not something they actually *need*: studies have shown that Americans are not made happier by more money once they reach $75,000 a year in salary. (A cost-of-living calculator would adjust that to about $150,000 in an expensive city like New York, or $55,000 in a smaller area like McAllen, Texas).

Though we have been told that money cannot buy happiness, by everyone from Ben Franklin to Daniel Pink, compensation continues to be a leading cause of career mismanagement among ambitious professionals. I know countless "successful" people not living their dreams right now because of the money. Here is how it happens. Alex is a top performer at a blue-chip company that pays her well. Her Impact Map and Happiness Matrix tell her she would love to help run a company, and she has been building up skills and experiences and contacts to make that a reality. One day the call comes in for her to take the president role at a smaller-growth company, overseeing all of the commercial operations—a big step toward her dream job. It is a pay cut, but she can afford to take a bit less salary for the next couple of years. She informs her employers, who do not want to lose her. In fact, they tell her, what a coincidence, they were planning on promoting her and giving her more money. And more stock. Stay, they say, and we'll give it to you now. A minute earlier, Alex was making the adjustments needed to live her happiest career path, but now she is comparing that path to more money and a more prestigious title . . . and she stays. Of course, she never tells herself, "I will forgo my dreams for money and title." She says, "With this money, I am creating even more options in the future; I can save it up and then I can take any offer. I'm buying freedom!"

We are all too smart to admit to ourselves when we are giving up.

Six months later, Alex has an upgraded wardrobe and is looking at bigger apartments. The money she promised herself she'd sock away has only served as impetus to increase her cost of living, making the start-up path now all but impossible. She and her significant other have always enjoyed Friday date nights, but the restaurants have become much more refined, the wine truly delectable.

A toast! To the death of Alex's career goals.

When comparing two options, most of us fall for choosing the thing that is quantitatively more, which is a mistake because, once your basic needs are met, there is nothing you can buy yourself that will make you as happy as living your purpose. Fortunately, there is a way for you to manage your career so that you do not fall into this trap. At this stage of our journey together, you are armed with a stronger sense of what is important to you and what makes you happy in life. It is not hard to calculate what that costs. Pick a point on the timeline, maybe when you are forty or fifty, and lay out what you need to have to be happy: nice home, health care expenses for two or three kids, money for colleges, vacations, and so on. If you want to retire at sixty-seven, you have to layer on the annual savings for that, too. Factor in money for a rainy day, unexpected illness, the boiler breaking, etc. Incorporate the financial contributions you wish to make to charity. Sum up the costs, then gross it up for your federal, state, and local taxes. This is your magic number—the exact amount you need to make to achieve the must-haves in your Happiness Matrix. If a career path does not get you to this number, either you need to revisit the inputs into the equation (maybe move to the suburbs, take fewer vacations, retire later, etc.) or you need to rethink your career plan. For instance, let's say you concluded that you want to work to enhance the health of people in the developing world and that you need a family income of $100,000 by the time you are in your late thirties. A Peace Corps salary is not going to get you there. On the other hand, the executive director of a leading nonprofit can earn into the six figures. A well-managed executive director career plan can give you the impact you desire and income that you need. As a nonprofit leader, you will be disregarding career paths that can pay more, but the point of the magic number is not to make the most money, it is to make enough money to be happy while pursuing your purpose.

Thinking today about the money you will need years from now ensures that you are putting yourself on the professional track that maximizes your impact and your happiness in a way that is sustainable for the rest of your life.

Exercise 3: The Eulogy

We have now thoroughly assessed the two elements of a purposeful life and career: importance to the world, and happiness. We have done this with our Impact Map, by first scoping out the impact we currently have, then the impact we could truly have if we removed our own constraints. Then, with our Happiness Matrix, we walked through a series of questions and thought exercises to identify what we really enjoy doing. By now, you should have a clearer, more specific view of what you want from your life and career. Now we are going to pull this together through one more exercise, one that takes very literally the advice of Stephen Covey in *The Seven Habits of Highly Effective People*: "Begin with the end in mind." We are going to imagine the moment, many years from now, when the doctors say they have done all they can, when you've stopped fearing the end and you think for one last time about your life. Do you have regret? Shame? Did you fail to pursue your path because you were afraid? Did you live a life that was prescribed rather than the life you wanted? Or will you smile, knowing that you spent this gift as best you possibly could, tried to have the most positive impact you knew how, struggled for what you thought was right, and never gave up?

What will you have to have done with the next decades to feel, in that one moment of truth, that you have lived your life as best you could?

The last exercise to help you understand fully what you want to achieve with your career and your life is this one: write your Eulogy.

> Alex Smith was a respected executive, a dedicated public servant, and a generous and caring neighbor who was always surrounded by her loving husband, children, and grandchildren. She is best remembered in her industry for the impact she had on the developing world as the leader of research and development for an important biotechnology firm. She is recalled by friends as a fierce competitor on the tennis court, even at eighty-five years old . . .

Write it and rewrite it and rewrite it again until it feels like yours, truly yours, and it makes you proud. The Eulogy should incorporate everything that you learned about your desired personal and career path in creating the Impact Map and the Happiness Matrix, and it may bring more clarity to those exercises, helping you to articulate a better answer. The things in your Eulogy are the things truly important to you. I suspect it won't mention a luxury car or how much money you saved or how many Instagram followers you had. You won't reflect on what other people thought of you, other than the people you love and the people you set out to serve. You won't remember whether you were promoted in two years or three years or whether someone else got one of the promotions over you. But you will know if you had the impact you set out to have on your family, your community, your friends, and the world through your work, and whether you spent your precious few moments truly happy.

Go back and underline the key parts of that Eulogy: *public servant . . . leader in scientific research . . . loving family.* These are the pillars of your life's plan, the things into which you will invest your time and energy, and the goals that we are going to achieve together.

If this book causes you to take only one action, I hope it is this one. Once you know how you want your life to go, you have done the hardest part, the most critical part, and the part almost no one else does. Now we just need to make a plan to make it happen: your Career Roadmap.

CHAPTER 4

⟶ Your Career Roadmap

*Oh but no one's yet explained to me exactly what's
    so great*
*About slaving 50 years away on something that you
    hate,*
About meekly shuffling down the path of mediocrity;
*Well if that's your road then take it, but it's not the
    road for me.*

—FRANK TURNER, "PHOTOSYNTHESIS"

In the previous chapters, you worked to determine the *why* of your life, identifying your unique purpose and sources of joy. You sharpened a sense for what kinds of organizations and roles fit your interests. Now you will establish *how* you will get there, and begin on the road to the career and life that you deserve.

I started this journey when I was twenty-five. I had a prestigious job at a highly regarded company analyzing potential acquisition targets for the executive team, regularly discussing our findings with some of the most important people in a very sexy industry. I worked with smart, cool people, and my parents were proud. But something about the job, deep down, didn't feel right, and it was making me unhappy, though I could not put my finger on why. The hours were lousy, but I had been working all-nighters since high school and that had never been a problem. I felt overdue a promotion (as usual), and couldn't help but notice the disproportionate money my friends in finance were making, so I assumed that was it, and that once I was finally made a vice president I would be happier.

Then a friend who was a kindergarten teacher invited me to speak to her class at career day. I told the kids that I helped "come up with big ideas," "buy companies," and "identify synergies." During the Q&A session, one little girl approached me and asked her prepared questions:

> "Do you work in New York City?"
> "Yes, I do—I love New York!"
> "Do you bring your lunch to work?"
> "No, I usually buy a salad, but that is a really good idea!"
> "Is your job important?"
> "What?"
> "Is your job important?"
> "Well, we guide overall capital allocation, which is a key driver of shareholder value. And, granted, the M&A deals do not always work, but we execute those deals and someone has to do that. And look, the business leaders don't have the overall view of the strategic landscape that we do, and—"
> "I'm supposed to write down yes or no."
> "Oh. Um . . . No?"

And there it was. All my ambiguous work anxiety, my fixation on the next promotion, the residual unhappiness that slipped from my workday to my personal life, and it took a child's simple question to illuminate the issue.

This was a perfectly good job. But I had always believed my best work would come when I was leading and executing, not strategizing. I felt that the world is moved forward by people who build, motivate, and direct great teams to do big things. I was not doing that, and I was not learning how to do it. It was a truly great job, and it was not the job for me.

I began a soul-searching exercise that would eventually lead me to develop the Impact Map and Happiness Matrix. I kept redrawing the Impact Map and redesigning my Happiness Matrix until I felt I had the direction my life needed. I faced the fact that I wanted to lead others, be accountable for the success of the team, and have an important impact on the lives of customers. I also knew that I wanted to do this in the context of marrying my amazing girlfriend, making a life in New York City, having kids and being a good dad, and giving back to my community by contributing to education and getting underprivileged people back to work. If I succeeded, maybe I would write a book. If I pulled all of that off, I would be proud of my eulogy.

Just one problem remained. I had virtually none of the qualifications or experiences I needed.

By this stage of our journey, you are probably in a similar situation. The career path you desire requires experience doing the job, but how do you get experience without getting that job? The average person is sitting in her role waiting for the person above her to retire or get fired to create an opportunity. But not you, not anymore—you create opportunities.

We are going to do a couple of exercises to build the Career Roadmap that will help you realize your dreams. This is how I planned the career path that I wanted, which guided me on countless occasions to take on the right new roles, volunteer for relevant additional responsibilities, seek out mentors and coaches who could teach me what I needed to know, read the necessary books, and so on. These exercises are simple, clarifying, and will light the way to your career destiny.

Let's pick an example, and pretend you have decided that your career purpose is to be a senior technology leader of a company in the e-commerce space, building an online shopping experience that brings lower cost and improved convenience to millions of people's lives while lowering the environmental waste of brick-and-mortar shopping. To clarify this picture in our minds, let's call this role chief technology officer (CTO), though you may figure that running a large technology team with any title would be a great career destination.

Write down the names of all the CTOs in your industry of interest that you can think of. Google something like "best CTOs in e-commerce." Study their bios and look for the patterns in their career paths to learn what skills, experiences, and achievements they have amassed. Start recording your observations. Seek other avenues to enrich this list, perhaps by talking to friends of friends who are in the higher ranks of technology organizations, reading books on the topic, and so on.

As your research is coming together, your list of needed skills, experiences, and achievements may look something like this:

- [ ] Ability to manage large numbers of people effectively
- [ ] Current on latest technology trends and new developments likely to emerge in the industry in the future
- [ ] Experience with large-scale engineering efforts with deadlines and budgets
- [ ] Tested problem solver who can understand the needs of the customer, convert that into product features, and create those features
- [ ] Excellent engineer who codes well
- [ ] Fluent in all functions of the business so as to make informed technology decisions

This list is going to form the foundation of what is essentially your career to-do list. Some of these items will appear clear and achievable, like staying current on latest technology trends, while others, like managing a hundred people, will seem insurmountable. Don't panic—when I first performed this exercise and reviewed the bios of successful CEOs, the only person I had ever managed was Felix, the summer intern. You just have to make a plan. As Henry Ford once said, "Nothing is particularly hard if you break it down into small jobs," and then he turned a horse into a car. For you, then, the next step is to break down each of these characteristics into the small jobs that are easier to visualize and plan to achieve. For instance, let's break down the first item from the list, "ability to manage large numbers of people effectively," into some of the components it might entail:

☐ Comfortable with management tools like budgeting, designing organizational structures, and performance management

☐ Can hire good people

☐ Can set clear goals for the organization that are aligned to the needs of the business

☐ Can delegate, motivate, coach, and provide effective feedback

So, while you may have struggled with the leap from where you are now to CTO-level organizational leadership, learning the component parts like "hiring good people" is not so daunting. Next, you are going to make a plan to learn and demonstrate each of these tasks in the coming years of your career. Again, we will break down the first item in the list above, "comfortable with management tools like budgeting, designing organizational structures, and performance management":

☐ Budgeting—read Eugene Brigham and Michael Ehrhardt's *Financial Management: Theory and Practice*

☐ Budgeting—have "knowledge exchange" lunches with your friend from accounting; learn organizational practices and insights from annual budgeting process

☐ Budgeting—when ready, offer to support your manager during budget process by preparing presentations, etc.

☐ Organizational structures and performance management—read Larry Bossidy and Ram Charan's *Execution* and Peter Drucker's *The Effective Executive*; share summary notes with interested colleagues

☐ Organizational structures and performance management—perform knowledge exchange with your friend in HR on how company's performance management system works

☐ General—explore MBA night classes; meet with three colleagues with MBAs to better understand the value

You will do this exercise for each item on the checklist. A few may be achieved just through the normal course of your work; for example, if you are currently a software engineer, your day-to-day work and hands-on learning may already support something like "excellent engineer who codes well." Others are learning experiences that will likely never present themselves to you unless you are magically promoted into the big job or you create the synthetic experiences, like those illustrated above, that will give you your first taste of the new skill. This checklist will inform the action items you tackle every week of your career. Write it all down, set deadlines, and commit. Each time you execute one, you will learn, grow, and demonstrate success in some way that helps advance your plot.

There are some keys to getting your Career Roadmap and its execution right. Here are a few snippets of advice that others have found helpful.

Commit to an unusual path. Achieving extraordinary outcomes will require unusual measures. Very few of your colleagues, classmates, and friends will have a Career Roadmap; most of them will be measuring their success in titles, compensation, and awards, and behaving accordingly, rarely with a clear-eyed plan for their future. Many of the people senior to you in your chosen profession will be guilty of the same—if enough people just do what is expected of them, eventually a few of them will be made senior vice president. Most people will find the idea of a big detailed plan for their future to be somewhere between odd and off-putting.

They will also find some of your career choices to be confusing. Not long after a kindergartner had shamed me for being misaligned from my career purpose, my team had begun negotiating the largest acquisition in the company's history. Everyone was salivating over putting this career-making deal on his or her résumé. At the same moment, a mentor of mine, who understood my Career Roadmap better than I did at the time, offered me a long-shot opportunity to develop and launch a new channel for the company, which would provide me with extensive operational and leadership experiences. For the next few months, the whole team worked excitedly on a deal that consistently graced the cover of the *Wall Street Journal*, while I played alone in the corner developing a new business plan. That channel became my first business launch, my first management experience, my first P&L responsibility—and it catapulted my career in the arc of my new Career Roadmap.[*]

I have yet to read in the autobiography of an important person, "I just did what everyone else did and, wow, here I am." If you do what everyone else does, you are going to get what everyone else gets. I want a lot more than that for you. Achieving your Career Roadmap requires a commitment to executing your own path.

Do your research. Your Career Roadmap calls for you to advance in your field well beyond your current scope of knowledge. By definition, that means you are making big assumptions and plans regarding a career and jobs about which you are at least somewhat ignorant. In ways you cannot yet see, your plan is wrong. Poring over books, articles, blogs, and TED Talks on relevant topics can help. And there is no substitute for talking to someone on the other side of the journey.

Delightfully, people are usually happy to share their advice; the successful tend to be motivated by service or by ego, and telling someone else the secrets of their success is consistent with both. With some hustle, you can gather a lot of insight and inspiration. For instance, in the exercise above, we strategized a CTO career path and collected a list of top CTOs in the industry. With some time on Google and LinkedIn, you could find a way to get in touch with each one of them and ask if you could visit or call them for fifteen minutes of advice, and if that would be too much trouble, could you email a question or two. At least one, likely more, will say yes. If you can find someone in your network who knows an individual on the list and agrees to make an introduction for you, your likelihood of success increases tenfold (more on networking in chapter 9). Ask them what propelled their

---

[*] Many of the folks who worked on the big deal have gone on to impressive careers. The point is not that there was one right project—it is that the right project depends on each individual's career roadmap.

career. Ask what they look for in top talent. Ask if the items on your Career Roadmap are consistent with their career observations. Ask them, if they had to go back fifteen years and do it again, what they would do, knowing all that they know now.

Will this feel awkward? At first, of course! You are asking intimidating strangers exotic questions about their success. But each of them can give you a piece of the map to the special place you are trying to go. Most every step of this extraordinary career path is going to require you to make yourself uncomfortable at first. Again, get comfortable being uncomfortable.

Enter into a career covenant with your manager. Your current manager can have a significant impact on your success. If advancement in your company is a component of your career plan, she can advocate for you at critical junctures, like when promotions are considered. Even if your Career Roadmap points in a different direction, your manager is someone who regularly observes your work and can provide valuable feedback and advice. Recruiting your manager to be a part of your Career Roadmap is key to success.

Michael Feiner writes in *The Feiner Points of Leadership* that a leader's responsibility is to deliver on a "career covenant," agreeing to provide skill development, performance feedback, advice, and career sponsorship to employees who deliver good work. You can initiate this relationship by asking your boss explicitly if she would be willing to provide this mentorship, and if she'd dedicate a fraction of your one-on-one meetings to coaching you on your career plan (more on feedback and effective one-on-ones with your manager in chapter 11). Here you could discuss elements of your Career Roadmap and solicit advice or introductions as you work your way through it.

Your boss's commitment to a career covenant with you also opens the door for you to take on "side hustles"—bonus projects that will develop new skills and experiences for you and benefit your boss. For instance, you may conclude that you need to become a better interviewer on the path to learning to be a manager, and you ask if it would be appropriate to join your boss for interviews and take notes for her and send her the summary. At some point in the future, you might be positioned to do first-round interviews for your manager and screen out candidates who are not worth her consideration. Or you may have a Career Roadmap action to learn marketing, so you are reading a few books on the topic and you offer to take a crack at producing a new marketing brochure for customers describing one of your team's services. If you deliver in your day job and in your side hustle, you will continue to build your manager's trust and receive more and more responsibilities. This has the added benefit of distinguishing you as a person who is learning the craft at the next level, which puts you on the radar for promotion.

Your side of this bargain is the heavy one: you need to do excellent work in your day job, keep your relationship with your boss focused on the work she needs the team to get done, and then create added time for the coaching and advice. You will very quickly lose your manager's support and goodwill if your assigned work appears to be slipping because of your focus on longer-term goals. You can be both Superman and Clark Kent, but you have to get your articles in on time.*

Be a giver, not a taker. Blatantly ambitious people often come across as needy, selfish climbers. There is a way for you to be ambitious without being that kind of person: frame your Career Roadmap and your career discussions in the context of what you want to con-

---

* An additional word of caution: your manager is not going to have all of the right answers and she may or may not always be able to be fully objective in her answers or advice for you. Firstly, everyone else's career advice will be somewhat intellectually dishonest, because it is, at its heart, career advice for themselves, not for you. For instance, the answer to the question, "Should I get an MBA?" is almost always determined by one single factor: whether the person you asked has or wants an MBA, in which case the answer is yes. Secondly, if you execute your plan, you may be well senior to your current boss someday, or on a different trajectory altogether. So, ask for input, seek learnings, request feedback, pursue new learning opportunities, and appreciate all of the feedback you get, but remember that only you can plan and execute your Career Roadmap effectively. As a mentor of mine used to say, "You have to be the CEO of your own career."

tribute and how you want to help. You could, using the interviewing example above, just go to someone in human resources and impose on his time to learn how to interview. Alternatively, you could say, "I have always respected professionals who value their people and understand HR and am hoping to be able to do the same someday. If this is something important to you, too, could I pick your brain? I don't know if you have interest in engineering, but I would love to repay the favor if you ever want to see how we do it." The latter is a sincere exchange and one to which an HR professional who cares about his craft will likely be excited to contribute.

There will be people upon whom you impose—for instance, the successful people in your field whose advice you solicit—to whom you can't really provide much value today. But you will someday, and it is important that as you progress along your path, you do not forget the people who helped you get there. In the meantime, there is always someone junior to you, who could use your help in one way or another. If you have read this far, you would probably make a good mentor to someone else. Pay it forward.

Change jobs thoughtfully and purposefully. Your job needs to be important to you, aligned to your Happiness Matrix, and challenging to you in ways consistent with the demands of your Career Roadmap. Unfortunately, many settle into jobs that do not achieve these principles. Some are aware that their job is not right, but are afraid of making a mistake, so they wait for the "perfect opportunity" to come along next. Others may not be comfortable pushing themselves to the next level, getting soft and lazy instead, convincing themselves that they have worked hard to get here and deserve to sit back and enjoy it for a while. The problem is, if you are not moving forward in your career, you are moving backward, because there are ambitious people all around who are gunning for the next challenge and are going to take your seat. The alternative to an extraordinary career is not an easy and comfortable career; it is failure.

Properly executing your career plan requires constantly assessing your current role and other potential roles in the context of your Career Roadmap. This does not mean opting instead for job hopping;

variety without a strategy is hardly better than sitting passively with the same old responsibilities. It does mean working relentlessly through your checklist of skills and experiences you need to achieve the next level. A well-managed career covenant with your manager can help to maximize what you are learning in your current role, but at times the next set of lessons will require a new job with your employer or with a new organization. For instance, your employer may not have management opportunities available for you, but another, faster-growing company does. Or your career plan may require you to work in a different industry or region, necessitating a move. Another company may be more willing to give you ownership of your own budget or some other broader responsibility. Or perhaps your Career Roadmap is leading you to starting your own business. Your job may change a dozen times over the next few decades; the key to a successful career is making those decisions proactively, with a focus on accomplishing the items in your Career Roadmap as quickly and successfully as possible, while continuing to honor your personal values.

With regularity, you should assess your current job as well as other jobs for which you may be qualified in the context of your Career Roadmap. As you do so, keep in mind the human bias to overvalue what you have and undervalue what you could have; when comparing opportunities, pretend you are already in the other job you are considering, and ask yourself if you would leave it to take the job you have now. If not, then it is time to think harder about making a move.

Fundamentally change how you think about time management. Most people see their lives in two parts: *working* and *playing*. Either they are required to be at work to get their job done, or they can do whatever feels fun. Executing an extraordinary career and life requires a radically different approach. Based on your Eulogy, you now know you have a handful of significant goals you wish to achieve and a plan for each. You have to set goals and action items and deadlines, and a good number of them need to be due this quarter. They must be in your calendar and you have to commit to them. You should be checking in on your plan regularly, assessing and adapting your plan based on your progress. We will talk more about time management in chapter 7, but for now I want to emphasize that leaving work on Friday for two days of mindless fun and returning Monday morning sleepy are for someone on a different path. To achieve your career goals, we are going to stack the calendar with the routines that are fundamental to your success.

Don't lose sight of the big picture. Examples throughout this book focus on work-related strategies and tactics because they are the most universally relevant (we all suffer from email overload and endless meetings). However, that is not meant to imply that work is more important than the other things you value in life—family, friends, and community may play a more prominent role in your Eulogy than anything you do at work this year. The goal of this book is to help you succeed in your career as part of an impactful overall life plan.

Therefore, your Career Roadmap should accommodate, and force thoughtful trade-offs among, the things that are truly important to you. You could spend all your waking hours working on your Career Roadmap, but that would come at the expense of your relationships with the people you love. A big promotion to a role full of international travel may fill important gaps in your Career Roadmap, but if that conflicts with your important responsibilities as, say, a new parent, you may be wise to decline. Being the first to reply to the boss's emails may earn you goodwill at work, but a life spent glued to your screen may not be the eulogy you were looking for. Having a clear plan for each of the things truly important to you, and investing the time and focus each deserves, is the balance required for an extraordinary life and career.

Now armed with a clear awareness of the important contributions you can make (your Impact Map), what brings you joy (your Happiness Matrix), what you want to achieve with your life (your Eulogy), and the checklist of skills and experiences that you need to get there (your Career Roadmap), we turn our attention to maximizing the successful execution of your plan. It is not enough to know what you want to achieve; you need to become radically more effective in your execution and efficient with your efforts. We are now going to rewire how you approach every critical element of your professional efforts. These next chapters are, essentially, the high-leverage systems and life hacks I wish someone had taught me fifteen years ago. Instead, I have learned them the hard way and am sharing them so you don't have to.

PART 3

Productivity: Get Ten Times as Much Done and Feel Great

When you opened this book, you were already awfully busy. Then we added to your to-do list discovering your life's purpose and creating a Career Roadmap whose execution, by itself, could easily be a full-time job. It feels overwhelming, but in these chapters you will learn the habits that will give you boundless energy, hyperfocus, rigorous prioritization skills, and enough time to achieve all your life's goals. You can do this. As a motivational poster at work reminds me, we all have the same number of hours in a day as Beyoncé.

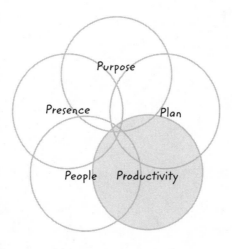

CHAPTER 5

⟶ **Confessions of a Productivity Psycho**

> *"He has a system for eating pancakes."*
> *"So the bottom pancake gets as much syrup as the first!"*
> *"He has a system for everything."*
>
> —MARGARET AND BARNEY COOPERSMITH,
> *MY BLUE HEAVEN*

Let me guess how you're probably feeling right now (and possibly every day):

- You are tired—a good night's sleep feels like a luxury you can rarely afford.

- You are distracted, as it seems there is always another priority pulling your attention away from the moment, demanding you do two things at once.

- You are frustrated, you always seem to be playing from behind, and the list never seems to get shorter.

- You feel overwhelmed or not in control of your time. Your day is dominated by other people's demands and meetings—endless, godforsaken meetings.

- You are out of balance, as time with family and friends, exercise, and a healthy diet always seem to take a backseat to keeping pace at work. The constant stress leads you to wonder if your ambition is worth all these costs.

If any or all of these feelings describe you, let me tell you this: it ends today.

I am going to provide you with the tools for getting done all of the things that matter to you. You are going to wake up refreshed, exercise, eat right, spend your day energized and focused, and accomplish your goals. You are going to achieve this through *good habits* that we are going to create together. Understanding the criticality of good habits for a successful life, and the science behind them, is the key to achieving the impact and happiness you deserve. We will start with a layman's summary of the science.

The Challenge

The human brain can be maddening; it is capable of solving complex mathematical problems, imagining other worlds, following the plot of *True Detective*, and, given six hours or so, assembling a miniature vintage kitchen set for my three-year-old. And yet, when we give ourselves a simple instruction, like, "Let's go to bed at ten tonight and get a fresh start to the week," we're still sitting there at quarter to twelve clicking links on the internet that say, "You will never believe which celebrity has hair plugs!"*

It turns out, we shouldn't be too hard on ourselves—a million years of evolution have conspired against us, developing the human brain into two complementary, but often conflicting, systems. In his

---

* Jeremy Piven

seminal book *Thinking, Fast and Slow*, noted psychologist Daniel Kahneman calls these System 1 and System 2.

System 1 works fast and automatically at a subconscious level. It doesn't calculate; it reacts based on patterns it knows. System 1 is constantly scanning the world for information, threats, opportunities, familiar faces, free pizza, etc., and making quick instinctual reactions. When someone honks their horn as you are about to cross the street staring at your phone, you don't calculate the meaning of the horn, you jump back to the curb—that's System 1. System 1 does not plan and prioritize for the future, and therefore takes satisfaction from binge eating and binge watching and impulsively reacting to every email and push notification. Jonathan Haidt, who wrote *The Happiness Hypothesis*, describes these two systems as an elephant and a rider—System 1 is the elephant, and it is very hard to control.

System 2, on the other hand, is the rider—the slow, effortful, logical part of your mind that you have to consciously engage. System 2 knows that you want to work out more, read *Infinite Jest*, call your mother more frequently, be a good person, and vote in the next election. If you are asked, "How many US presidents had facial hair?" it is System 2 that starts pulling mental images of James Garfield and Abraham Lincoln.* System 2 is your smart, conscious mind, while System 1 is the impulsive wild animal that seems to be in charge of much of your life.

There is evolutionary benefit to a mind that can process and react to everything happening around us in the world. Most of the things happening in a day—a customer extends her hand to greet you; the barista says, "That will be $3.75"; your six-year-old screams, "Give me back my Legos!"; someone sneezes; and so on—do not justify extensive calculation, they just need a reaction from System 1. If you

---

* I know you're wondering: John Quincy Adams, Martin Van Buren, Zachary Taylor, Abraham Lincoln, Ulysses S. Grant, Rutherford B. Hayes, James Garfield, Chester A. Arthur, Grover Cleveland, Benjamin Harrison, Theodore Roosevelt, and the big man, William Howard Taft.

had to stop and slowly calculate every one of these incidents, you would never get through the day.

But there is a real downside to this structure, too. Because System 2, which thinks about the long term, calculates cost versus benefit, and so on, plays second fiddle. While System 2 contemplates New Year's resolutions and knows we are going to lose ten pounds this year, System 1 could not care less. Instead it just reacts: *There are doughnuts in this meeting? Yeah, baby!* Behavioral psychologist Kelly McGonigal summarizes it best when she refers to System 1 as the "immediate self" and System 2 as the "future self." And System 1 is the first activated, the one that is always going, while System 2 kicks in only when necessary and when actively engaged.

There is also research suggesting that System 2, beyond just being second in line to activate behind System 1, takes greater effort to use, and your capacity to engage System 2 effectively is exhaustible. One lab experiment found that subjects who had resisted the urge to eat a cookie subsequently surrendered more quickly when tackling a difficult math problem, suggesting that their willpower had been depleted by eschewing the cookie. In another study, a team of psychologists examined the decisions of a parole board and found that they were more likely to make the difficult decision to grant parole to a criminal first thing in the morning, when the board had not suffered from a day of "decision fatigue." This phenomenon, referred to as "ego depletion," is much debated in scientific circles. It is, however, obvious to anyone who has tried to resist a bowl of candy for a nine-hour corporate off-site meeting, or who has asked me for additional budget at six p.m. on a Friday, that our ability to resist temptation wears down as we use it.

That in a nutshell, my friend, is your brain. System 1, with all the characteristics of an impulsive child, runs the show and is conspiring against you. System 2, the keeper of your best interests, is generally weak and exhausted. The good news is that once you understand this structure, you can manipulate it to your advantage. System 1 can be beat.

The Importance of Good Habits

The first, and most important, key to winning this battle is forming good habits. System 1 thrives on habits; it lets them kick in all day long without consulting System 2. A Duke University researcher found that more than 40 percent of the actions we perform each day are not the result of decision making—they are habits. Backing the car out of the garage without heavy calculation, going to Starbucks when you're bored at two o'clock, reacting defensively when someone questions your actions, turning on the TV when you come home from work—all are habits. We are each a walking collection of habits.

To illustrate, imagine I gave you a challenge of two tasks: polish some silverware for a few minutes twice every day, and every time someone misappropriates the word "literally," reply, "I'm sorry, that is not what the word 'literally' means." How long could you successfully stick to these two tasks? Maybe a day or two? But if the charge instead was to brush your teeth twice every day, and anytime someone says, "Thank you," say, "You're welcome," you would deliver with a 99 percent success rate for the next fifty years. The tasks are similar, but doing one feels impossible, while doing the other is so automatic it would be hard not to do it. The latter are habits. They were not easy habits to form when you were a kid—take it from the family enforcer of dental hygiene and good manners—but once you had those habits set, you owned them for life.

Well-established habits do not require willpower. You just do them. System 1 loves habits, and therefore our path to successfully executing anything that we resolve will not be through a lifetime of suffering, it will be through a deliberate approach to replacing old, bad habits with new, positive habits. Doing so, at first, will take effort, so we are going to set a plan to ensure you get through this habit formation stage successfully.

The first step is to examine the old habit that you want to replace. In his book *The Power of Habit*, Charles Duhigg describes the "habit loop": a cue, a habit, and a reward that reinforces the habit. The cue triggers your brain's craving for a habit; think of Pavlov's dog, salivating the instant he hears a bell ring, believing food is about to be served. The reward is some pleasure received by your brain, such as the endorphin orgy that follows eating a bag of Sour Patch Kids. To fix our bad habits, we have to examine the cues and the rewards that support them.

I drink a lot of coffee. Granted, caffeine is addictive, but, come on, it's not a crack habit. And I get plenty of sleep. Yet there I am at 10:30 a.m., unable to face the next meeting without a coffee. Why do I crave coffee? The cue, usually, is not that I am tired and need caffeine to solve it. More often than not, walking to the coffee machine and getting my blood flowing is enough to wake me up. But there is something I crave. Looking closer, 10:30 follows about ninety minutes of focused work in the office, or the end of the first hour and a half of meetings of the day, after which my brain seems to want a break. The coffee is not the caffeine per se; it is a break from looking at my computer or sitting through another budget review. The cue for this habit is being enervated by the first batch of work at the office, and the reward is the refreshing feeling that follows a break in the action.

The science suggests that we cannot actually erase an old habit. To wit, ask any reformed smoker what he would do if the world were ending today—he is likely to tell you he would smoke a cigarette. However, we can *replace* the old habit with a new one. If I wanted to reduce my caffeine intake (which I do not, for the record—caffeine is fantastic), I could switch to a different habit, like a green tea, a decaf coffee, or a walk outside. Same cue—batch of work—but different habit—tea—equals the same reward: the brain gets a little break. After a week or two, System 1 will stop screaming for coffee and will obey the newly formed habit.

So that's the setup. Your brain is two systems, the impulsive child System 1 is in charge, and fighting it exhausts your willpower, ensuring that you can never consistently beat System 1 over a long period of time. But System 1 loves habits, and if you form good habits, or replace bad habits with good ones, you co-opt System 1 and those habits become yours for life.

You may have to go to extraordinary lengths to develop the new habit. Every year for over a decade, I made a New Year's resolution to exercise more. Every summer, I found myself wondering why my bathing suits had mysteriously shrunk over the off-season. I am not someone who lacks for willpower, but, more often than not, the gym alarm would go off, I would be exhausted, and I would convince myself that I would definitely work out that night instead . . . but work or life would interfere, and I would punt to the next morning, when I would again be exhausted and fail to get up. And repeat. Every morning I was trying to *will* myself out of bed, at a moment when System 1 was firmly in charge. I had no habit to rely on, other than the habit of self-loathing that comes from consistently failing to achieve a goal. However, thanks to much study of this topic, I took a new approach that worked.

First, I diagnosed the root cause of my failings: simply, I was tired and reluctant to get out of bed. Step one, I started going to bed early enough to ensure good sleep (we will cover the importance of this in more detail in chapter 6). I did so by setting an evening alarm that would interrupt my work and compel me to bed. I would hit the sack in my gym clothes and mentally walk through the morning's exercise routine, both serving to increase my commitment. The next morning, when it was time to wake up, the alarm would *not* be sitting next to my bed where I could reach it and hit the snooze button—it would be across the apartment at the front door, tucked inside a pair of gym sneakers. When the alarm went off, I would no longer be lying in the warm comfort of my bed asking System 1, "What do you think, should we work out?" I would be standing with my gym clothes on, facing the front door, only one step away from heading to the gym.

Once over the biggest hurdle—getting out of bed—the next key was forming the habit: going to the gym no matter what. If I was tired, or not up for it, I would still go to the gym, and just do some low-impact cycling and stretching, a completely half-assed workout but one that maintained the habit of going. After a few weeks of this, going to the gym became my habit, and *not* going became the uncomfortable option that would have required willpower. Fitness was no longer a resolution, it was a natural part of my day, like showering and wearing pants. I have subsequently applied the same principles and practice to personal productivity, reading daily, healthy eating, expressing gratitude, not watching TV, limiting social media, working in focused intense bursts, and so on. It only took some planning, and some self-trickery.

Your Career Roadmap runs straight through the path of good habits. They will be the foundation of everything you want to achieve. Think about two or three habits that you have long desired, resolved to do, but ultimately failed. Maybe it is better time management, eating well, calling your parents every week, investing time in your professional development, or learning to play the ukulele. Lock these in your mind as you review the following steps that will help you take control of your life and establish permanent habits for a better you.

1. **Set an "if–then" formula.**

   You cannot successfully commit to notions like "try to eat better," "work out more," or "be a more polished speaker." Those are concepts that require your System 2 to constantly process, depleting your willpower and inviting System 1 to take over. System 2 will be struggling to assess: *Am I being a more polished speaker right now?* while System 1 is talking full speed: *Like, I was, like, oh my God, and, like, he was literally, like, what??* Instead, you need crisp, clear, measurable "if–then" rules that become habits. Instead of "eat better" try "If I crave sugar, then I will eat an apple." *If:* crave sugar, *then:* eat apple. The task is clear and obvious and doable. Just do that thing until it becomes your habit. You may not have completely fixed your diet with that one rule, but you have built a new habit on which the next one can be stacked, and significantly improved your diet and your health along the way. Similarly, instead of "become a more polished speaker," just try "Never say the word 'like.'" *If:* feel urge to say "like," *then:* don't say "like." Or instead of "spend more quality time with my friends," start with, "When I am with my friends, turn off my iPhone." *If:* with friends, *then:* no iPhone. Or try *If:* alarm goes off, *then:* go to gym . . . *If:* it is ten p.m., *then:* open a book in bed . . . *If:* meeting a new person, *then:* smile warmly, extend hand, introduce myself. It will only take a couple of weeks until you have won an important battle and created this new habit for yourself. Once you get it right, string together more related habits that build on your success.

2. Create habits that are important to you.

Initially, creating these new habits requires commitment. And the habits you create will, typically, use up precious minutes of your day for the rest of your life. So these resolutions better be personally meaningful to you. What do you want to change and why? What reason do you have for doing this that is bigger than just you? A lot of people say, "I'm going to get fit," but they don't have a clear incentive, other than they just know they should or they want to look a little better. That is probably not enough motivation to get you through the grind of creating a new habit.

A few years ago, I hurt my back badly enough that I could not roughhouse with my son, which deprived him of his favorite activity for two months. Through physical therapy, I realized that my back felt best when I exercised consistently. So I started the habit of exercising virtually every day. And I knew that if I missed two days of the gym, my back might tighten up again. For me, it became much easier to exercise by motivating myself for the purpose to "be a good dad" rather than to "drop a few pounds."

Go back to the Eulogy you wrote in chapter 3 and work backward to this year. What habits would help you achieve those goals? If you want to be remembered as a mentor, then your resolution this year may be "Read ten books on mentoring and leadership, mentor one person, and help her get to the next stage of her career." That is much more inspiring than "Read more business books." If you keep reminding yourself of the purpose behind your struggle with a new habit, the next time your System 1 would really rather read *US Weekly*, you will have the extra motivation you need to power through.

3. **There is only one way to eat a whale: one bite at a time.**
   Your willpower is exhaustible, so you cannot try to do everything at once. You want to get enough sleep, go to the gym, read more, eat right, learn chess, and lose fifteen pounds? Try to do it all and you will crush your willpower reserves. Start with one; for instance, "I will go to bed at ten and wake up at six. If I want to go to the gym at six, great; if not, it's okay, I will get to that next." In a few weeks, those sleep patterns are your new habit and no longer take willpower. And there you are, bright-eyed and bushy-tailed at six a.m. ready to take on the next bite of the whale: going to the gym. And once you get into the pattern of going to the gym, you will find you have a real desire to eat right, because you will be well rested and in the mood to feed your body healthy foods. While doing them all at once would overwhelm you, doing them sequentially is not only easier; one habit actually supports the next.

4. **Round up your posse.**
   Peer pressure is a powerful force. Once, years ago, before I had fully embraced Hard Thing 2—thinking for yourself—I jumped off a rather high bridge in a small town in Pennsylvania because my friends did it, too. This human weakness for peer pressure can be used to our advantage by involving other people in our resolutions. For instance, if you have committed to creating the habit of

reading thirty minutes each night before bed, and want extra motivation to follow through on the commitment, start a book club with your friends. Now your friends are counting on you, and you are less likely to let them down than you are to let yourself down.

A contest can be fun, too. Each January, the same friends from the bridge incident do a workout challenge. We group text our progress ("Ran five miles today") and keep track of who is winning and who is losing. We are very competitive with whomever is winning, and generally insult and harass whomever is losing. Good fun, and it works—our first year, six guys lost fifty total pounds in sixty days, and two logged their longest runs. Try not getting out of bed to go to the gym when you know that your friends will beat you in a contest and then bring it up for the rest of the year.

Another tactic is to find a resolution buddy. My kids and I write down our resolutions together. (Theirs include some tough ones, like "Stop skipping baths.") They know I want to run a race and are really excited to come watch. I know that if I run it, they will believe that they can do things they set their minds to, and if I don't, they will learn that it is okay to be a failure. I *might* have run that race for me; I am *certainly* going to run it for them.

5. **Bribe, con, and lie to System 1.**

Recall that System 1 is not the deep-thinking system, it is the impulsive one. You can find ways to manipulate those impulses. Say you are in a meeting and there are cookies. If I am just staring at these cookies, my willpower is declining fast. So I lie to myself. I just say in my mind, "Someone sneezed on them." (I am able to do this because I once saw an employee at Au Bon Pain sneeze into her hand before handling baked goods.) Now I just put that memory to work; I tell myself she didn't wash the hand, she touched those cookies, there is sneeze all over them, and the cookies probably have norovirus. The cookies are no longer very attractive to either System 2 or System 1. That's my deranged trick; you will have to come up with the ones that work for you.

A related judo move you can use is this: when your System 1 is telling you to eat the cookie now, and be good later, counter with "I'll just wait a few hours; maybe I will have it this afternoon, just not now." Studies have shown that we are more likely to avoid temptation altogether if we say we can have it later—it seems to give us the dual satisfaction of staying on resolution while also maintaining the option of having the thing we crave. Usually the craving goes away and we don't cheat later.

Avoidance is another easy trick. If you don't want to eat cake, don't walk by the conference room with cake in it. If you are cutting back on drinking, go to a movie, not a bar. To watch less TV, unplug your cable box or log out of Netflix, so you have to go through a minor annoying process to watch something. Candy at the office that is less visible and out of reach is 60 percent less likely to be eaten than candy sitting visibly on your desk. Candy you have thrown in the toilet is 100 percent less likely to be eaten. Remember, fighting System 1 is hard, so if you can re- move the temptations in the first place, you are much more likely to succeed.

Similarly, if you want to eat healthy, plan ahead. If ev- ery time you get hungry you have to go find healthy food or starve, you will be in trouble, because you are busy, and hungry, and in a hurry, and the only source of food around here is a vending machine, which usually has some almonds in it, but of course right now it doesn't, and now you are on the wrong side of the glass at Willy Wonka's Chocolate Factory. You promised to eat apples, and now you are eat- ing a Twix. Instead, on Monday morning—fresh and full of energy and willpower—stop and buy enough apples and almonds and turkey jerky to survive a nuclear winter or a corporate off-site meeting. Then, when you get hungry, there is no need to go to the vending machine.

6. **"What gets measured gets managed."**

System 1 is a sneaky bastard. It says things like, "Listen, let's just break the resolution this once, and then tomorrow you can be really good; you can have the candy *and* the resolution!" Or it says, "Listen, this one is a special occasion, it's not like you go to a nice restaurant every night, right? Tomorrow back to the grind!" System 1 seditiously convinces us that the resolution is great, it's just that *this particular moment* is an exception. But there is a way to counteract this weakness: record your progress. Numerous psych studies have shown that when participants write down their daily performance, they are less susceptible to System 1's chicanery. Remember when you were in school, you paid attention to every assignment and every test, not because you were so motivated in that moment to learn the subject matter, but because it was going to be calculated into your final grade. Keeping score makes it count every time.

I use an app called Daily Tracker and each night before bed I spend fifteen seconds entering the day's data. I view each resolution at the end of the week on the app's chart and see where I am succeeding and where I am failing. Because I know that any time I give in to System 1 I will have to face my own disappointment in myself later, I am less likely to succumb "just this once."

7. **Support yourself with positive emotions.**

Humans are notoriously bad at valuing long-term benefits over short-term rewards. This has been demonstrated in studies where people are given the choice between, say,

$50 now and $75 in a year. The right answer, with a massive 50 percent risk-free return, is $75; but most people opt for the quick fifty bucks. However, in one study where subjects were prompted to express gratitude at the beginning of the exercise, they were much more likely to make the long-term-oriented choice. There is some connection between the emotion of gratitude and our ability to resist short-term urges. Studies have also shown that expressing gratitude as a daily habit—in the form of making a list of things for which you are grateful or sending an email to someone expressing appreciation—makes you happier and more productive. Researchers have made a similar case for the power of personal pride. Psychologists have shown that when people are congratulated for success, they subsequently work harder at that task (echoing Dale Carnegie's timeless advice from *How to Win Friends and Influence People*: "Give the other person a fine reputation to live up to").

So consider reinforcing your emotional strength by regularly expressing gratitude (a pretty good habit to add to the top of your list), or, when faced with a temptation to stray from your resolutions, reminding yourself what you already have in life and how fortunate you are. And give yourself the big reputation you deserve—don't think of yourself as someone who is "trying to watch less TV," think of yourself as someone "who reads every night, because I am an intellectual."

Remember, you are human, and you are going to have setbacks. When you fall off the wagon, don't hate yourself; give yourself the positive energy you need to get it right next time. As the poet Rainer Maria Rilke wrote, "The purpose of life is to be defeated by greater and greater things."

CHAPTER 6

→ Never Tired Again

Success isn't earned. It is leased. And the rent is due every day.

—From Rory Vaden's *Take the Stairs*,
as popularized by J. J. Watt, NFL linebacker

At this stage of your journey, you have a sense of where you want to go with your life, and the scientifically proven techniques for how to create the right habits for success. The execution of your Career Roadmap requires you to have the mental and physical stamina to face challenging work every day, to learn incessantly, to maintain self-awareness, to be patient and kind to others, and to do the Hard Things. The keys to maximizing your energy to achieve all this are simple, generally well-known, and patently ignored by 97.2 percent of Americans. If you really want to achieve your life's goals, it begins with a commitment to the following habits that will give you the energy and longevity needed for the battles ahead.

This chapter is going to feel like a bit of a non sequitur, as I spend a few pages encouraging you to adopt a set of healthy habits that may seem entirely unrelated to your career and life goals. However, following these strategies will not only increase your stamina and brain power, it can extend your life by a decade or more, and is therefore the single most important thing you can do next to improve your odds of having an impactful life.

Sleep

Have you ever had a conversation with someone who fervently rejects evolution? Someone who steadfastly ignores centuries of scientific study and endless evidence? The way that conversation would make you feel is the way I feel when people tell me they do not need seven to eight hours of sleep per night. The science is clear, comprehensive, and definitive: you need seven to eight hours of sleep per night to feel your best and do your best work. Every time you stay up late working or binge watching TV or scrolling through Facebook, you have seriously damaged your productivity for the next day, and possibly even the day after. If you sleep six hours a night or less for two weeks, you have the same cognitive and physical functionality as someone who has pulled two consecutive all-nighters, roughly the equivalent of a drunk nine-year-old. If you want to succeed, you have to commit to a full night's sleep in the same way that you commit to showering: it is not a luxury, it is a basic requirement to start your day.

Here is how to reclaim the power and glory of sufficient sleep and enter each day with the energy you need to win.

1. **Set an alarm to go to bed.** You have a natural circadian rhythm that regulates feelings of sleepiness and wakefulness. Keeping your sleep times consistent maximizes the benefit of this internal body clock. Set an alarm to go off at the same time every night, forty-five minutes before you need to be asleep. When it goes off, immediately stop whatever you are doing and begin your go-to-bed routine. Honor this alarm like it is a superior being; it is the way to stop the evening cycle of time wasting and sleep procrastination. If you go to bed on time every night, you will have enough sleep, and you will feel fantastic for the rest of your life.

2. **Plan the next morning the night before.** Before you go to bed, review what the next day's schedule looks like. It

settles your mind and makes waking up the next morning easier. An easy hack for this is to rename your smartphone alarm every night for what you need to know when you wake up the next day; for example: *Run six miles. 9:00 a.m. meeting with client at Bassett Street. Wear a suit.* If you also take two minutes to prepare your clothes for the next day, you will have one less thing to think about in the morning.

3. **Plug in your phone away from your bed.** This will reduce the temptation to use your phone in bed, as scientists have proven that using electronics before bed suppresses melatonin (the hormone that controls your circadian rhythm), stimulates your mind, and undermines the quality of your sleep.

4. **Read in bed.** This is your chance to settle in, relax, and absorb some information. (For the reasons stated above, read a physical book or an e-reader, not your phone or tablet.) As soon as you start feeling sleepy, close your eyes and give in to your body's primal yearning for sleep.

5. **Plan for margarita night.** Perhaps, even though you have an ambitious life plan, you do still like to go out and drink margaritas. It's okay—your author also likes margaritas. But here is the rule, and it is nonnegotiable: you are still getting up at the same time tomorrow morning. This rule keeps your sleep cycle in sync, reinforces your sleep habits, and encourages better life choices as the night gets later and you know the alarm clock will be calling for you the next morning.

6. **Make up for lost sleep.** Whether due to margaritas or other factors, there will be times when you underdeliver on your sleep quota. Each time you sleep less than the seven to eight hours you need, you accumulate sleep debt,

which you must repay to achieve your mental and physical potential. It is a common misconception that one really good night of sleep will make up for days or weeks of sleep debt. As Dr. William Dement, a preeminent expert on sleep health from Stanford University, describes it, each hour of sleep you miss is like a brick added to a backpack you carry everywhere, and each hour of sleep above the seven to eight hours you require removes one brick. You need to make up for your lost sleep. To do so while maintaining a consistent wake-up time, give yourself the gift of an early night to bed, or, if it is a weekend, try what sleep researchers call "a big-ass nap."

Set Yourself Up to Win the Morning

Some of the most important hours in your day are your productive hours away from the office. This is the time you get to exercise, clear your head, plan, learn, and execute. Unfortunately, too many people get little value out of these hours because they attempt to utilize them in the evening. But the night is dark and full of terrors: team projects that run into the late hours, spontaneous social plans, exhaustion, ego depletion, and so on. It is very difficult to consistently exercise and be productive after a full day of work, one of the reasons most people end up spending their evenings decaying in front of their phone or TV.

However, the morning is completely yours. In the early hours of the day, the unplanned client dinner or emergency project cannot preempt your gym schedule. Your boss cannot bother you. The exhaustion of a long workday cannot undermine your plans to accomplish your key priorities. There is nothing good on TV. No one is texting you. For someone committed to making every day a productive one, the early morning is the most valuable and important time of the day. But most people are sleeping right through it. Now that you have committed to getting enough sleep, you are ready to follow these simple steps to win the morning.

1. **Commit.** If you are not naturally a morning person, it takes a few weeks to change your biological sleep rhythm. It gets better; just stick with it. And give yourself some help: set your coffeepot to be ready for you when you wake up. If you don't drink coffee, now would be a great time to start.

2. **Use a smart alarm.** Devices and apps can measure your body movements and wake you when you are in your least deep sleep. At the time of this writing, the Sleep Cycle alarm app, various smartwatches and exercise bands, and the Hello Sense device are all fine products for helping you wake up at the most pain-free moment.

3. **Do not snooze.** Hitting the snooze button resets your sleep pattern and makes you feel much worse once you do wake up. Again, put your alarm far away from your bed to avoid the temptation.

4. **Stand strong.** Your posture directly affects your emotions, a concept scientists call "embodied cognition." In a 2009 study, psychologist Richard Petty had college students sit either straight up with their chests out or slouched forward with their heads down, perform a short exercise, and then rate themselves on how well they thought they would perform in the future. The ones sitting confidently were more optimistic and confident. A confident posture causes the release of testosterone, the dominance hormone, and suppresses cortisol, the stress hormone, mimicking the hormonal makeup of alpha primates and powerful human leaders. (For more on this topic: Amy Cuddy's 2012 TED Talk, "Your Body Language Shapes

Who You Are," is terrific.) Start your day on the right foot by immediately sitting or standing up straight, stretching your hands out to the sides or over your head, and taking a deep breath. You are a badass, ready to tackle the day.

5. **Hydrate as soon as you wake up.** Have a tall glass of water waiting next to your bed. Your body needs water and you haven't had any in eight hours.

6. **Express gratitude and reiterate your purpose.** Focus for a moment on something for which you are grateful, like a loved one, your health, or an opportunity ahead of you. Scientists have shown that people who express gratitude live happier, healthier lives (more on this in chapter 13). It is a great way to start your day. Couple this with thirty seconds reciting to yourself the things you intend to achieve with your life or your week or your day to orient the day's activities.

Now you're awake, confident, hydrated, grateful, and focused, and it only took ninety seconds. Next, you get to go win the day before most people are even out of bed.

Sweat

We all know we are supposed to exercise. Virtually everyone has made a New Year's resolution to work out more and has failed. For you, it is about to become an ironclad habit. Exercising to start your day pumps up your energy, builds your confidence, and improves your cognitive and emotional function, literally growing new brain cells for you. Exercising makes you live seven years longer than if you did not exercise. In fact, every hour you exercise adds nine hours to your life. If looking good in your jeans isn't motivating enough for you, how about a ninefold return on your time investment? If you do not have a good habit of exercise, here are some basic tips to get you started.

1. **Exercise in the morning.** Big data from companies that make wearable technology have shown that people who work out most consistently work out in the morning, and people who work out least consistently work out in the evening. Win the morning, my friend, win the day.

2. **Exercise every day.** The American Heart Association, an organization completely dedicated to keeping you from having a heart attack, recommends at least thirty minutes of exercise five days a week, including two days of strength training. Making a plan to exercise every day creates a strong personal habit that, after a few weeks, requires virtually no willpower to execute. If you set out to exercise seven days a week, life will interrupt once or twice a week (work, travel, kids, etc.), leaving you at the AHA-recommended levels. The energy and mental clarity you earn from daily exercise will help carry you through the rigors of an ambitious daily schedule.

3. **Exercise vigorously.** Exercise is supposed to be hard. More intense exercise, like running fast, lifting heavy weights, and performing high-intensity fitness intervals, increases your cardiovascular capacity, burns more calories during and after exercise, and, on average, makes you live longer than if you perform moderate-intensity exercise. Strength training improves muscle mass and bone density, boosts endorphins, and improves your mood, giving you the energy and positivity to manage an ambi-

tious daily routine, a calendar full of work, and each new obstacle that stands in the way of your goals.

4. **Track your results.** As we discussed in chapter 5, tracking your performance helps you stick to your goals. Mark off the calendar each day you exercise, weigh in at least once a week, and compare your performance over time (increased strength, running speed or distance, etc.). Apps like Runkeeper and MyFitnessPal are great tools for this.

Eat Smart

Given the enormity of your personal ambitions, it's important to fuel them in the right way. And that starts with the food you consume. You have to stop thinking of lunch as a special indulgence. For a person on a mission, food is fuel, and getting that fuel right will maximize your energy, endurance, mental function, and longevity. Every Frappuccino and every pasta dinner is detracting from your mission. Here are some simple rules and tactics to ensure you are well fueled and healthy for the adventures that lie ahead.

1. **Eat only as much as you need.** For healthy living, you can replace every book on fitness ever written with one sentence: *eat no more calories than you burn.* Unfortunately, it takes your brain about twenty minutes to register how much you have eaten; by the time it catches up, you have devoured way more calories than needed. To ensure your diet is aligned to your proper energy needs so you can maximize your success in all parts of your life, try taking a smaller plate and filling it with less food than usual, and when you get to where you feel about 80 percent full—not stuffed, not completely satisfied—stop eating. In the rare case that

you have stopped eating prematurely and are still hungry twenty minutes later, you can always eat some more.*

2. **Employ simple strategies to eat for good health.**
   These tips for healthy eating are not carefully hidden secrets, but honoring them is hard, especially since the least healthy foods are the most readily available and short-term rewarding. Leveraging what we learned in chapter 5, here are some simple techniques to ensure you have only the food you need to serve your mind and body.

   • *Eat the same thing.* It is hard to constantly have to exert willpower to turn down delicious chicken parm, French toast, or that pint of Ben and Jerry's. Your best bet is to remove them completely from consideration by choosing among the same few healthy meals every day. For breakfast, maybe Greek yogurt, or peanut butter and an apple. For lunch and dinner, cook something healthy if you have time, or save a few healthy lunch options in your favorite food delivery app and order one of them each day. Successful people tend to routinize their food to save time, reduce decision fatigue, and maintain a healthy diet.

   • *Fill your desk with healthy options.* Every time you have to make an effort to eat well, your odds of maintaining a smart diet decrease. Give yourself the advantage by purchasing fruit and vegetables on your way to work on Mondays to enjoy whenever you are hungry. Fill a drawer of your desk with peanut butter, almonds,

---

* 2500 years ago, Confucius preached a healthy life habit called "hara hachi bu" (which roughly translates to "stomach 80 percent"), urging people to stop eating before they become full. Citizens of the Japanese island of Okinawa often greet a meal by intoning Confucius' adage, reminding themselves to stop eating before they are satiated. Coincidentally, Okinawans are famous for their lower caloric intakes, lower BMI, and extremely high life expectancies.

roasted chickpeas, turkey jerky, and other healthy snacks. Now, when you get hungry at your desk, you can reach for one of these instead of the leftover doughnuts in the communal kitchen.

- *Plan ahead.* When you are going out, think about your likely food options. A child's birthday party is going to offer chicken nuggets, a cake, and nothing else. A dinner that starts at eight will greet your completely empty stomach with alcohol and a two-thousand-calorie bread bowl. One of the terminals at LaGuardia Airport has barely anything to eat other than two-day-old muffins and bags of candy. Plan ahead by having a healthy snack or meal so that you do not show up hungry for one of these unwinnable situations.

- *Make value judgments.* I have it on good authority that many people have eaten a cookie and still had a successful life. Of course you are allowed to treat yourself. The goal of this section is to make you aware of the trade-offs between short-term pleasures and the energy you need to achieve your long-term goals. It is okay on occasion to have a big uninhibited dinner out or to crush an ice cream sandwich. Just stay committed to healthy habits and smart routines to ensure the exceptions remain exceptions, and that the vast majority of your meals remain focused on fueling your ambitions.

Sleeping, exercising, and eating right will ensure that you have the energy to win your day and will maximize the number of days you are likely to live. The next step to accomplishing ten times as much and feeling great is eliminating from your life the things that occupy your time but are not helping you achieve your goals. In the next chapter, I am going to give you back five hours a day to invest in success and true happiness.

CHAPTER 7

→ Five More Hours to Live

Never confuse movement with action.
—ERNEST HEMINGWAY

You are out of time. From when you wake up until you go to sleep, the demands on you will be greater than your capacity to satisfy them. Meetings, obligations, chores, and distractions tiptoe into your life, innocently take root in your calendar, and then spread like a weed, choking your precious hours and stealing your days from you. How many times a day do you think, "If I only had a few more hours"? In this chapter, if you open your mind to a new way of operating, I will give you back five hours a day, every day, for the rest of your life.

Imagine for a moment you were in some fantastic crisis and were at risk of running out of food. (In my mind, Matt Damon and I are trapped on Mars, two unlikely friends working together to survive this interplanetary disaster . . . but you have to come up with your own scenario.) Would you just eat whenever you felt like it? No, you would not waste a crumb. You would treat every morsel as the most precious thing in the world—because once you run out of food, you die.

That is your life. But you are not in a space station with my best bud Matt Damon, you are in your home on Earth. And you are not running out of food—you are running out of a different scarce resource: the hours in your day. And when all the hours in your life are spent, friend, you are dead.

Yet, if you are like most people, you do not treat those hours like they are precious and scarce. Instead, you regularly agree to join some weekly meeting or another and, just like that, lose fifty hours a year—a full workweek, gone! You start watching a new TV series you heard is good, and a hundred hours are vaporized. Every day you spend time as if it were never going to run out.

To succeed in your life's plan, you have to make every hour count. Here's how.

Zero-Base Your Calendar

Zero-basing is a popular management thought exercise for resource allocation, in which every business initiative and every department mentally starts with zero resources, then builds up to the investments needed to achieve the outcomes that are important for the company. Teams that use this approach escape incremental thinking, free themselves of the cognitive bias of sunk costs, and find that they end up moving investment from parts of the business that are less important (but have traditionally been resourced) to newer or potentially more valuable parts of the business that can create more upside with those resources. Companies that approach resource allocation in this way outperform their peers in revenue growth and profit growth. We are going to use a similar approach and zero-base your time allocations, applying your limited hours and energies only to the things that matter most to your impact and personal success.

To zero-base your calendar, let's begin with the basic requirements: you need to sleep for eight hours; you need to perform essential personal tasks, like eating, bathing, performing personal hygiene, and getting dressed, which in the aggregate should take you about two hours a day; you need to exercise. That is eleven nonnegotiable hours. Presuming your career plan involves a traditional job, and you are striving for high performance, you probably need to work around sixty hours a week, or an average of eight hours a day not including your time for lunch (for this exercise, we're treating all days as equal, even though you will likely invest more hours in your work on a Monday than on a Saturday). Five hours remain. Five precious hours a day, teeming with potential to change your life.

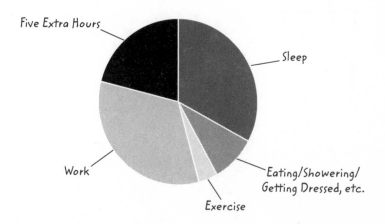

Your 24 Hours

"Now wait," you are thinking, "those hours are spoken for, too—I have tons of stuff going on." This is exactly the point. You have five hours of discretionary time a day, and now that you have set your life's goals and your Career Roadmap, it is time to zero-base those last five hours and invest them in the way that has the highest return on the impact and happiness you are pursuing in your life. Cooking, cleaning, volunteering, spending time with your family are all demands on that precious five hours. So are your social media obsession, your adult kickball league, your commitment to watching every episode of *The Bachelor*, and your repeated urge to play Temple Run on your phone. Let's walk through a few steps to ensure you are getting the best life imaginable out of your limited time.

1. **Make the fixed hours count.** In the previous chapter we talked about the importance of really working up a sweat

and making your heart pound when you exercise; this ensures that you get the most health benefit for the half hour or hour you invest in exercise. Similarly, you need to maximize the intensity and the return you get from the hours you invest at work. It is quite easy to fill a day at work with easy-to-do, low-value activities, like attending optional meetings, replying to every email in your inbox, reading all the articles people send you, and so on. Though it might feel like you are being productive, performing activities that are not critical to the achievement of your goals wastes your most precious resource: time. Your calendar fills up because you are afraid you might miss something in that informational meeting or forwarded newsletter, not leaving you the time required to excel in your work assignments, build your relationships, manage stakeholders, secure resources, invest in your Career Roadmap, and so on. Go through your calendar and ask, for every activity, "Is this critical to achieving my team's goals and my goals?" If not, kill it.

2. **Get a calendar buddy.** Have you ever asked someone else what is keeping them busy, and when they describe all the important things they had to do that day, they didn't sound very important to you? Guess what: the same thing happens when you describe your day, because our appointments always seem more critical to us than they really are. A great exercise for ensuring that you are making the fixed hours count is to have a friend who understands your goals review your calendar. There is no greater gift than to hear direct feedback on your time allocation, like, "Why are you meeting with Aiden every week? That's a waste of time. Why do you attend the marketing cross-functional meeting? Nothing gets done there. Why are you attending a two-hour HR benefits seminar? Max out your 401(k) and get back to work." You can reclaim at

least an hour a day from a regular calendar audit performed by a good friend at work.

3. **Outsource.** You have a big plan for your life, and your most valuable resource is your time. Whenever possible, you need to buy yourself more time. For instance, you can spend twelve hours doing your taxes, or you can pay an expert. You can spend two hours a day cooking, cleaning, and shopping, or you can buy your groceries and meals online. You can address your holiday cards, or you can pay a service to do it.* I do not take this recommendation lightly; I know that for most Americans money is scarce. I also know that having time to pursue your career growth and achievement of life goals is extremely valuable and worth sacrifice. Personally, I outsourced meal preparation early in my career when I was living in a five-hundred-square-foot apartment and driving a fifteen-year-old car with a coat hanger for a radio antenna—time is far more precious than the frivolities people usually buy with their money.

4. **Eliminate distractions.** A friend told me recently that he did not have time to exercise, see friends, read books, or invest in his career. I asked him to open the battery settings on his iPhone for me, which revealed the exact amount of time he spent in each app the last week: YouTube 6.1 hours, Facebook 4.1 hours, Instagram 2.6 hours, ESPN 2.9 hours, and so on. "Great news," I told him, "you have more time than you thought." The same is true for most of us.

---

* As of this writing, handy.com, GrubHub, FreshDirect, Postmates, and TaskRabbit all offer reasonably priced services. I am sure one or more of them is out of business by the time you are reading this, and I am equally sure someone else has stepped in to offer an app that delivers these services, because everyone hates doing these things for themselves.

Of those five precious hours we can invest each day, the average American spends all five of them watching TV or playing with his or her phone for entertainment. Every single person wants to have more professional success, more knowledge, better and closer friendships, invigorating hobbies, positive impact on others, and so on, and yet takes the hours that could be used to achieve those things and throws them into the sinkhole of mindless clicking and binge watching. Think of all the amazing books that you might not read before you die. Remember all the people you care about in your life but with whom you haven't spoken in a long time. Imagine how cool it would be to learn to make a soufflé or play piano. Consider the vast opportunity waiting for you in your Career Roadmap. None of it happening.

Worse, sitting around vegging out during your Five More Hours to Live not only wastes the valuable moments of your life, it reduces them: scientists have estimated that every hour of television viewing after the age of twenty-five reduces your life expectancy by 21.8 minutes!

So unplug your cable box; cancel Netflix; remove Instagram from your phone. Those are not proactive investments of your time, they are bad habits, habits which you have the power to break. On your deathbed, you are not going to look back longingly on all that time you spent reading celebrity gossip, so eliminate it, and let's find a better way to invest your time.

You are now five hours a day richer. By eliminating everything in your work schedule that is unnecessary to your success and happiness, outsourcing activities that do not require your precious attention, and eradicating time-wasting activities from your personal life, you have made room for hours of highly productive and meaningful time every day. Next, we schedule those hours with activities aligned to your true priorities.

Proactively Allocate Your Entire Calendar

Return to your Impact Map, Happiness Matrix, Eulogy, and Career Roadmap. Think, with precision, through the activities that are truly important and rewarding in your life. Let's redesign your calendar to reflect these priorities.

Invest Your Hours

How much time do you want to spend with family and friends, and which ones? Which books do you desperately want to read this year?* Do you wish to own a dog that needs to be walked for thirty minutes every day? Do you want to learn Mandarin? These are not isolated decisions; they are allocations of your most scarce resource: your time. Each one is a trade-off, costing you the opportunity to spend your time on something else. Treated well, this time can be used to execute your Career Roadmap, strengthen your personal ties, build your skills, and live the life of your dreams.

When you have no plan for your time, it will be allocated passively and reactively. Without a plan, the next stimulus—the powerful attraction of your phone, your TV, internet click bait, or the bottle of wine in the fridge—is almost impossible to ignore. You give in to it, and to the next, and next thing you know your time has been spent, wasted.

I find enormous value in allocating my Five More Hours to Live based on my current priorities. I write them down, allocate minutes, and list them in order of importance. When my professional or personal responsibilities surge (a sick kid, school events, board meetings, extensive travel, etc.), I can work to keep to the items at the top and sacrifice the ones at the bottom. Just to illustrate, here's how I allocated each day's five hours last week (on average across seven days).

---

* Pro tip: the average book has roughly the same number of pages as there are days in a year . . . so if you want to read 20 books, you simply have to read 20 pages a day.

Priority	Example	Minutes per day
Focused time with my kids	Art, sports, reading, homework, outdoor adventures, urban culture	120 minutes
Time with loved ones, friends	Date night, dinners, texts	45 minutes
Writing	This book, blog posts, brainstorming	60 minutes
Nonprofit work	Helping run and fund-raise for a literacy nonprofit and a high school scholarship fund	15 minutes
Reading and personal development	Alternating fiction and nonfiction	30 minutes
Personal network	Helping others*	15 minutes
Relaxation	Guitar, chess, news	15 minutes

In proactively assigning my time, it is clear that I do not value watching a nine-inning baseball game or playing Xbox enough to schedule it over my other priorities. Of course it would be kind of fun to play Call of Duty for three hours tonight, but life is a series of choices, and I am happier and more productive when I choose the more fulfilling, energizing, and impactful activities. I want the same for you. How will you spend your Five More Hours to Live tomorrow?

Make Your Calendar Your Operating System

To cement these proactive commitments of your five hours, we employ a simple system: your calendar, on steroids.

If your boss scheduled a meeting with you for four p.m. tomorrow, would you show up on time? Yes. If you had to drive a loved one

---

* More on this in chapter 9.

to a doctor's appointment, would you pick her up as expected? Of course. Because these things are important to you, so you put them in your calendar, and you honor them. You can create the same effect for the other important things in your life outside of work: sleep, exercise, reading, time for your Career Roadmap. So far in this chapter, I have implored you to eliminate everything from your schedule that is not important to you and repurpose those minutes for things that are important to you. To ensure you honor those commitments with the same dependability with which you would honor a court date, put them in the calendar and obey that calendar zealously, not just during the workday, but all twenty-four hours of the day. This will change your life.

To start, open your calendar and schedule your fixed daily time commitments: sleep, food, hygiene, exercise, family obligations, travel time, etc.* Next, layer in your detailed work schedule, starting with meetings, then blocking all other time to achieve your work priorities, such as dedicated time to do your work, dedicated time to investigate competitors or best practices, time for thinking and brainstorming, etc. Finally, schedule your Five More Hours to Live,† based on the exercise on investing your hours you just completed in the previous section. Block off every hour for something necessary or important to you.

For example, having trouble sticking to a consistent bed schedule? At exactly, say, 9:45 p.m., your calendar will alert you it is time to close your computer or put down your art project and get ready for bed. Having a hard time staying focused and getting your work done on time? Knowing that you have a scheduled period for a focused burst of effort will make you more productive. Never can find time to call your parents? If your calendar tells you at seven p.m. on Mondays

---

* If you are embarrassed for your colleagues to see that you intend to sleep eight hours a night, you can mark these events "private" in any calendar software; many calendar programs also allow you to make separate, co-operable calendars, of which one can be shared with others, another kept private.

† Some days, such as weekends, the Five More Hours to Live will be more than five hours; for others, like busy work days, they will be less. It should average to 5 per day over the course of a week.

to call your parents, then you will call your parents at seven p.m. on Mondays. You have the time to achieve your life's most important ambitions; you just need the system to help you do it. This will feel awkward and difficult for the first week or two, and then it will be a habit on which you will build unprecedented success in your life.

Be Spontaneous . . . on Schedule

"But wait!" your now terrified System 1 is screaming. "What, we can't have any fun? We have to live like robots?" Of course not. The purpose of a clear plan for investing your time is to maximize the impact and joy you get from your hours. Whenever new opportunities arise, you only need to assess them in the context of your priorities and how you want to spend your time. Spontaneity is a feature of this system. If you are scheduled to work on your Career Roadmap tonight and a few work acquaintances are going out for drinks, you simply ask yourself what would be a better use of your Five More Hours to Live, given your goals. If drinks with a few colleagues is not a priority of yours, you can pass. On the other hand, if a dear friend is in town unexpectedly, a loved one needs you, or you just scored Taylor Swift tickets, you very well may prioritize that above your other uses of time. What is important is that you reach the decision intentionally, with your priorities and trade-offs in mind.

Five hours a day are completely yours to deploy for the achievement of all you desire. That is 1,825 annually, more hours than the average Frenchman spends at work all year. That is 91,250 hours over the next fifty years, enough time, according to the ten-thousand-hour rule,* to become a world-class expert in nine different fields or en-

---

* This is a mostly unscientific maxim by pop psychologist Malcolm Gladwell from his book *Outliers* identifying ten thousand hours of deliberate practice as the threshold level at which one becomes an expert in a field. Like all of Gladwell's research, the rule is controversial, but I think it is fair to say that if you practiced pottery for ten thousand hours you would be able to make some damn nice pots.

deavors. But most people let these hours slip away, never deploying them to achieve their full potential. You can fix that in your own life by zero-basing your calendar, deliberately allocating your hours to align to your life's priorities and Career Roadmap, and making your calendar your operating system for spending your time wisely.

There are your five hours. Now tell me you don't have time.

Next, we will make all of your hours twice as productive.

CHAPTER 8

→ Get Sh*t Done

Efficiency is doing things right; effectiveness is doing the right things.

—Peter Drucker

Every day, we do battle with a modern-day Lernean Hydra, the mythical monster of Greek mythology, an undefeatable beast that sprouts two new heads every time you strike a blow. It has been growing, morphing, and winning battles against us since sometime around middle school.

We call this scary son of a bitch our "to-do list."

Our to-do list plays host to more work than we could ever hope to complete. It is fed by our boss, our colleagues, our families, our neighbors, and ourselves. It contains everything from a project due at work Monday to the books to read on our Career Roadmap to a missing 1099 that we need to complete our taxes. It is constantly growing, springing eternal from the anxious lizard part of our brains: *Don't forget to call Aiden back . . . I owe my boss those numbers and no one has gotten back to me yet . . . I have to remember to update LinkedIn . . . I really need to stop eating so many carbs . . . I think I want bangs . . . Is Mother's Day next Sunday? Get Mom a gift . . . Tonight I need to do that PowerPoint presentation I should have done already . . . I'm going to return this shirt; it makes me look like I'm pregnant . . . I think it's time I took out renter's insurance . . .*

Every day, our ambition calls us back to the battlefield for the hopeless task of defeating this monster.

You and I are about to take a new approach. We are going to tame this beast, put a saddle on it, and ride it to Mount Olympus. We are going to establish a process for assessing, defining, and prioritizing your tasks, based on the goals, impact, speed, and timing of each; we will set you up with a no-stress system for filing the tasks as they bombard your life; and I will propose the essential practices that will help you do the right things well. We will even fix your broken relationship with email. You are going to slay your to-do list.

First, a Reset

I am going to tell you something that you will reflexively reject, but I want you to suspend your disbelief for just a few minutes and work with me. Okay? Okay, here it is:

You don't have to do anything.

I'm serious. Every project, every meeting, every email in your life is optional for you. You are free to choose to do it, or not.

The key is not to view your to-do list as a mandatory list of instructions you must follow but as a series of cost-benefit trade-offs. Understanding these costs and benefits will be important, as it will help you decide if you want to do something, when you want to do it, and how much energy you want to invest in it. Doing some tasks will accrue benefits to you, which can range from "save 15 percent on car insurance" to "close big deal and exceed most important professional goal for the year." Not doing some tasks will have costs, which can range from "miss out on potentially interesting information shared in quarterly finance update meeting" to "be fired for failing to deliver critical project in time for board meeting." Every minute you spend on one task is a minute you are not spending on another, so it's important to determine how to best spend your time for maximum positive impact.

What follows is a system for applying the same "zero-base" approach we discussed in chapter 7 to all items on your to-do list. This system will ration your energy for the actions that will have the most leverage on your goals and life's plan. It turns meetings into opportunities to have impact at work, not prison sentences; makes email a tool for connecting with people to help achieve your goals, rather than an incessant and miserable task list; and converts all action items into possible next steps, to be judged against the other tasks in your life, with only the truly important ones ever seeing the light of day. Here's how you do it.

Getting the GIST (Goals, Impact, Speed, Timing)

Evolution wired our brains to survive a bear attack, not navigate the mundane complexities of modern human existence. To our brain's System 1, almost every new task is another bear: an urgent, stress-inducing threat, requiring our immediate attention and the maximum of our abilities. This section will help you put each of your action items in its proper context and prioritize it appropriately by assessing the *goals* it is intended to achieve, the *impact* it will have on that goal, the *speed* with which you can get it done, and the *timing* required of it. I gave the system a clever acronym—GIST—because that makes it more likely you will remember it and I will get invited to talk about it on *Good Morning America*.

GOALS

The more frequently you assess and prioritize your goals, the more effective you will be in choosing the right tasks to achieve those goals. Start with your big life goals (your Career Roadmap) and break them down into the ones you have to achieve this year, then this week, and finally the critical goals you want to tackle today.

Over the course of your life. Dedicate regular time to review your Impact Map, Happiness Matrix, and Career Roadmap. Assess your progress toward your life's goals and continuously reassess them.

These will be the big things you imagined in your Eulogy. Carry these aspirations in your heart and use them to set your goals every year, week, and day.

Each year. In the context of your life's goals, each December, write your annual plan for all you intend to achieve personally and professionally in the next twelve months, with specific and measurable outcomes. Use your professional team's targets to orient your work goals, and your Career Roadmap as a guide to setting personal milestones. For instance, if one of your life's goals is to run a successful nonprofit, and your Career Roadmap calls for you to learn how to be a good charity executive director, one element of your annual plan may be to meet with six nonprofit leaders, learn how they succeed in their roles, and hone your development plan. Write it down and commit to doing it this year.

Every week. Every Sunday evening or early Monday morning, review and reorganize your calendar and your to-do list to make significant progress toward your yearly goals. Demand that every meeting and every task align with your aspirations for the year; every week needs to get you at least 2 percent closer to achievement of your annual plan. On many high-performing teams, each person writes up a punch list of important goals and tasks for the week and emails them to the rest of the team every Monday morning. Articulating the week's activities ensures that each person's focus is consistent with the team's goals, and deepens everyone's commitment to each other's success.

Today: the big three. Ben Franklin's day planner had printed at the top "What good shall I do this day?" and at the bottom "What good did I do this day?" I love this way of framing your day. You know your goals for your life, your year, your week—now ask yourself, "What two or three things will I get done today to come closer to those goals?" Write them down and prioritize them above everything else today.

Frame your goals and to-do list tasks with outcomes and actions ("achieve–by" framework). For a goal or a task to be useful, it needs to state the exact outcome to be achieved and how it will be accomplished: *achieve* [specific outcome] *by* [specific action]. Whenever possible, state the outcome numerically, so that its accomplishment is unambiguous. A goal to "get in shape" is vague and tough to execute, but "*achieve* 15 percent improvement in mile time and squats per minute *by* performing *The 30-Second Body* routine six days a week" provides clarity, direction, and motivation. Similarly, "discuss sales performance with team" will get some people together to chat about sales, whereas "*achieve* 10 percent of $500,000 incremental revenue goal *by* brainstorming ideas for new products we can sell, assigning owners, and enforcing deadlines" will lead to action. Applying the "achieve–by" framework to all your goals and tasks will ensure that your efforts are driving to an important and successful result.

With your goals clearly articulated, the first step of GIST is complete. You are now in a position to judge each task as it attempts to invade your life by first assessing those possible actions against the impact they can have on your goals.

IMPACT

Everything feels like a big deal when it first hits your list, but to be effective, you have to assess the true impact of each action item with the cold detachment of a task assassin.

Importance. Your potential tasks range from "achieve $50,000 budget approval by preparing PowerPoint for quarterly business review" to "achieve new pants by going to the Gap." The former is, overall, more important, but if you never do the latter, you will be giving that presentation in your underwear. Your success in identifying which actions will truly have the biggest impact will largely determine whether you achieve your goals.[*] For every task, ask yourself:

- "If only this gets done, how much closer am I to achieving my goal?"

---

[*] The ability to focus on important items is one of the critical habits Steven Covey identifies in *The Seven Habits of Highly Effective People*, a book that has near biblical status with ambitious people and that I highly recommend.

- "If this does not get done, how much further am I from achieving my goal?"

Assess and mark each action's importance #low, #medium, or #high based on the impact it will have on your goals (we will get to the tools you will use to record and organize these later in this chapter, as well as the reason for the # marks). For the moment, ignore the urgency of the task—the fact that the presentation is due Monday or next quarter is addressed later. For now, focus only on how important the task is to your goals.

Leverage. Some tasks are the gifts that keep on giving, as they pay off repeating or compounding benefits. Imagine you have these two actions on your list:

- Achieve 10 percent improvements to next year's sales by completing commission data entry, comparing results, and recommending improvements.

- Achieve 10 percent improvement to team productivity by completing negotiation with data entry outsourcing firm.

The first task produces a single output and requires data entry. The second task, however, creates a new capability and can do your data entry for you. If you do the second task first, it will make the first task take much less time. The second task has *leverage*. When a task has high leverage, and is aligned to your goals, its impact is likely to be #high. Here are some other examples of tasks with leverage:

- **Reducing.** Eliminating that which wastes your time pays off perpetually, whether it is setting email filters to lessen time spent in email (more on this soon), canceling unnecessary meetings, or removing distractions that tempt your System 1 away from your goals.

As Antoine de Saint-Exupéry wrote, "Perfection is achieved not when there is nothing more to add, but when there is nothing left to take away."

- **Organizing.** If you clean your apartment, but your drawers and closets are disorganized, the place will be a mess again in no time. However, if you create a system for where things go, they will go there, and they will stay there, and you will do a lot less cleaning in the future. You'll find the same with effective systems and processes at work. If you are going to do something like this task again, consider a system or process to facilitate or replace the activity.

- **Automating.** Rather than pay your bills, set up each of your bills to be automatically paid on your credit card or from your checking account—now you never have to pay bills again. Similarly, if you find yourself repeatedly making the same reply to emails, create canned responses or an autoreply (more on email later this chapter). If you are reading this book sometime after the year 2040, please refer to the operating manual of your personal humanoid robot assistant for more great ways to automate tasks that currently consume your personal time.

- **Networking.** Building your network offers all kinds of compounding benefits, as we will discuss in chapter 9. Similarly, contributing to the recruiting, interviewing, and training of great teammates makes the entire team more effective. Investing in people tends to have high leverage.

- **Learning.** Picking up skills that improve your overall productivity—whether a hard skill, like memoriz-

ing the quick keys in Gmail, or a soft skill, like
learning how to read microexpressions in people's
faces to better understand what they are thinking—
can increase the impact or decrease the time required
for hundreds of actions you will take in the coming
months.

Setting clear goals and understanding the impact that every potential task can have on those goals ensures you are working on the
right things. Another consideration is how much impact you can get
from the time you invest in something, i.e., the speed with which you
can finish the task.

SPEED

The impact of a task on your goals is not the only consideration—
how long it will take to complete that task and when you will have
time to do it are also critical considerations.

Time to complete. Because we were raised by a school system
built on lengthy tasks—writing a paper, completing a project, studying for a test—we tend to associate these longer-cycle tasks with our
most important work. And while that is sometimes the case, it is often
true that quicker actions have just as much impact. Asking someone
for advice, walking down the hall to change someone's perspective,
proactively calling a cranky customer, or spending a few minutes using a new competitor's product are just a few examples of quick, high-
impact actions in your arsenal. Moreover, you can accomplish a
number of these actions in the time it takes to complete one long task.
Knowing which tasks you can complete quickly is a powerful tool for
organizing your time.

Matching the task to the moment. Thirty free minutes between
meetings is a valuable block of time for accomplishing your goals. For
some reason—poor planning, naïve optimism, or masochism—people
regularly try to use these thirty minutes to complete the ninety-
minute project at the top of their to-do list. They get started, slowly at

first, then, just as they get a little momentum, they're pulled away to the next meeting. They come back, get reoriented, make a little progress, and then the next obligation interrupts. Somehow, over three or four thirty-minute blocks of time, almost no work gets done.

Context switching—i.e., moving from thinking about one topic to thinking about another—is massively destructive to your productivity, costing as much as fifteen incremental minutes each time you try to pick up where you left off. To avoid this pitfall, the GIST system matches your projects to the appropriate blocks of time. When you have only a few free minutes, you will focus on quickly completing easy action items, like replenishing your deodorant supply from Amazon (which, I hope, you will make a recurring delivery so you also get *leverage*). When you have longer periods of time, like the few hours between dinner and bed, or your early morning, you will focus intensely on more involved projects. As each task hits your radar, assess whether it will be a #quick one, a #long one, or something in between.

TIMING

When your to-do list task has to be completed and where it must be done are also important factors we will note in this system to optimally sequence tasks.

Deadline. If there is a deadline, such as your boss wants it before close of business today, or the Nick Jonas tickets go on sale at eight a.m. sharp Friday, then you will have to do it in that time frame or decide not to do it at all.

Time and location. Some tasks, like calling on a customer, must be done during business hours. Some, like fixing the garbage disposal, need to be done at home. Duh.

With the GIST framework in mind, we are ready to handle the first step of getting sh*t done: managing and organizing inbound action items in the most efficient manner possible.

Getting Organized and Capturing Your Tasks

The tasks come nonstop, and you need a system to handle and prioritize them. The average person receives eighty-eight business emails per day, checks email nearly every hour of work, uses her phone more than 150 times per day, and attends sixty-two meetings per month (with 90 percent of us multitasking or daydreaming through them). Rarely do five minutes pass without more tasks added to our pile. Here follows a simple, cheap, and elegant system to capture and organize everything.

You will need three simple tools to organize your life:

> **Index cards.** Tasks, ideas, important facts, and inspiration strike throughout the day, whether from a meeting with your boss or a serendipitous discussion in the elevator. You need to capture these notes quickly, without the socially off-putting act of pulling out your smartphone or computer while someone is talking to you (yes, it is off-putting; please stop doing that). I carry three-by-five-inch index cards, conjoined with a mini binder clip, and a small pen in my jacket or back pocket all day. The notes for each meeting are recorded here, as are tasks that need to be sorted and handled later when I'm in action mode. (If you want a classier option, Levenger.com sells leather index card holders and thicker index cards.)*
>
> I strongly advise index cards over a notebook. A notebook takes up space, needs to be schlepped everywhere, and, if lost or forgotten, robs the owner of months' worth of notes. Index cards, on the other hand, fit elegantly in your jacket pocket, jeans pocket, or purse. When scribbling in your notebook, you look like an undergraduate in a history seminar; when you pull out your discreet index card to take a quick note, you look like a baller.

---

* I do not get paid for endorsements of these apps or any other companies or products I recommend in the book, FYI.

Evernote. Evernote is, as of this writing, one of the leading products for storing notes. It has been downloaded over 100 million times and is a favorite among the productivity minded. Like its competitor products Google Keep, Microsoft OneNote, Simplenote, Springpad, Basecamp, and whatever else has been invented since I wrote this, Evernote allows you to save notes typed directly in the app, written in the app, scanned, or photographed and uploaded. It is easy to organize, sort, and search notes, and it can even search out words you wrote by hand. Evernote is where your index cards go at the end of each day. You can use the app to scan each note you take and save it as its own note, or add it to a collection of other notes. When I walk into, say, a monthly product review, I simply open Evernote and pull up the collection of past notes for that meeting for easy reference. This system is also convenient for storing whiteboard drawings, receipts, tax documents, and all the pictures my daughter has drawn of ninjas, firemen, and ninja firemen.

Wunderlist (Microsoft To-Do). In 2011, a German start-up team launched Wunderlist, an exceptional app for tracking action items that gained fame among the organizationati and grew to be used by over 13 million people. Microsoft later acquired the company for $100 million, discarded its playful German moniker, and gave it the cheeky and fun-loving name Microsoft To-Do. We'll just call it MTD from here on out.

I love MTD, but there are numerous similar products that you may prefer, like Evernote's list feature, Remember the Milk, Google Tasks, Astrid, Things, and others. (This is a serious commitment, so you are going to want to find the app right for you.)*

---

* If you want to shop around, Appcrawlr.com is, at the time of this writing, a good source for discovering and comparing apps.

MTD allows you to capture action items, manage multiple to-do lists, create folders to organize to-do lists by goal or other organizing principle, set reminders for time-sensitive items, assign tasks to people, and use hashtags to easily search and review action items that share characteristics.

That's it: a few bucks' worth of index cards, a pen, and these two apps on your smartphone and we are ready to go.

Applying the GIST Method

Next, we will create a pile of index cards, covered in new tasks, and quickly turn it into a prioritized, sorted, easy-to-manage list of action items.

1. **Take simple notes on your index cards.** In each meeting, format an index card by writing the date, meeting name, and attendees at the top. Jot down any important information you would like to remember throughout the meeting. Most importantly, quickly capture any action items that arise (shorthand is okay for now; you will process and prioritize these later), indicated with an unchecked box, like this:

   ☐ Call Tom re: project deadline extension

2. **Save important notes to Evernote.** Many of your index cards will have notes you will want to refer to later. Scan them into Evernote and save them. You can use folders to sort top-level categories (Marketing, Sales, One-on-Ones, Tax Receipts, etc.), and then set up subcategories to keep a running list of notes for each specific meeting or initiative. For instance, you might have a folder called "One-on-One Meetings," under which is a note called "Meetings with Jordan," within which you store the index cards

from those meetings with Jordan. Later, you can retrieve these notes by poking around in the folder, by searching for "Jordan," or by searching for any of the words you jotted down in that meeting (the software recognizes handwriting as well).

3. **Capture action items in MTD.** A couple of times each day, transfer action items from your index cards to MTD. First, add them to the main checklist, called "In-Box"— this is the waiting area, where tasks are sort of like planes circling the runway, waiting to be prioritized and sorted. Then apply the GIST method.

4. **Apply GIST.** Rewrite each action item so that it expresses the goal you are trying to achieve ("achieve–by"). Add a hashtag for the impact this item can have on your goal (#low, #medium, #high), the speed with which it can be done (#quick, #long), and, if applicable, the necessary timing (needs to be done at #work, #home, #weekend, #morning, etc.). For instance:

   - Achieve 10 percent sales productivity improvement by identifying best practices to implement in sales training. #high #long

   - Achieve 5 percent app performance improvement by sending top five bugs to engineering and requesting plan to resolve. #medium #quick

   - Achieve a suit that fits properly by bringing it to the tailor. #low #quick #weekend

(These hashtags will act as simple filters when we return later to complete these action items.)

5. **Tag #owner.** Many action items will be gated by someone else, either to whom you have delegated the work or

from whom you are awaiting a response. Mark that person here. Try to use the same naming taxonomy for people, so that later it is easy to find all the action items involving a given person. This tactic is especially helpful in preparing for a meeting with someone, as you can pull all related action items by clicking on his or her name in MTD. For instance, before my meeting with Sarah Jones from sales operations, I can quickly pull up:

- Grow top accounts 5 percent by increasing account support; first, get customer list from sales ops. #high #quick #sjones

- Win back 10 percent of lapsed accounts; review historical customer spend analysis with sales ops, identify best targets. #high #long #sjones

6. **Add detail if helpful.** You can add subtasks, additional notes, and attachments to an action item in MTD if it will be helpful to you to have that additional detail when it comes time to tackle the action. You can also set an alarm, though it is probably best to do this only when there is an actual deadline. If you try to put the date by which you would like to do each task, in order to prioritize them, you will spend half your life resetting the dates you set too ambitiously the week before.

7. **Create separate lists.** I find it valuable to file to-dos into different lists and arrange those into folders for quick reference. An example follows, though you should tailor the categories to the needs and focus areas of your own life.

WORK: *To-do list tasks and professional priorities*

- Focus This Week—Tasks to achieve this week's goals go here.

- Delegated—Action items that other people owe to you are tracked here.

- Later—Things that do not need to be addressed soon but you don't want to forget go here.

PERSONAL: *Anything related to my personal life and my family*

- Activities—If you hear there is a new polar bear at the zoo you want to see, you can note it here. Check this list before laying out your calendar for the upcoming weekend.

- Books to Read—Keep track of all the interesting books recommended to you here, and refer to the list when you are ready for a new book, so that you may pick the one most relevant to your current areas of challenge or interest.

- Gift Ideas—If you, like me, always think of good Mother's Day gifts the week after Mother's Day, put them here and refer back later.

- Home—Sexy action items like "get sink fixed" and "buy Parmesan cheese" go here.

FEEDBACK: *Coaching opportunities for your teammates and yourself*

- Team—Capture feedback for your teammates in real time and share it in a future one-on-one meeting, such as "Stop yelling so much in meetings, #jerry." When you sit down with Jerry and pull up action items assigned to him, you will see his feedback in the same search results.

- Self—Self-criticism and feedback from others goes here—check it regularly to make sure you are constantly improving.

Just tapping in MTD the word "#quick" or "#sjones" will pull up every open action item that has that hashtag, making it easy for you to prepare, sort, prioritize, and execute. Next, we will take a detour to focus specifically on handling the work that comes to you via your most challenging channel—email. Finally, we will turn to how to best prioritize these actions and optimize your day to get the most done.

Email

You now possess the tools for recording notes on index cards, saving notes in Evernote, and capturing and tagging action items in MTD. Next comes a simplified approach to the true bane of your existence, that digital hellhole called email.* Employed Americans spend 6.3 hours a day checking business and personal email. That is because they are using it wrong. As a key tool in your productivity toolkit, it is important that you deploy email effectively, using these primary approaches and pro tips for email air traffic control.

Email is not your job. Go to your employer's job openings page and read some of the job descriptions; you will see that none of them includes the phrase "incessantly check email." Email is not your job—achieving your personal and business goals is your job, and rarely will you come out of an hour of email self-loathing and think, "I've really nailed my goals today." It is a distraction, a necessary evil, and some-

---

* "But our start-up uses Slack!" Congratulations, here is a cookie. Eighty percent of the advice in this chapter still applies. The other 20 percent will be helpful to you when you get bought by a big company and they make you install Outlook on your computer.

thing that needs to be tamed and controlled for you to maximize your productivity.

Email is not your to-do list. MTD is your to-do list. If you also use email as your to-do list, saving every email in the in-box until you do the job, then you have two to-do lists, and it is nearly impossible to prioritize between the two. Every time you check your email you look again and again at the big items that you need to tackle over the next week or so and have a heart attack. Instead, treat email the same way you treat all other inbound tasks: assess each one in the context of your goals, file and tag it in MTD, clear it from your email in-box, and deal with the action item at the appropriate time.

Email should be a batch process. Very few jobs require that you respond to an email in less than eight hours. So why are you checking your email every thirty minutes? Or, worse, allowing your email to present a pop-up distraction on your computer or push notification on your phone while you are working on your actual priorities? As we will discuss in the "Focus!" section of this chapter, you work best in intense bursts of sixty to ninety minutes with no distraction. You will be most productive if you set aside a few blocks of time each day to focus on resolving your email, then, at all other times, shut it off.

There are five kinds of email. Quickly and accurately identifying which type of email you have received will allow you to deploy strategies to achieve your goals with maximum efficiency.

1. *Junk*—Whether it is an email from Banana Republic telling you that turtlenecks are now 20 percent off or a mass email from a colleague telling everyone something that they really don't need to know, this stuff is wasting years of your life. *We are going to eradicate junk emails.*

2. *Waste of Time*—These emails are not junk per se, and each was sent to you by a well-meaning individual, and you feel an urge to respond, but it is a waste of your time. These

emails come disguised as interesting information, updates on initiatives, and requests for follow-up on initiatives that are not directly related to your business or personal goals. *We are going to quickly resolve or ignore waste-of-time emails.*

3. *Quick Win*—These emails are related to your goals and can be handled in less than sixty seconds. Responding to them gets you closer to achieving your plan. They say things like "Yes, I would love to discuss budgets with you—can you do Friday at 2:00?" or "You asked for a marketing expert to help with your project—would Lisa Walker work?" *We are going to bang out these quick-win emails in a way that leads to clear and rapid action.*

4. *Project*—These emails are related to your goals and come heavy with instructions from important people, hairy problems, insights that will take time to understand, and/ or gigantic attachments. Resolving will take some time, from five or ten minutes to hours. *We are going to transfer the action items related to these project emails to MTD.*

5. *Article*—People send you articles they think you will find interesting or, more often, that they think will make you find them interesting. At this very moment there are millions of articles on topics relevant to your goals that you are not reading. Odds are, the one you just received is not the most important one. *We are going to file this article and read it when it is the most important article in the world relevant to your goals.*

Strategies to master each kind of email. Each time you approach email, plan to move through your in-box as fast as possible and direct each plane to the runway where it belongs. Identify each email as one of the five above and apply these simple techniques to eliminate it, delegate it, or put it on your MTD. Your goal is to get out of email and get back to the highest-impact priority actions on your to-do list by executing the following tactics.

1. **Eliminate junk**. Ever notice how many of these promotional emails are marketed to you with the phrase "Don't miss out on . . ." You know, I have yet to have one of my goals undermined by the fact that I do not receive regular updates from my telecom provider or local wine store. There are myriad tactics for getting rid of these. You can:

   - *Unsubscribe:* It takes a few steps, but saves you hours of time in the future. Do this for the vast majority of the third-party emails you receive.

   - *Filter:* Most email providers offer you this ability to set rules to move certain emails to other folders or to skip your in-box altogether. So if you cannot bear the thought of not having Tory Burch coupons in your life, set up a filter to send them to a coupon folder that you can check when you have the urge to splurge. This is also a great tactic for emails you receive from someone at work that are not useful. As it is socially frowned upon to ask a colleague, "Can you please stop emailing me? I'm not interested in your project updates," instead you can set a filter to have a certain person's emails with certain keywords or characteristics skip your in-box.

   - *Mute:* When you are one of fifty people copied on an email thread that repeatedly moves to the top of your in-box with yet another person replying, "Way to go, Janette!" you can mute the conversation by selecting the email and selecting the mute or ignore feature that is available from most email service providers.

   - *Alter ego:* Some dirtbag websites not only spam you, but sell your email address, making it hard to ever eliminate all the junk. The best solution is to limit giving out your email address to only credible sites. You can also consider having a secondary email account that you use just for signing up for websites. Alternatively, if you are a Gmail user, you can take advantage of a little-known feature that allows you to customize your email address by adding the plus (+) symbol and some text between your email handle and the "@ gmail.com" part. So, if your email address is johnny .santiago@gmail.com and you sign up for a website by using the address johnny.santiago+junkmail@gmail .com, you can then set up a filter to have all emails to your "+junkmail" address go right to the trash.

From now on, be a merciless destroyer of these junk messages that are clogging your in-box and robbing you of the focus you need to achieve your goals.

2. **Ignore or quickly resolve waste-of-time emails.** The majority of emails in your in-box are these waste-of-timers. Most often, they come in the form of something that someone else wants or cares about, but is not relevant to your goals. There are hundreds of varieties, but three easy ways to handle these:

- *Just say no:* Unwanted solicitations, like "Hi, Mike, I was wondering if I could have a fifteen-minute call to tell you about our industry-leading solution for creating massive shareholder value with better HR tools . . ." warrant a kind no: "Thanks so much for thinking of us, but we're not looking to change our HR tools at this time. If things ever change, I'll definitely reach out to you. Have a great day!" If the person follows up and presses you further for a meeting, just treat it like junk.

- *Assign it and say good-bye:* Many emails that come to you are useful but better placed with someone else. For instance, the note may say, "I'm interested in an advertising partnership with your company," but you do not handle advertising partnerships. In this case, forward it to someone who does: "Val, I know you guys are often looking for advertising partnerships, so I am sending this in case you are interested. No response is necessary to me nor the inquirer, but if you are interested, feel free to contact him directly." And to the original emailer, say good-bye: "Thanks for thinking of us. I have forwarded on to the right folks in advertising partnerships and encouraged them to get back to you if there is interest. Have a great day!"* If you receive further solicitation, treat it like junk.

- *Pocket veto:* You feel an urge to respond to every email, but, again, many emails sent to you are not aligned to your goals. And every time you reply to an email, you receive two more emails in return. It's like getting a gremlin wet.† So, for each email, before you react, ask yourself if replying will actually help you achieve your goals, and if not, just clear the email from your in-box. More often than not, people forget that they sent it to you and it never comes up again. The opposite of the pocket veto is the dreaded "reply all." According to

---

* Pro tip: The Canned Response—Some email programs let you save a canned response, like the ones above, and quickly insert them into an email. If your email provider doesn't, you can just save your favorite canned responses as a draft email and copy them as needed. This can save you hours a month.

† In the '80s hit movie *Gremlins*, a gremlin is an adorable Muppet creature that a lonely boy bought from a mysterious elderly gentleman with the promise that he would not get it wet, feed it after midnight, or expose it to bright light. Of course, he gets the gremlin wet, which makes it multiply, and allows it to eat late, which turns it evil, and then uses bright lights to save the town from the marauding hordes of evil gremlins. Obviously, *Gremlins* is a Christmas movie.

one study, every hundred people needlessly copied on an email results in eight hours of lost productivity. So, next time you get an email congratulating Jim on closing a big deal, please consider sending directly to Jim some heartfelt congratulations on his efforts and success, rather than replying, "Great job, Jim," to all eighty-five people on the email thread.

3. **Bang out the quick wins.** You've quickly evacuated the unimportant emails, now on to the ones that you can quickly handle to advance your march toward your goals. This email exchange is how *not* to do it:

"Mike, I am glad you reached out. I would be glad to meet with you to hear your pitch and consider a partnership. Floyd."
"Thanks so much, Floyd—would it be okay if I bring my head of partnerships, too? I know she would be a valuable addition."
"Mike—you are welcome to. Thanks."
"Great! How is this Friday at 9:00 a.m.?"
"I'm sorry, I am not in New York on Friday."
"Anytime Monday?"
"It is a long weekend away with family. Could do Tuesday."
"Oh, man, we are on the road Tuesday. How about Wednesday at 10:00 a.m.?"
No reply.
"Hi, Floyd, I haven't heard back from you about Wednesday. Can we meet then? Another time?"
No reply.

You can see what went wrong here, and everyone does it. It is important to remember that email is not live chat, and the counterparty is often not standing by waiting for your reply, especially if he or she is a senior professional or has read this book. The key to turning a potential quick-win email into an actual quick win is to deliver clear instructions that get the job done. Rather than the train wreck above, try:

"Floyd, thank you. I will make myself available anytime Friday morning, Monday after 2:00, or anytime Thursday. If any of those times works for you, just reply your confirmation and I will be there. If not, let me know a time or two that does work for you and I will accommodate. I will come to you at the fourth floor of 111 Eighth Avenue, unless you suggest a different location. I will bring my head of partnerships, unless you prefer I come alone. I look forward to connecting in person. Warmly, Mike."

"Mike—Tuesday 10:00 a.m. at 111 Eighth is perfect. See you both then. Floyd."

The difference between these two exchanges is obvious. When you reply to a quick-win email with clear next steps that minimize the back-and-forth, you shorten the distance to successful completion, saving time and maximizing the likelihood of achieving your objective.

4. **Transfer project emails to MTD.** How many times has it happened that you get an unexpected assignment sent to your email and jump right in to execute it, only to reach the end of the workday and realize that your higher-priority tasks are still waiting for your attention? Project emails can consume your day. To effectively manage one of these items, simply:

    - *Capture it in MTD:* These emails are tasks like any other and should be handled using the GIST method as we discussed earlier: restating the email as a goal and assigning the impact, speed, and timing.

    - *File it in "Active Projects":* Move the email out of your inbox and into an Active Projects folder, where you can grab it quickly when you need it, but where it will not clog your in-box.

5. **File articles and read later.** You have an ambitious set of goals for your day and a number of important meetings. During a thirty-minute break you turn to email to quickly scan for quick wins that can help advance your goals. But, wait, what is this you see? A colleague has sent an article titled "Seven Ways to Be a More Effective Leader." You want to be a more effective leader—and had no idea there were seven different ways to do it! This must be read right now!

Ridiculous. And yet we are all guilty of doing it. Of course, many articles are valuable and insightful, but what are the odds that one you did not even request is suddenly the highest-priority use of your time at the moment you opened your email? Rather than feel compelled to read it, file this article away in any of the popular apps or browser extensions that are out there for saving articles. Personally, I use Pocket, which has around 20 million users and works seamlessly with news apps like Flipboard and Twitter. With the Pocket browser extension in Chrome and Safari, you can open any article and click the "save to Pocket" function, and the article will be tucked away for when you are looking to spend a dedicated period of time reading articles.

Later, when you open Pocket, you will notice that some of the articles that you considered reading on the spot are, in fact, far less important than others that you have saved. Seeing all the articles in one place gives you the ability to prioritize what you read and maximize the value of your reading time.

DON'T FILE. DON'T DELETE. ARCHIVE AND SEARCH.

In the beginning, there were only two email programs for work, one called Lotus Notes, the other Microsoft Outlook. They had terrible search functionality, so it was very difficult to find an email unless you meticulously saved it in the right place in your folder hierarchy and could hunt it down later. Work email also had very limited storage, so human beings in those days spent many hours clearing out old emails and feeling conflicted over the decision to delete certain emails forever. Today, even though most email programs have an excellent search function and virtually unlimited storage, some people still feel the pain of this phantom limb and waste time filing their emails in special folders named for each initiative. To be much more efficient with email, do the following:

Archive—You can save any email you like forever by archiving it instead of deleting it. In some email programs, archiving is the default option. For email programs that do not offer archiving, you can replicate the feature by creating a folder called "Archive" and moving emails there instead of deleting them.

Search—Most email programs use standard logic that makes searching highly effective. You can just search for keywords when the content is very specific—for instance, "incriminating photos from Cancun" will likely do the trick for that case. Other times, you are looking for something more generic and you need the search to work harder for you. With a few minutes of practice in your email search box you can nail this invaluable skill; here are a few examples to help you along:

- Looking for an exact phrase? Use quotes to return only exact matches—search: "Kanye West tickets"

- Looking for something someone sent to another person? Search: from:jon to:debbie

- Looking to make a search more specific by eliminating irrelevant results? Search: "Red Hot Chili Peppers" -recipes (i.e., don't return any results that include the word "recipes")

- Looking for a presentation someone sent prior to 2017? Search: "has:attachment before:2017/01/01"

The more effectively you can search and archive, the easier it will be for you to clear messages from your in-box and retrieve them later, as needed, avoiding the hassle of filing, and improving your productivity significantly.

LEARN QUICK KEYS AND MESSAGE THREADS

Imagine if, in order to navigate the screen on your smartphone, you had to reach a foot or two away from the device for a tethered mouse that controls a cursor on the screen. Your productivity would suffer greatly, not to mention your sanity. And yet most of us are in the habit of using a mouse when at a desktop computer, repeatedly pulling our fingers from the keyboard, breaking our flow, and losing precious hours, two seconds at a time. By learning the quick keys of your email program, you will, over time, process email much faster. For instance, if you use Gmail and enable quick keys, and you want to return to the in-box to respond to the second email in the list, simply do this: type *g i* [go to in-box] *k* [go to next message in thread], hit enter [open email], type *r* [reply].

Another option in most email programs: rather than receive each reply to a message thread as a separate item in your in-box, view entire chains of emails as a single conversation thread. This is the default format in Gmail and an option in most other programs. It is significantly more efficient to view all the related emails under the same subject as one conversation view. Once it is archived, the emails under that subject stay together, making it easier in the future to search for them.

Are we having fun now or what?

BOOMERANG IMPORTANT MESSAGES

Boomerang is a browser add-on that allows you to send delayed emails and reminders from Gmail, Outlook, and other Web-based email programs. You can set emails to reappear in your in-box at a certain day or time or to come back to you if no one responds in a certain period of time. You can also compose emails and have Boomerang hold them to be sent later. This eliminates the need to leave emails in your in-box that are awaiting further action from others without worrying that something will fall through the cracks.

WHEN THINGS GET UGLY, TRIAGE THE IN-BOX

Remember that show *Grey's Anatomy*, where these abnormally attractive doctors would repeatedly perform acts of medical and romantic excellence with charm and grace, until the writers would mix things up, with something like a plane crashing into a submarine, and the doctors would have to scramble to intubate or defibrillate every extra the studio could afford?* Sometimes that happens to your email in-box. You're concentrating your energy on handling your normal inbound traffic, organizing your to-do list items, nailing quick wins, when suddenly a day of twelve meetings coincides with an urgent request from your boss's boss, and next thing you know, you have 115 unread messages that all appear vaguely career threatening. In these situations, even the most productive and focused among us can lose control of the situation: the in-box becomes overwhelming and unmanageable and can no longer be handled in short-burst sessions as recommended. To get back on track, create a temporary folder called

---

* I know, you are thinking, "didn't you say to stop watching TV, Mike?" I saw *Grey's Anatomy* a couple of times and I'm not proud of it.

"Triage," scan quickly through your in-box for anything that looks like it needs to be handled but is not urgent, and move it to your new folder. Set a task in MTD to handle your Triage folder, prioritized as appropriate. In the meantime, you can return to the relative calm of a more governable in-box.

Now Let's Get It Done!

The average worker, according to one study, works nearly eight hours a day but is only producing useful output 1.5 hours a day. As a result, the average worker does not achieve extraordinary results in his or her career. To achieve our goals, we have to be much more efficient with our time. Here is how.

DO THE RIGHT THINGS

Applying GIST to each of your action items has set you up to be highly productive when you tackle them. Now turn to your MTD and follow these steps to determine what to do next:

Goals—Reflect on your goals for the day and the week. Challenge yourself to focus on your true goals. "Empty my in-box," "catch up on reading," "attend team off-site event" are activities, not goals. "Achieve $500,000 of new business by completing Marriott deal" is a goal, as is "Achieve insight into career in design by meeting three designers." Identify which goals you plan to tackle today, and give first-priority attention to the action items aligned to these goals.

Impact—Identify the items on your list that will have the biggest impact on those goals. This should be easy, as you have already marked each item #high, #medium, or #low. Search MTD for "#high" and start there.

Speed—Match the length of project to the time you have right now. You marked your tasks #quick or #long in MTD. If you are sitting down for a quick thirty minutes of work before a meeting, focus on the items aligned to your goals that are #high and #quick. If you have carved out a few hours, now is the rare window of time you have to resolve those that are #high and #long.

Timing—Do what's due. Items that are aligned to your goals, that have high impact, that match the length of time you have available to work, and that are due this week are your highest priorities. If the item does not align to your goals, is not high impact, or does not fit well into the amount of time you have to dedicate to it, you have to use your judgment—you may need to deprioritize it. It may be true that your taxes are due Tuesday, but if you have other urgent matters that have more impact on your goals, then your taxes should wait or, better, be outsourced all together. (Before you freak out: 80 percent of taxpayers will receive a refund, which means there is no penalty for late filing; the other 20 percent face about a 2 percent penalty if they file two weeks late.)

FOCUS!

Now you've got your goals clear and the right task identified, you sit down, ready to conquer the world.

Let's see, here's our first task: Achieve $500,000 revenue goal by writing detailed proposal to boss to get budget approval for two new hires. #high #long

Okay, awesome, here we go. Starting our task, computer open . . . Oh, wait, the game is on, let's just check ESPN real quick, will only take ten seconds . . . Okay, got the score, good stuff, ready to get working . . . John—I am writing to request . . . Oh, my phone is buzzing, what do we got here, ooh, push alert from New York Times, let's check that out . . . Great article! Glad I read that, and all the other most emailed articles of the day. Okay, where was I? Oh, right: Dear John, I would like to . . . It's been half an hour, I wonder what the score of the game is . . .

Most of us naturally suck at focusing. It's not our fault, it's our System 1 lizard brain running the show up there. We have to create the right environment for our System 2 brain to kick in and help us do our important work. Here's how to do it:

Feel the flow. The first few minutes that you work on a task are the hardest and least productive; your mind constantly wanders, your System 1 pulling you away to the short-term relief of various distractions. But the longer you stay focused, the easier it becomes for you to stay focused. Your brain houses a chemical called norepi-nephrine, which increases arousal and alertness, promotes vigilance, enhances formation and retrieval of memory, and focuses attention. Studies have shown that, as you remain focused on a task, your brain rewards you with the release of this powerful chemical. You know this feeling: your thoughts become clearer, the words come faster, your fingers or thumbs start banging out more and more words per minute.

Start "single-tasking." One of the themes of this book is that we do not know our brains as well as we think we do, and high per-formance requires adapting our habits and operations to maximize the productivity of our brains. One of the most blatant examples of this is multitasking: you think you are a good multitasker, but you are not. Don't believe me? Let's ask renowned neuroscientist Earl Miller:

"People can't multitask very well, and when people say they can, they're deluding themselves . . . You're not paying attention to one or two things simultaneously, but switching between them very rap-idly."

Dr. Miller has been studying the brain for over thirty-five years, so how about rather than continue to delude ourselves, we believe this brilliant scientist, and stop trying to surreptitiously check emails while sitting in a staff meeting?

Multitasking makes you less productive because the cost of switching between tasks is high. Researchers from the University of Illinois teamed with Microsoft to track the productivity of their workers in the face of multiple simultaneous tasks: jumping from spreadsheet work to email. They found that when a user switched from the serious task that required their focus to another, say, an email alert, it took them, on average, fifteen minutes to return to the original task. In another study, Stanford University researchers gave a challenging task to a group of people who were active online multitaskers and a group who were not. The group with a history of multitasking showed a diminished ability to control their attention and to distinguish more important information from irrelevant information.

There is a very high cost to multitasking. It is time to rethink how you work and focus if you want to have the productivity needed to achieve your goals. It's time to commit to single-tasking.

Block interruptions. External interruptions are as damaging to your productivity as self-inflicted multitasking. Researchers asked subjects to complete a series of tasks on a computer that required them to remember their place in the sequence. The researchers measured the subjects' performance, and then started interrupting them and measuring the performance again. The error rates of the volunteers in the study doubled following a 2.8-second interruption and tripled following a 4.4-second interruption. The shorter interruption, 2.8 seconds, is the time it takes you to silence your cell phone; to say, "I'll call him back"; or to dismiss an alert that someone has just liked your status. So close the other windows on your computer, put your phone out of reach, turn off your notifications, go someplace where no one will walk up and bother you, and flow through your work. Like a boss.

Breathe and stop. Multiple times while writing this chapter I have had an itch to do something else, just for a quick second. System 1 is a strong and persistent force. If you give in to that urge, you fall into a downward spiral. When the urge comes, stop, take a breath, remind yourself what you are trying to accomplish, and recommit to your actions. Giving in to distraction is a habit; so is not giving in. Trust me, it's worth it to develop the latter.

And with that, you have the best tools I know for capturing potential action items, organizing them with index cards and digital tools like Evernote and Microsoft To-Do, sorting and prioritizing them using the GIST method, avoiding or extricating yourself from the trap of email, and focusing until you get the right things done. Thanks for sticking with me through this; it will pay off in spades for you and your career success. And the next chapter is a lot more fun, I promise.

PART 4

People: Achieve Impact with Others

No matter your Career Roadmap, your success will depend upon your ability to positively affect other people. Developing your network, influencing others, managing stakeholders, and executing effective meetings will be foundational to your success.[*]

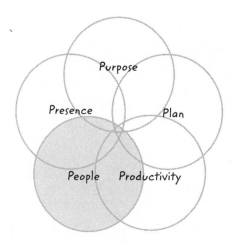

---

[*] Unless you are a hermit or the lone survivor of the robot apocalypse, in which case you may skip this part of the book.

CHAPTER 9

$\longrightarrow$ Networking for a Cause

I tend to think of myself as a one-man wolf pack. But when my sister brought Doug home, I knew he was one of my own. And my wolf pack—it grew by one. So . . . there were two of us in the wolf pack. I was alone first in the pack and then Doug joined in later. And six months ago, when Doug introduced me to you guys, I thought, "Wait a second, could it be?" And now I know for sure—I just added two more guys to my wolf pack.

—ALAN GARNER, THE HANGOVER

Consider this for a moment: who are the people you personally care about, who in turn care about you?

That is your network. And the opportunities for impact in your life will spring from the strength of those relationships.

If you are like most well-adjusted people, the word "networking" evokes images of awkward meet and greets, uninvited solicitations, and disingenuous interactions. Networking, the way many people do it, is kind of gross. Like this:

————Forwarded message————

From: Fred Smith <fmsith@crapleadgencompany.com>

Date: Thursday, January 26, 2017

Subject: Reconnecting with a Fellow Quaker and Disruptive Innovator!

Hi, Michael,

We went to Penn together and are both innovative and disruptive thinkers in our industry. Go, Quakers! Isn't it great that our basketball team just won the league? Also I just realized that we both know Carrie Jones from GE. I am writing because we have a customer solution just perfect for your company to better monetize your content through innovative lead-based b2b . . .

Ugh. I don't know Fred Smith, I don't care about basketball, and I don't really like Carrie Jones from GE. But Fred is deploying these superficial connections to try to get me to buy his lead generation product. It is clumsy, self-interested, and symbolic of how people misunderstand and abuse the concept of networking. People often mistakenly visualize their "network" as a list of names that they can utilize to achieve a personal end goal, which is a mistake. Networking isn't a one-sided thing, and no one is required to help you get what you want simply because you happen to know them, know someone in common with them, or share a common profession.

As networking expert J. Kelly Hoey defines it in her book, *Build Your Dream Network: Forging Powerful Relationships in a Hyper-Connected World*, "Networking is an ongoing process of establishing and strengthening relationships. It is not confined to a single activity such as email introductions or cocktail receptions . . . Networking is always about the people—who they are, how they engage, how they want to be reached, how they cluster—and until you truly internalize that, your networking efforts won't be effective."

If you want to get anywhere, you have to build a good network, and if you want to build an effective network, you must focus on the people on the other side and what you can do for them, rather than what they can offer you. So contrast Fred Smith's out-of-the-blue email request with the people who contacted me in the same week who already had taken the time to establish our relationship before they needed to ask me for anything: the valued former colleague who needed a strong reference for a new job; the work friend who was struggling with her business strategy; the friend on a new career path who needed some introductions in his new field; the mentor who needed help finding his daughter an internship in my industry. For each of them I was willing to drop what I was doing to help because we had an authentic and lasting connection *before* they ever thought to request a favor. These connections are special, valuable, and symbiotic. They constitute what I call a Meaningful Network.

You have four types of personal networks, as the illustration below shows.

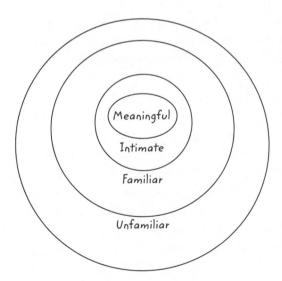

First, there is your Unfamiliar Network of strangers whom you have not met (the largest outer circle). Next, there is your Familiar Network of acquaintances whom you know, but either barely or not all that well. Then, you have an Intimate Network of people you have gotten to know rather well. Finally, there is your Meaningful Network, your true personal network of deep relationships and friendships. Your Meaningful Network will make it possible for you to have the impact with your career and life that you desire. You welcome people into your Meaningful Network in three steps:

1. Bringing people from your Unfamiliar Network to your Familiar Network by making initial contact and forming a connection. Strangers become people you know a little.

2. Bringing people from your Familiar Network to your Intimate Network by getting to know them well and finding some way you can be helpful to them. People you know a little become people you really know.

3. Bringing people from your Intimate Network to your Meaningful Network by investing in making their life better in some important way. People you really know become people you have helped in an impactful way.

A critical element of this process is that you are building a network based on a desire to know, appreciate, and help other people, not a desire to get them to help you. This may be counterintuitive to some readers, especially to the Fred Smiths of the world, but this is the only way to build real and lasting relationships. Think back to your Impact Map, and to all the ways in which you have imagined you can positively affect the world. That map emanates from you *out* to other people, not from other people in to you. The help that you provide others defines your impact and your life. And then something fascinating happens: the relationships you build germinate over the years and come back to help you in some unexpected, often life-changing ways.

So let's get started.

From Unfamiliar Network
to Familiar Network

If you are blessed with being one of those naturally bubbly, friendly extroverts who chats up every stranger in sight, you can probably skip to the next section of this chapter. This section is for people like me who find chatting up a stranger to be one of the most awkward or unnatural acts in the world. Sadly, I spent years encountering people with fascinating and enriching knowledge, insights, and life experiences . . . and failing to even say hello to them. You wouldn't know it today: I have worked for years to develop the simple tools for connecting with others, and I can share some advice.

Let's start with the relatively easiest group of people, those with whom you already share some connection, like working in the same company, attending the same school, or living on the same block. It should be easy to be acquainted with these people; you have a lot in common, and they are eager to meet you. People at work or on your block will be glad, even relieved, when you have finally introduced yourself and eliminated the awkwardness of nodding as you pass each other by. To make the giant leap with someone from Unfamiliar Network to Familiar Network, just do these three simple acts:

1. **Appear warm and friendly.** Albert Mehrabian, professor emeritus of psychology at UCLA, identified in a study that human communications are 55 percent visual (appearance, body language), 38 percent vocal (the tone, volume, cadence of your voice), and 7 percent verbal (what you actually say). So, to initiate contact and welcome someone in from your Unfamiliar Network, give him or her the proper greeting by:

   • opening up your body physically (uncrossing your arms, standing tall, widening your shoulders, exposing your heart to the other person),

- bringing warmth to your face (lifting your chin, making and maintaining eye contact, and smiling),

- stretching your right hand forward (warmly, not aggressively),* and

- saying in a confident voice, "Hi! I'm Mike Steib.† I work down the hall in corporate overhead."

I know, it sounds very basic, but most people, especially introverts, get this wrong, physically closing off their body, pasting on a slightly pained-looking smile, darting their eyes around, and offering a hesitating arm that suggests they're not sure if this encounter warrants a handshake. Or, worse, the discomfort of initial contact leads them to avoid a greeting altogether. If you don't believe me, spend a few minutes watching the pained human interactions at the beginning of your next external meeting at work. Most people are modestly afraid of coming into contact with each other.

You might need to work on the proper greeting in the mirror, and it will take repetition before this feels natural. Maintaining eye contact with a warm and welcoming look when you are dealing with the discomfort of meeting people can take practice. Try it on the person in the car next to you at a stoplight, behind you in line at the grocery, or walking toward you on the sidewalk, and you will be amazed—if you warmly smile at people, they all instinctually smile back.

2. **Initiate a brief but enjoyable conversation.** This begins with how you introduce yourself. If you just say,

---

* It has been written that claiming the top position in a handshake, by twisting your thumb in and facing your palm down, subconsciously communicates to the other person your superiority or dominance in the newly formed relationship. If you do this, you are a douchebag.

† It's most effective if you use your actual name, not mine.

"Hi," a person will just say back, "Hi." If you say, "Hi, I'm Mike Steib. I live in apartment three—I'm the one with the two little kids always tearing down the hallway," he will say back, "Hi, I'm Joe Carlon. I live in apartment six—my girlfriend and I have the boxer terrier you always hear barking." Take one of the things you hear back and turn it into a quick conversation by asking an open-ended question. "It's nice to meet you. Have you always had dogs, Joe?" Keep the conversation positive and simple—don't ask your new acquaintance yet if he believes in true love or climate change.

Without practice, ending a conversation can be just as awkward as starting one. A local politician with thirty years of service once told me that the key to success in politics is saying hello to each person for thirty seconds, and then making "the slip"—off to another voter for another thirty seconds. So, following an exchange of one or two questions and answers, after your new acquaintance finishes a sentence, you can simply stretch out your hand again, smile, and say, "I am really glad to meet you, Joe. I hope I see you and your dog Roosevelt around here again soon."

(If you need more tips on the art of making acquaintances, I would encourage you to read the seminal *How to Win Friends and Influence People*, the obscure but fascinating *It's Not All about "Me,"* and the very fun *How to Make People Like You in 90 Seconds or Less*.)

3. **Remember the person's name.** I am terrible at this. It has taken a ton of practice to get it half-right, so I can at least tell you where we all go wrong. First, in the adrenaline of a new encounter, we just don't hear the name; the person says it, but it doesn't register. You have to make a habit of listening for it, and if you miss it, you just have to ask—"I'm sorry, would you say your name again?" Once

you have registered the person's name, you have three tactics for remembering it, and their relative success for you will depend on how you best learn.

- **Repetition.** For some people, this works. "It's nice to meet you, Joe." "And tell me, Joe, is it hard having a dog in the city?" "It was great to meet you, Joe." As Dale Carnegie writes in the aforementioned *How to Win Friends and Influence People*, "Remember that a person's name is to that person the sweetest and most important sound in any language." Just be careful not to overdo it; it can sound weird if you say someone's name every sentence you speak—I think that in a short conversation you get three, max.

- **Visualization.** Repetition does not work as well for some people, who soon find themselves thinking, "Shoot, what was that name I just kept repeating? And now how am I going to ask him his name again? I just said it to him three times in one conversation." Another option is visualizing the name. If you are a visual learner and you imagine the person's name written on her forehead or on an imaginary name tag or in lights over her head, your likelihood of remembering it goes way up. It depends on what works best for your brain.

- **Associative memory.** The human mind does not function like a filing cabinet, tucking away interesting facts for future use. The mind makes associations and uses those associations to retain important information. For example, try to memorize these words: monkey, train, supermarket, robot, fedora, window, Pepsi.

Right now you're saying them over and over again in your head, trying to force your brain to store them. It's not working. Who won the War of 1812? Where is the

Rock and Roll Hall of Fame located? What was the fifth word in the list I just gave you? See, you forgot. The human mind is capable of operating a particle collider, and yet it can't seem to remember seven words that a three-year-old can say.

Now try this: visualize each of the seven words in association with the next word. A monkey is driving a train. A train rolls past a supermarket. A supermarket has robot store manager. The robot wears a fedora. The fedora blows out the window. You are sitting next to that window, drinking a Pepsi. If you carefully imagine each item interacting with the next item, you will remember it. People who compete in memory championships use similar methods, sometimes also picturing each item in a different room in a mental floorplan (called the method of loci). Joshua Foer's *Moonwalking with Einstein* is an interesting study of how the mind retains information, if you are curious.

Back to remembering our neighbor Joe and his dog Roosevelt with the associative method. Neighbor Joe has a great head of thick black hair. Like Joseph Stalin. Joe Stalin. Joe Stalin put Russians in gulags. Bad guy. But Teddy Roosevelt protected American workers from unfair labor practices. Good guy. Here comes my neighbor with that thick black hair . . . what was his name again? Oh, right! "Nice to see you again, Joe, how is your dog Roosevelt today?" It takes practice, but it works consistently.

Through use of these techniques, you can break down the uncomfortable barriers that separate you from the other people around you, the hundreds of potential acquaintances and future friends who pass through your life each day. By simply smiling, making eye contact, extending a hand, having a brief friendly conversation, and remembering the person's name, you have moved this stranger to your Familiar Network, putting yourself in a position to build a more intimate relationship with the person if you so desire.

From Familiar Network to Intimate Network

You now have a strategy for exuding friendliness, overcoming the awkwardness that exists between strangers, making people comfortable, and remembering their names. The more you do this, the easier it will become, and you will notice the overall positive energy your new approach brings to nearly every situation. But this is only the first step. Next, you have the opportunity to really get to know a subset of people with whom you would like to have a closer connection.

Just about everyone gets this next part wrong. When faced with an interesting new person in our Familiar Network, we tend to make one of two fundamental mistakes. The first is talking about ourselves. We go into overdrive trying to convince him that we are interesting, too. We do not know how long this conversation will last, and have so much to tell him about our fascinating job, impressive college degree, training for the Chicago marathon, and so on. If we don't get to it all, how will he know to like us? As a result, most of us have developed an incredible ability to pivot any conversation back to ourselves. "Oh, you work for the Treasury Department? I majored in finance and economics at Tulane . . ." "You do CrossFit? Cool, I run every morning . . ." And so on. After five or ten minutes of conversation, we know very little about our new friend, other than that he seems to do a lot of things that are somewhat related to the even better things we do. We live up to the expectations of the old joke: *How do you know if someone is a vegetarian? Don't worry, he'll tell you.*

We make this mistake because it feels good to talk about ourselves, to indulge the natural human desire to be understood and appreciated. (After a few filler terms like "and," "the," and "be," the most commonly used word in the English language is "I.") When we do all the talking, we rob our new friend of the opportunity to perform this most essential act. How does that make him feel about us?

How did you feel the last time someone you just met kept interrupting you to tell you all about how wonderful and successful he is? You likely developed, at minimum, a low-grade envy and dislike for the person. And what a sad missed opportunity. We expend all this energy trying to get someone to like us, when all he really desires is the opportunity to get us to like him.

So don't talk about yourself. From now on, rather than approach every interaction as a chance to be known and be impressive, use it as a chance to appreciate someone else by investigating that person's work and interests. "How long have you been doing CrossFit, Jordan? . . . Are you enjoying the results? . . . What are the primary exercises? . . . As a vegetarian, is it hard to get enough protein to support all that weight lifting? . . . People struggle with having good exercise habits—what's your secret? . . . You sound like a determined person—tell me more about what you do at work . . ." Every nugget of information is an opportunity to let the other person tell you all about him- or herself. Approach the conversation with the mind-set of being the batting practice pitcher in your new friend's home run derby of personal greatness. Avoid all temptations to talk about yourself, pivot those questions back to your new friend, and watch how eagerly this person takes the chance to tell you more about his or her passions. The person will love you for it. As famous adman David Ogilvy said, "If you want to be interesting, be interested."

The second mistake we all make, after solipsism, is conversational cowardice, keeping the discussion safe and limited to the surface:

"Have you enjoyed the event?"
"Oh, yes, it's very nice."
"Do you go to many events, Margaret?"
"Three or four a year."
"How nice."
"Yes, it's nice."
"You're right, this one is very nice."

Small talk is a fine way to break the ice with someone in your Unfamiliar Network, but you will never get to know someone until you move into conversations of substance:

> "So did you hear anything at this event relevant to your work, Margaret?"
> "The piece about consumer drone technology was interesting."
> "Do I remember that you work for a defense contractor? How do those small drones fit into the broader national security picture?"
> "Oh, it's a big deal. Imagine a network of internet-connected drones outfitted with sensors that . . ."

Same person, different outcomes. With the first approach, we learned that we both thought the event was nice; in the second we got to learn all about a cutting-edge new technology and more about our new friend's work. By bringing genuine curiosity to our interactions with others, we get to know them better.

People are afraid to have these more intimate conversations, because the counterparty has so much more knowledge on the subject, and we are afraid to look ignorant:

> "Todd, you said you work at a Swiss bank—what do you do there?"
> "Debt capital markets."
> "Oh, cool."

And then you spend the rest of your life not knowing what debt capital markets are and what your new friend actually does for a living because you're too afraid to ask. Guess what? If Todd is worth getting to know, he won't care that you may or may not be familiar with his line of work; in fact, he may be surprised or disappointed when you don't ask him about it—or he may even take that to mean you're not interested in him (and thus why should he bother investing his time in getting to know you, either). Liberating oneself of that fear will open the door to thousands of fascinating conversations:

"I have to admit, Todd, I don't understand the finance industry as well as I would like. Tell me what you all do in debt capital markets."

"Oh, sure! When a company wants to borrow money, we provide capital by selling bonds to investors as part of a syndicate on behalf of the company."

"Syndicate?"

"The company will usually appoint a small group of Investment Banks to aid in the capital raise, and the group is called a syndicate. The group will offer bonds to investors that compete over price."

"Like when I get a mortgage through a mortgage broker?"

"Yes! Similar dynamic, except these mortgages tend to be a couple billion dollars apiece . . ."

Now you are getting a basic understanding of a new business and your new friend is doing something he enjoys, which is talking about his work. You are nodding and smiling and being interested, which is encouraging and satisfying to Todd. You can take this conversation in any number of directions next. Here is a set of questions that are almost always applicable to someone else's work:

- Tell me the business model—who pays whom and who is delivering value or goods or services to whom?

- What advantage do you offer over your competitors that get your customers to choose you?

- What drew you to work in your particular industry, field, company, etc.?

- How big a piece of the overall business is your division? What are the other divisions?

- Are there new technologies that are affecting your business?

- It sounds like you've been successful. What tends to make someone successful in the role?

- How do you think the business will be different in ten years?

- What is your favorite part of your job and why?

And so on. Once you begin to practice this, you will find that you lose the fear of sounding ignorant to someone, because you are able to enter into fun and mutually fulfilling conversations that build your rapport and understanding with your new friend. Each subsequent time you connect, you can get to know more detail and can ask insightful questions about his or her success at work. "How have you been, Todd? I just read in the *Financial Times* that bond prices have been erratic; this must be affecting your business in some way, right? . . . You were working on a big new account when I last saw you, did you land it? . . . So what are you working on next? And what do you think the Fed is going to do next about interest rates?"

There is another hidden benefit of this approach: you become more knowledgeable and interesting to other people based on all the fascinating things you are learning from your new friends, and you never know where the knowledge you glean could come in handy later on. Based on conversations I have had with new friends in just the last week or two, I could now tell you about the regulations governing the import of wine, how large diamonds are bought by wholesalers (a monthly payment of $50 million for a nonnegotiable box of assorted rough stones), the exercises that can suppress cold symptoms (light resistance training), the debate over the cognitive benefits of writing versus typing in childhood development (pro-writing studies have been funded by the pencil industry), and how to kite surf (hold on to your ass).

But if we have just met, I won't tell you any of this; I'm only going to ask you about you.

From Intimate Network to
Meaningful Network

You have drawn people into your Familiar Network by being friendly and engaging, then into your Intimate Network by investigating their work and their passions with great interest. As you get to know these new friends, some you will really like, and you will want to build a lasting relationship. You can now bring them into your Meaningful Network, in the only way I know possible: you are going to do something important for them. And whereas the previous two steps required only what could be considered superficial social skills, bringing someone into your Meaningful Network requires effort and a genuine caring for the other person. By taking a personal interest in the success of someone in your network, not only will you build a valuable bond with them, you will be growing the reach of your Impact Map, as the people you help are able to help others and so on. I would like to suggest three ways you can help others, and in the process grow your Meaningful Network.

1. **Share knowledge.** As you get to know someone's work, interests, and passions, you will find areas of overlap in your sets of expertise and opportunities to share things that you know they will find illuminating. The act can be as simple as relating an interesting and relevant insight that you know, emailing an article, or sending a book with a note, but it is only useful when you have thought hard about it and are sharing an insight that will be important to the other person. It is not hard to imagine yourself doing this on a daily basis:

   • "Todd, you told me about your interest in technologies affecting commercial banking. I just read this great white paper on bitcoin and blockchain. I feel like you would get a lot out of this, so I'm emailing it to you . . ."

- "Judith, congrats on your new job. Enclosed, please find a copy of the best book I have read on starting a new job, *The First 90 Days*. Call me anytime if you want to compare notes. I found it super helpful."

- "Jordan, I just got an invite to a private class to celebrate the opening of the new high-intensity fitness gym they just opened off of Route 40 but cannot go; you mentioned you love CrossFit—maybe you'd like my ticket?"

And so on. When your knowledge can help other individuals you know be more successful, they are going to appreciate it and value their relationship with you. Over time, that sharing will become mutual, as they have the urge to repay the favor and to ensure that you stay in their network, because you tell them interesting things, and they like you.

Now, one thing: don't overdo it. There is a line between helpful and desperate or clingy. The insights you offer a new friend should be casual in nature ("I saw this and thought of you") rather than creepy ("You said your favorite author was Tolstoy, so I read all of *War and Peace* to see if you would like it, and I think you would!"). Someone I recently met and did not know very well sent me an expensive gift basket later that week, leading a colleague of mine to say, "Congrats, you have your first stalker!" Remember, you are not trying to get something from this person, you are just trying to be helpful. So be cool.

Social media is another way to share useful insights with your network. But take care to make sure what you say is valuable or contributing something new or interesting to their lives. Rather than using Facebook, Twitter, etc., to share the trifling minutiae of your day ("So hungry, but can't eat at Chipotle, too gross!") or to try to convince others how terrific your life is ("OMG, what is someone like me doing at the most exclusive party in the city, I mean, right?"), share interesting things that you know that others don't: analysis of what is going on in the news; book recommendations; things that inspire you; insightful articles on science, technology, the arts; and so on. If you are going to invest time in social media, invest it in enriching the lives of the people with whom you are connected, not self-aggrandizement. Until you have a baby or a dog; then you can just post their pictures. Everyone wants to see those.

2. **Make connections.** One of the best ways to help others in your network is to expand their own respective networks. Put two people together who end up doing business or being friends and your impact compounds. This takes on all kinds of forms:

- "Jesse, I heard our marketing team is looking for a new director of acquisitions. I don't know if you are looking, but it is a killer job at a really fun company . . ."

- "Amy, you mentioned your daughter wants to apply to Penn State. I happened to run into a friend who went there who told me the admissions office heavily emphasizes the essay in the admissions process, and that they love athletes like your daughter, so play that up in the application. My friend would be happy to talk to your daughter, if she would like . . ."

- "Anthony and Claire, you are two of the most forward-thinking people I know working in nonprofit workforce development—I can't believe you haven't met. I am connecting you in the hopes you meet sometime. I feel like something really good would come of it . . ."

Early in your career, your network is relatively weak, so it takes some additional effort to get started. Seek to get to know and be useful to folks who sit at important network center points; recruiters are a great example. Find out who the headhunters are who fill roles around your level in your industry and reach out to them. Tell them you know a bunch of great folks who are always asking you for career advice, and you want to be able to help the recruiter fill roles when she needs an assist, so to keep you on her call list. Each time you connect a recruiter to a good candidate, you have helped two people in your network, and have made it likely that the recruiter will call you again, creating more opportunities to help.

Other key people you may want to try to get to know to jump-start your network include:

- The people who run the alumni network for your alma mater; they can be very valuable in connecting you to other graduates from your school with interests, skills, or insights that you are seeking.

- Trade magazine journalists, who tend to know key people across the industry. They are often happy to meet with you off the record if you have interesting insights on the industry that can become stories for them in the future. (Just be careful never to share anything about your company; that can get you canned.)

- Consultants, bankers, and advisers who serve your industry. They know key decision makers, trends, and opportunities at countless companies around your industry, and they will often be happy to make a connection, as they are always looking for angles to develop new business.

- Social connectors who run clubs or affinity groups that draw impactful people. Sometimes, the most interesting folks you will meet are hanging out in a local book club. And sometimes not.

Each time you have made a valuable connection, you have expanded the power of your network, helped someone you like, and made the universe a slightly better place.

3. **Offer support and friendship.** When you get a new job, a promotion, a big win or major recognition, or other good fortune, you are very popular. The emails and tweets and likes pour in, congratulating you on your new success. Some are happy for you; others see your success as a possible opportunity for themselves. When these moments happen for you, enjoy them, because when things break the other way, when you get passed over for a job or your business fails, your in-box gets a lot quieter. That is when you only hear from your true friends.

Make a decision to be one of those true friends, both in good times and in bad. People in your network need you when they are struggling as much as when they are doing well.

- "Johnny, I heard you just left the company. I doubt you need it, but I'm sending you the info for three headhunters I have found most useful. Feel free to tell them I sent you. I would love to get a coffee anytime if you like . . ."

- "Martina, I wanted to reach out and check in on you, as I know you've got a ton on your plate and can tell you are stressed and overloaded. Last time I felt that way I had a friend go through my calendar and help me cancel the things that were adding to my stress but not helping me achieve my goals. It was really helpful and a big relief! If you're interested and would like a calendar buddy, I'm here for you . . ."

- "Keric, I know you wanted that job. You should have gotten it. Want to grab a drink tonight?"

Of course when things are going well, be there, too. Be good company, be a positive person, be a good listener, if you're witty be witty—be someone who people like to have around. You are building a network of people you like and want to see succeed. The more you contribute to the interactions you have together, the more people will look forward to them, and the more likely they are to think of you when they need advice, help, and so on. This is all basic stuff that the average American second grader knows, but somehow we all forget it and apply a selfish model to the idea of networking: we seek out people who can help us, and we think of them only when we need something. If you really want to create value with your life, seek to help others; as your network grows, your ability to help multiplies, and when you least expect it (and perhaps need it most), one of those favors will come back to find you.

Let me share one last anecdote to bring this all together: A couple summers ago, my wife and I took an outdoor high-intensity interval-training class that we really enjoyed. After the first class, I exchanged pleasantries with the instructor—introduced myself ("Great class! I'm Mike"), remembered his name (Adam), and asked him a bit about his business as a trainer. He turned out to be an entrepreneur, and we had enough in common in our work that we found ourselves slipping easily into each other's Familiar Network and talking again after the following class. After a few interactions one of us suggested we get a drink with our significant others that night before dinner, and we all got to know each other more; my new friend had just launched a production company and just sold his new book, two interesting subjects that I enjoyed getting to understand in a lot more detail, which also happened to bring Adam into my Intimate Network. A couple of weeks later, I found myself in need of a production company for a small video project and called Adam, to our mutual benefit. Soon after, he called me with a business idea relevant to his work and mine that we explored together; it didn't quite click, but was a fun attempt. His book *The 30-Second Body* was coming out and I suggested that, to help sell more books, I organize an event at work, knowing that a lot of my colleagues would love his approach to fitness. Again, win-win.

Though we were relatively new friends, we found ourselves proactively looking for ways to help each other, which brought us into each other's Meaningful Network. If Adam called and asked for a favor, I would do it without hesitation. Other than that I liked Adam, there was no hidden agenda here. Then one night we grabbed a drink after work and I found myself giving Adam unsolicited advice on his business. He cut me off and said, "You know all this stuff—why haven't you written a book? You should talk to my agent." Of course I had always had the idea for a book—this book—and had been developing material for it in bits and pieces for years. I just didn't think it would happen now. But creating great leaders is a core tenet of my personal Impact Map, and a book would help to do that, so I took the introduction and the meeting, and then the meetings with the publishers, and now here we are, you and me. Because I invested in getting to know and possibly helping someone I liked, without any express expectation of getting something in return.

The same approach has given me the privilege of countless friendships, business deals, career opportunities, social invitations, even a reception with the president at the White House. But all those benefits of my Meaningful Network are worth less than when a friend told me recently: "Your advice when I needed it on work-life balance has really helped; my wife says to me all the time, 'I don't know what Mike said to you, but whatever it was, keep doing it.'"

When you set out to help other people, helping them is, in and of itself, the reward. Amazingly, it also has the by-product of yielding connections and opportunities that will likely help you and your career, too.

CHAPTER 10

⟶ If Someone Asks You If You're a Sales God, You Say Yes

Oh, no, no. You can do better than that, Jerry! I want you to say it with me, with meaning, brother! Hey, I got Bob Sugar on the other line; I bet you he can say it! . . . Show me the money!

—Rod Tidwell, *Jerry Maguire*

Earlier in one's career, the world seems it can be divided into two groups of people: salespeople and everybody else.

For many of us, our experience with sales has consisted of being on the receiving end of a hard sell for new tires by a mechanic, or struggling to escape the clerk at the clothing store who is convinced that we would look literally so amazing in the most expensive sweater in the store. We have met salespeople who clearly want something from us and are armed with tricks to get it. These extreme examples make sellers seem greedy or even dishonest.

The stereotype is unfair. When done right, sales, quite simply, is *helping to solve someone's problem by tailoring your solution to her needs.* Sure, pushy telemarketers are in sales. But so are public health advocates, prosecuting attorneys, diplomats, elder care nurses, and the parents of four-year-olds who refuse to brush their teeth. Sales, done right, connects people with products, services, or information they need. Sales makes things better.

You, faithful reader, work in sales. You may not carry a quota, but you will have to convince a business partner to work with you, persuade management to resource your project, or make the case for your next promotion. If you work in the nonprofit world, you will have to fund-raise. If you are in politics, you will have to ask for votes. If you are a writer, you will need to connect with audiences and sell your book. If you are to be successful in your career—no matter what career—you must be great at sales. I have had the opportunity to personally learn, practice, and teach sales at all levels. What follows is a framework that I have found consistently puts you in a position to best match your audience with the solution they need. This is crafted with a traditional big-pitch sales meeting in mind, but can be tailored to any kind of interaction where you hope to positively influence another person's decision.

There are three steps to a successful sales engagement: prepare, pitch, and propose and close.

Prepare

You can't solve someone else's problem until you are an expert in her industry, goals, and authority; prepare a killer presentation; and define roles for the engagement. So, before the meeting, here is how to get your act together.

Study the Customer

What are the trends affecting the industry? What are analysts, journalists, and people who work in the industry excited about? What are they worried about? What are competitors doing in the space? What does your company's proprietary data tell you about trends in the industry? Let's pretend you are hoping to sell more environmentally conscious packaging materials to a warehousing company. To walk into that potential customer's office and say, "I don't know much about your company; here is my product; it is good for the environment," is virtually worthless to her. However, if you've studied the industry and the company and found that half of the leading players have switched to green packaging materials, that they have noted improved customer satisfaction and retention since going green, and that this company you are selling to has a shareholder initiative on its proxy ballot to invest in reducing its carbon footprint by 10 percent, then you might be in a position to present an actual solution to this company's problem.

Know the Goals and Motivations of Your Audience

Most people have the unhelpful tendency to assume that the key to selling their product is extolling all of its many features and benefits. Not true. For example, let's say you wanted to sell me a cat. There are many wonderful things about cats. They keep you company. They have a dignified indifference to humans who have not earned their affection. They teach your children responsibility and a love of animals. They go to the bathroom indoors. They are natural predators that kill birds, mice, and any other small critters they can find in or around your home. In forty-four states in America, it is legal to eat them.* Technically, all true benefits. But if you're selling to an animal lover, just running through that list (especially that last one) is not going to help you sell your cat. On the other hand, if you are selling to a bodega owner with a storage room full of cheese half eaten by mice, you'll really only need to focus on that predator one.

You need to know the goals of the person or people to whom you are selling. Understanding the challenges and opportunities of their industry and goals of their company before you walk in the door is a good start. Next, you need to learn which of the company's goals are relevant to this individual—the enterprise may be focused on growing profit, but this person might only be tasked with cost reduction. Then, once you understand the goals, you have to get your arms around what actually motivates this human being. If it is

---

* It's true, guys. Call your congressperson.

money, you will want to figure out what affects his or her bonus. If it is long-term career trajectory, then learn what things get people in her industry promoted. Alternatively, she may be motivated by thought leadership, altruism, popularity, curiosity, standing out, or fitting in. Studying the person's professional profile, cruising through her public social media feeds, and asking mutual connections might tell you a lot about what motivates your potential customer. Here are some examples of what might be motivating your customer, and how it would affect your pitch for those aforementioned environmentally conscious packaging materials.

Customer is motivated to:	The pitch you need to prepare:
Do anything it takes to make her customers happy	"Using environmentally conscious packaging materials has been shown to improve customer satisfaction and retention by 15 percent."
Relish in the joy of improved warehouse productivity	"These thinner packaging materials take up 15 percent less storage space, increasing your usable warehouse floor plate and making your inventory management more efficient."
Get a bigger bonus by reducing costs	"My product uses 30 percent less paper, which will reduce your storage and handling costs by 10 percent."
Impress the boss by improving employee retention	"Our research shows that when a company actively adopts green solutions, employee pride in their employer increases 20 percent, which leads to 5 percent lower employee churn per year."
Be recognized as an innovator in the industry	"We were really proud to see our first customer in a similar industry recently recognized as an environmentally conscious business leader by the Tulsa Chamber of Commerce."
Achieve some goal that your product doesn't actually solve	Cancel the meeting. Don't try to sell something that someone doesn't really need. It is unproductive and unethical. And if no one truly needs your product, then you should get a new job, because you're scamming people.

There are countless other examples, and the more you practice sales, the more intuitive other people's motivations will become to you, and the better you will be at helping them achieve their goals. *Understanding the goals and motivations of your potential customer is the single most important element of executing a good sale.*

Understand the Authority of Your Audience

I've seen countless sales calls where a potential customer is just eating up the pitch, the team struggling not to start high-fiving right there in the meeting, when the customer then says something along the lines of, "This is so cool; we really have to get you in front of our agency— they control the budget for these things." Aaaand there's four hours of your life you won't ever get back. Because you're not actually on a sales call until you are in the room with the person who can say yes and sign the order. Before you put on your dancing shoes, make sure your date is allowed to go to the party.

Coordinate Roles

Many sales calls involve a group of people from your expanded team. The owner of the meeting should ensure that each person has a defined role. The roles can include:

- *The point person:* This is the meeting owner. Generally, she is assigned to the account, project manages the meeting, creates the agenda and presentation, and handles the follow-up. Relatively speaking, the point person is the person who has the most to gain or lose from the outcome of this meeting, which is why she was up all last night replacing stock photos in the deck with different stock photos that feel more "on brand." This chapter assumes that you are, or someday will become, the point person.

- *The table setter:* This is often the senior person with the most impressive title and most expensive suit. He or she tends to know something about the golf game or the children of the senior person on the other side. The table setter kicks the meeting off with authority and chimes in from time to time to say things like, "We hear that concern all the time, but trust me, it has never been a problem." The table setter often has very little idea what we are pitching today.

- *The special expert:* The special expert usually comes from another division and has deep knowledge of something cool, like new pharmaceutical develop-ment, computer science, big data,* the Fed's plans for raising interest rates, or the purchasing habits of baby boomers. This person's role is to impress the customer by presenting one or two very technical slides that, in the end, deliver an insight like, "Baby boomers are 50 percent more likely to buy all-white sneakers." For reasons that seem appropriate but have never been discussed, this person is not held to the same standard of dress code for the meeting, and is under no obliga-tion to make small talk before the meeting.

- *The junior employee:* "Mike, can you make sure we have eight copies of the deck? No, Mike, color cop-ies! . . . Mike, do we have a car to the meeting? An SUV, Mike, Table Setter is coming! . . . Mike, make sure you get the Wi-Fi password for the client's of-fice . . . Should we bring doughnuts? Hey, Mike, can you run and get doughnuts?" The job of the junior

---

* Pro tip: if you call it "big data," people will assume it is more important than if you just call it "data." For some reason this does not work with other business jargon, so avoid the temptation to start referring to "big artificial intelligence" or "big social media."

employee sucks, and I have been there. If this is you, make sure you get the details right and use this opportunity to study the meeting and learn.

Pitch

You're ready for the show. You've prepped, studied your audience, and spent hours crafting your presentation. Now the hard part: it is time to stand and deliver.

Build Rapport

Lab experiments have shown that subjects are more likely to accept a deal from someone they like, even if they are being offered a better deal by someone they do not like. Therefore, your first job when you walk into a pitch is to be likable. The awkward first few minutes before a meeting, while people are trickling in and the room is being set up, are critical to your success. Before you even open your mouth, people are subconsciously deciding whether they like you and if they should really listen to you. The psychologist Daniel Kahneman has shown that people can, with surprising accuracy, predict election outcomes based only on a brief view of the candidates' faces, and correctly assess a teacher's end-of-year ratings based on a silent ten-second video, because human beings are so susceptible to come to, and stick to, snap judgments. So dress well, stand straight, carry yourself confidently, and employ the tactics we discussed in the last chapter for welcoming someone from your Unfamiliar Network to your Familiar Network (introductions, remembering names, initiating conversation, etc.).

Open Strong

Once everyone is seated, the point person needs to take control of the situation by announcing the beginning of the meeting. Doing so quickly and firmly will start the meeting on the right track; failing to do so opens you to the risk that someone else speaks first and throws the meeting into chaotic motion before you have laid the essential foundation. That foundation includes the following:

- *Just the TIP:* Begin the meeting by announcing the topic, importance, and purpose (TIP) of the engagement. "We are here today to talk about your new vehicle launch, and how we might be able to contribute to the success of that initiative with our marketing programs [topic]. We recognize the importance of this launch to your team, as it is your first full-size hybrid SUV launch, and raising awareness among young families is critical [importance]. The purpose of today's meeting is to propose and customize a marketing program that will contribute meaningfully to your success and assign the right people to make it happen [purpose]. Does that sound like a good investment of everyone's time?" Heads nodding, they can already tell you did your homework. I think they like you!

- *Make the introductions:* The goal of introductions is threefold: get names, identify people's authority, and break the ice. It sounds simple, but introductions can get away from you quickly. If the first person to give an intro also gives some biographical information ("Hi, I'm Andrew, I grew up in Philly and have been in content for twenty years; before this I worked at . . .") there will be no stopping the twenty minutes of personal narratives to follow. Nobody cares. To avoid this mess, as point person make sure you make the first intro—"I'm Mike Steib, and I am responsible for all marketing solutions for the team." Prep your team to give introductions in the same way. Just as we discussed in the networking chapter, whatever information you provide, your counterparts will reciprocate with the same.

- *Collect the goals:* Despite all your prep work, you can't be sure of the counterparty's expectations for the meeting until you ask them. "Quickly, before we start, I would like to hear from you your goals for the meeting, to make sure we have the right agenda. John, what would you like me to make sure we accomplish in our time together today?" Nine out of ten times, the customer will reinforce your plan for the meeting, giving added credibility to your presentation. But every once in a while, you will learn here that the client is hoping for something different from what you were planning to present. And while that may feel momentarily like a setback for you, it is a million times better to learn it now than after you have wasted everyone's time for an hour or two. You'll adjust the pitch accordingly.

- *Agree on the agenda:* If collecting the goals reinforced your agenda, just read it off and ask if anyone wants any changes (they won't). If your client's goal was inconsistent with your agenda, this is your chance to adapt. "We came today prepared to talk about our brand marketing solutions, but John, based on the goals you stated, I feel we should skip most of this and instead share with you some of our performance marketing options, some of which I can pull forward from the appendix. How does that sound?" Here, your client will either agree, and love that you have tailored the agenda to his needs, or backtrack by indicating that he had raised only one of his goals, but he is also very interested in your initial presentation. In which case you return to your original pitch, but with a heightened sensitivity to the other goals of the customer.

Tell Your Story (Situation, Complication, Resolution)

Your presentation may be PowerPoint, Keynote, a live demo, a video, a scripted whiteboard drawing, or an interpretive dance. Regardless of your medium, the point is to tell a simple and clear story that lays a contextual foundation, indicates the challenge or problem or opportunity that your customer has, and presents a good solution *that you would honestly drop everything to buy if you were the client.* If you are not convinced, you won't convince someone else.

To articulate your story, I am fond of the "situation, complication, resolution" framework.* Let's continue to torture our earlier example, selling environmentally friendly packaging materials. Imagine you are talking to a senior leader who cares about top-line sales, profits, and the public perception of the company. You might lay out the top level of your story very simply like this:

- *Situation:* Americans are increasingly concerned about the environmental impact of their purchasing decisions.

- *Complication:* Companies that have taken visible green efforts have grown sales significantly, while those who haven't are losing market share.

---

* Barbara Minto offers a version of this in her terrific book on communication, *The Minto Pyramid Principle.* Highly recommended for helping to organize your storytelling.

- *Resolution:* Packing materials that kill 30 percent fewer trees would put you among industry leaders, thus growing sales and profits for you.

An effective presentation would follow that narrative, supporting each of those primary points with a few pieces of evidence. For instance:*

Situation: Americans are increasingly concerned about the environmental impact of their purchasing decisions:

- According to Google Insights, searches on "going green," "environmentally friendly," "conservation," and "climate change" are all up over 30 percent in the last three years.

- Sixty percent of voters recently listed the environment as a top factor in which presidential candidate they will support.

- When asked to choose a $100 shoe or a $125 shoe that was ethically manufactured to create a 30 percent lower carbon footprint, the majority of consumers choose the $125 greener shoe.†

Chances are, you have plenty of charts and examples and data points. The mistake is in pummeling your audience with all of them. Instead, create your presentation by first writing your narrative as I did above, summarizing each point in a succinct one-liner at the top of each page, then paste in only the chart or graph or other evidence that is necessary to prove that one-liner point. Put everything left

---

* For the record, this example was concocted to illustrate the point. I don't know anything about cardboard boxes—I work at an internet company.

† These stats are fake. Again, this is not a good book for those interested in insights about cardboard.

over in the appendix; you can reference it in the meeting if needed to buttress a point or handle an objection.

Instill Confidence: The Six Ps of a Money Pitch*

The head of a major news network once told me that you can tell who is going to win an election by watching the debate with the sound off. (Try it; it works.) People buy *you* as much as they buy the product. If you are confident in your product and your pitch, they will feel more comfortable and more welcoming of your recommendation. There are some simple strategies you can practice to present masterfully. I got them all to start with a *p* so they are easier to remember. I did that for you.

- *Posture:* If you are a mortal, presenting makes you feel nervous and exposed. We have such an urge to hide behind something when we present that someone invented podiums. Because you are anxious, your physical posture becomes closed and protective. Your shoulders slump, your chin tucks closer to your chest, and your gestures diminish. Your subconscious has figured that if it can just get you to roll up into a ball, you have a chance of rolling out of the room unnoticed before this goes any further.

  You need to learn to fight this urge. A wide-open posture communicates to the room that you are reputable and to be reckoned with. Watch any address by an important person and you will see the same characteristics: the chin held high, shoulders back,

---

* Not to be confused with Jerome McCarthy's Four Ps of Marketing: price, product, placement, and promotion. The Four Ps are the ingredients that a marketer uses to articulate and promote a brand's unique selling points. There, I just saved you six months of business school.

pronounced gestures. A confident body posture tells the subconscious of an audience, *Follow this person, she knows what she is doing.**

- *Pause:* So, like, you know that way people rush to talk who are, like, obviously not, um, a successful senior executive because, like, they, like, sound like a teenager? The cadence and confidence of your voice will communicate more to your audience than your slides. Contrast this example with the CEO of your company, whom I suspect speaks much more deliberately and precisely. The primary difference between the two is the use of filler words, such as "um," "like," and "literally." To be a successful communicator, you will need to practice eliminating such words from your vocabulary. The key is becoming comfortable pausing silently to think when you are speaking. It will feel horribly awkward to you, but to your audience it will make you sound measured and confident. Try saying each of these out loud: "Our research shows that millennial customers are . . . um-mmmm . . . like . . . a skeptical consumer." Now try: "Our research shows that millennial customers are . . . [pause to think, silently] . . . a skeptical consumer." The latter makes it sound like you took the time to find just the right word, which must mean your point was very important, which is why we all trust you already and are going to buy what you are selling.

- *Punctuate down:* For some reason, some of us speak as if there is a vestigial question mark at the end of each

---

* It is not lost on me that the advice, "stand up straight," like much of this book, is what your mother told you when you were thirteen-years-old. We should all listen to our moms more often. I love you, Mom.

sentence. "And we did a lot of research? And we found that six out of ten customers prefer cornflower blue? So we should change the packaging?" If you want to influence people, you've got to sound like you believe it yourself. End each declarative sentence the way it was designed to be spoken, on a downward note, not an upward inflection (unless you are giving a toast at a sweet sixteen in Beverly Hills and really want to, like, totally fit in?).

- *Precision:* Be concise. Every word you speak in a meeting should matter. An amateur says, "Thanks, everyone, for coming, um, I know this was really hard to schedule, and Pam's not here, but we should really have a great meeting, we're really excited about this . . ." A pro says, "Thank you for coming—let's begin." Examine your presentation and see what you can eliminate. The moment when you transition from one slide to the next is a terrific opportunity to hone your presentation. Rather than saying, "Aaaaand . . . as you'll see on the next slide," like everyone else does, jot a note at the bottom of each slide reminding you what the point of the next slide will be, and just make that point as you advance to the next page. For example, "The cost of corn has been declining for eight consecutive quarters [flip to next slide, containing fascinating corn charts] because global food supplies have become more plentiful, while ethanol demand has diminished in the face of competition from fracking."*

- *Proper English:* Have you ever claimed that something was growing exponentially? If your intention was to

---

* I don't know if this is true. Why are you so obsessed with corn and cardboard facts?!

say "growing a lot," but you were referring to something that was actually growing arithmetically (as most things in business do), then the person in the room who took math in college certainly concluded that you are not to be trusted with numbers. Have you ever said something was orders of magnitude bigger when you really meant "way bigger"? If it was not actually one hundred times bigger (two orders of magnitude), then that same mathlete thought, "Good grief, not again with this guy." Or perhaps you have said that something coincidental was "ironic," or used the word "less" when you should have used "fewer," thereby torturing the fancy senior manager in the room who studied English at Princeton. It's okay, you are not alone—language misappropriation is common and it is contagious. It only takes one person at work to start saying "extrinsic" without proper license and, before you know it, we're all saying it. But if you want to present yourself as a trustworthy and confident champion for your company, product, or service, you have to be the exception. The next time you hear someone claim, "Those two topics are orthogonal," and you are tempted to start saying "orthogonal" yourself, ask Siri or Google to define it for you first.*

• *Practice:* We're talkin' about practice.† Everyone mistakenly assumes that because they wrote the presentation, they are ready to give the presentation. To do it really well requires rehearsal. Set up your phone where your audience would be sitting and record

---

* or·thog·o·nal—ôr'THägənl/—adjective—of or involving right angles; at right angles; statistically independent.

† That's an Allen Iverson reference for the sports fans out there.

yourself giving the pitch. Then watch it and brace yourself for something between intense disappointment and mild disgust. You will notice your lousy posture, fumbling gestures, and soul-crushing tendency to read right off of the slides. You will hear every "um," suffer through each time you say "literally," and realize that for some inconceivable reason you say "tremendously" ten times per presentation. All of which can be fixed with just a little bit of practice. Write down your worst presentation style errors, pick one, and try again, this time focused on getting this one technique right. Once you've nailed it, go to the next item on the list. It takes consistent effort to be a great communicator, but the payoff is that you will be able to win other people's trust and open their minds to what you truly believe is the right solution to their specific problem.

Look. Listen. Ask. Adapt.

Now here we are—you studied the industry and the customer, practiced your pitch, got everyone's buy-in on goals and the agenda, and are methodically laying out your narrative. Look at you! But, wait, the client is checking her watch and fidgeting a little. She wants to leave. No! Failure! Great anguish of failure! You suck at sales!

Hold on, it's not too late. Let's find out why you are losing the audience, and get this sale back on track.

- *Look:* Know how to read the room. People will tell you more with their eyes and their body language than they ever will with their words. Some signals are clear. If someone is frowning, has her arms crossed, is clutching her bag in her lap, or otherwise closes off her body language, she disagrees with you or, worse, doesn't really like you. If someone is nodding, smiling, holding a physically open posture, or leaning in to focus on your words, you have engaged this person's interest and are on the right track. Other signals are less obvious, like a person's eyes. If you are doing introductions and the senior client looks at your laptop, she is eager for you to open it and get started with your presentation. If, during your pitch, a member of your audience keeps glancing over at another person in the room, he may be looking to that other person for validation. The corners of someone's mouth are another subtle but clear signal of someone's reaction: most people will form an almost imperceptible smile or frown at the corners of their mouth for a brief second after you have said something, indicating to a careful observer whether or not they agreed with or welcomed the comment. You can even read someone's feet: if they are turned toward the door, she might be fantasizing about leaving the room (you'll especially see this signal when two people are standing in conversation—you can always tell by the direction of their feet which one wants to escape). Observing the small details in your audience's body language will tell you who agrees, who disagrees, who has something to say but is holding it back, and so on. A fun book on the topic is *How to Read a Person Like a Book* by Gerard Nierenberg. This is also a skill you can practice when you are not the point person: note body language and try to predict whose comments and questions will be positive or negative later in the meeting.

- *Listen:* If you have given a pitch a few times, you will have heard a few questions or objections repeatedly, leading you to form quick and effective responses to those objections. Soon, those responses will sit at the tip of your tongue, waiting for the slightest excuse to disabuse your audience of their misperceptions. While it is helpful to be prepared for likely objections, this is also a dangerous crutch, because you will be at risk of incorrectly concluding that this customer's question is just like everyone else's.

Him: "I'm worried about the cost . . ."

You [jumping in immediately with your brilliant canned response]: "The great news is our product is the lowest cost in the industry, 10 percent below our closest competitor!"

Him [thinking silently to himself]: "I meant the cost to our operations to make a major change in our production cycle, you arrogant putz."

Every question deserves the honor of your full consideration. Most times, you should investigate the question further before answering it. "Tell me more about your production cycle and how your current supplier fits in. And what would be the possible cost of a change? . . . Have you changed suppliers elsewhere in your production chain before? What worked and what didn't work?" This is where the sale is really won: not in the talking, but in the listening.

- *Ask:* Amateur sellers think it is a great sign when the customer doesn't object or ask hard questions, and are later surprised to not get their calls returned. If someone is seriously considering your pitch, he will be thinking through what it would take to make it happen, and how it might go wrong. Probe for concerns; dig until you find the objections. There is one question you can ask in a job interview to dramatically increase your odds of landing the offer: "We have talked about your requirements for the job and some of my experiences and abilities; can I ask you, what hesitations would you have trusting me with this important role?" By asking, you then get to explore and handle each objection and resolve your interviewer's concerns.

- *Adapt:* One of the hardest things in the world is to convince someone he is wrong. And if you successfully do convince someone that he is wrong, he will probably really dislike you for making him feel like a fool. So what is one to do when the counterparty's objections stand in the way of a successful sale? Simply explain that certain facts have changed or new facts have come to light. A useful framework for this is "feel–felt–found." "I can see why you *feel* changes in your supply chain will be too costly to make a change. We have two other clients with very similar domestic supply chains who *felt* the same way when our product was new. However, what they *found* was that our high-touch client engagement team was able to help them anticipate and preempt any possible disruptions, and as a result they had minimal switching costs and total cost savings of over 10 percent." Your audience wasn't wrong—your audience was right, based on the facts that he had. And now, with new facts in hand, he has the chance to be right again.

Propose and Close

It is time to bring it home, with the hardest and most essential part of your sale: closing the deal. Imagine there is a restaurant that I know you would love and I am trying to convince you to eat there. I prepared, finding out that you are a health-conscious foodie and that you and your significant other like to have a big date night once a week. I lay out my "situation, complication, resolution" pitch:

> "I know you are always looking for a good place for dinner. And it can be hard to find someplace fun and healthy. There is a great new restaurant downtown called Calcetines* that offers five delicious entrees under five hundred calories and is a great date night place. You should go!"

Pretty good, right? Good preparation, good pitch. Maybe you will go. But, then again, it's all the way downtown, and how do you know it's really great? Food is so subjective, right?

Okay, we can do better than that.

> "I know you are always looking for a good place for dinner. And it can be hard to find someplace fun and healthy. There is a great new restaurant downtown called Calcetines† that offers five delicious entrees under five hundred calories and is a great date night place. *It has been given four stars by the* New York Times *and was recently called by Eater.com 'the best date night in town.' Our good friends Jeff and Doug ate there last week and are still raving about it. You should go!"*

Well, that really does sound great. Next time you are making plans for dinner, there's a good chance you'll think about our conversation and go to Calcetines. Unless you forget, or inexplicably lose your enthusiasm, or if someone else pitches you another restaurant and you go there instead. Ugh!

All right, let's close this sale.

---

* FYI, Calcetines is not a real restaurant. "Calcetines" means "socks" in Spanish.

† Why would anyone name a restaurant Socks?

"I know you are always looking for a good place for dinner. And it can be hard to find someplace fun and healthy. There is a great new restaurant downtown called Calcetines that offers five delicious entrees under five hundred calories and is a great date night place. It has been given four stars by the *New York Times* and was recently called by Eater.com 'the best date night in town.' Our good friends Jeff and Doug ate there last week and are still raving about it. *The only problem is there is a six-month wait for a table. I have a table this Friday at seven o'clock for two, but something came up and I can't use it. I want to give you my table, but I need to know now or cancel the reservation. Will you go?*"

Guess what? You're going to Calcetines, because I made you feel better about the choice, and then I made you feel urgency to make the choice. I closed. If you want to sell, you have to close. Here is how you do it.

Leverage Experts and Crowds*

There is a reason toothpaste ads have a man in a white lab coat telling you that four out of five dentists recommend Crest toothpaste. The next time you shop for toothpaste, and are gripped by the fear of picking the wrong toothpaste, you'll be comforted knowing that Crest has the support of all these experts. (Of course, it does not even occur to us that the man in the ad is an actor, that any of us can purchase a lab coat, and that, apparently, one in five dentists thinks you *shouldn't* use Crest toothpaste. What evil toothpaste secret does that silent minority know!?) We are equally likely to just follow the instructions of train conductors, uniformed crossing guards, construction workers

---

* *Influence*, Dr. Robert Cialdini's seminal book on this topic, is a must read for any aspiring leader. Some of the advice in this chapter is inspired by his research.

with an orange vest and a stop sign, and pharmacists (again, lab coats). We look to experts to know what movies to watch this summer, what not to wear, and the latest tech trends. We have been conditioned to obey authorities, and good marketers and closers know how to use this to influence our decisions.

We are also susceptible to following a crowd, as evidenced by such social catastrophes as saggy pants, Cabbage Patch Kids, the Macarena, and hipsters. It is why brands brag to us that they have millions of fans, are the most downloaded app in a category, or have sold trillions of hamburgers. Hearing that others have done something makes us want to do it as well. Direct-response TV ads used to say, "Call now, operators are standing by," but learned that more people called when they said, "If the lines are busy, please try again."

Sadly, these psychological tricks can be used to manipulate people into choices that are not in their interest by less scrupulous actors, such as drug dealers, or the marketing people at McDonald's. But you can deploy these lessons ethically, referencing the viewpoints of authorities and crowds when their endorsements are relevant to your audience and can help them to make a better decision. If Dr. Sanjay Gupta says to take vitamin D, we probably really should take vitamin D. If a billion people use a particular social network, it probably really is the best social network. If the *New York Times*, Eater.com, Jeff, and Doug all love this restaurant, it probably really is a great restaurant. Sharing those insights will help your audience make the right decision.

Take It Away

As we discussed in our chapter 8 productivity recommendations, our highest-priority actions should be those that are important and urgent. You have approached a potential customer with a solution that you believe is important to her success. However, as we know, human beings are conditioned to prioritize that which appears urgent. We see this every day: *30 percent off—last day today!* (as if Gap pants are never going on sale again); *while supplies last!* (right, your diet pills are so pop-

ular, your factory couldn't possibly keep up). If you are going to pro-
voke action with your customer, you have to compete with this daily
cacophony of false urgency. You have to make your offer important
and urgent. Here are a few simple examples of the many ways to create
urgency:

- *Important dates:* Implementing a solution that saves expenses or increases revenue can have a measurable impact on someone's business. "If we execute an agreement
  today, we can have the product up and running in sixty
  days, which means millions of dollars of savings in the
  fourth quarter, which I know is your most important
  quarter."

- *Expiring resources:* The availability of enabling resources can come and go, and it is important to take
  advantage of them when they are available. "Our
  technical product management team just rolled off of
  a huge project and has another coming in October. If
  we partner now, we can get their full focus on this as
  a top-priority initiative; if we delay too long, we may
  not be able to launch until next year."

- *Expiring offer:* There are often short windows of time
  when certain economic or other benefits are available. "We are allowed to offer this feature for free for
  the first six months to customers who come on board
  before the end of January. After that time, it will
  only be available as part of our premium-priced
  package."

- *First-mover advantage:* Some people are afraid to take
  an action without the validation from others that it
  has worked. Some others value first-mover advantage, fancy themselves pioneers, or just like the acco-

lades that accrue to people who try successful things first. "We have other teams pitching this around the industry, and there is a lot of interest. We have authority to grant you a six-month industry exclusive if we get our order in before anyone else."

- *Probably not for you:* I once sought advice from a friend who ran one of the world's largest advertising agencies on how to close a sale with a notoriously tough customer. He said, "Just tell him you are showing it to him as a courtesy, but 'this is probably not for you'— he'll start to wonder why you are keeping it from him, and then he'll really want it." It is counterintuitive advice that turned out to be right on. People are so conditioned to expect everyone to be selling to them, that when something is held back, they immediately fear it is highly desirable and being offered to someone else. You can do this honestly by preemptively pointing out your customer's possible objections. Compare these two examples:

  - You: "We have this great new software that can really accelerate revenue." Them: "We really don't like to work with third-party software."

  - You: "Your company rarely takes on third-party software, so it probably does not make sense to explore one of our most important new revenue-accelerating technologies. We should just talk about our available consulting services." Them: "Hold on, we can work with third parties if the value is compelling enough—tell me more."

- *Oh, look what you found:* I just have to tell you this story. An old man in my neighborhood repairs watches, and I went in to see him one day to replace a battery. He works in front of a display case with a hundred junky watches that have, presumably, been left at his shop over the decades by people who did not pay or pick up after their service. I noticed, sitting discreetly to one side of the case, somewhat hidden by deceased Casio and Mickey Mouse watches, an expensive luxury watch with a broken band. I asked about it and the man took it out and looked at it, as if he had not noticed it in years, and he said simply, "A hundred dollars." I informed him that it was a fancy watch and asked how it ended up there, and if it was authentic. He just shrugged and went to put it in his pocket. I told him that he should get it appraised, but if he still wanted to sell it, I would take it. He just shrugged again and sold it to me. I wore this beautiful watch for months, receiving daily compliments, dumbfounded by my luck in attaining it, until I went back to his store for another battery and noticed in his display case, tucked innocently in the exact same spot, the exact same watch. That sly old son of a bitch sold me a knock-off watch without saying two words! I have to admit: I was impressed.

You can create the same dynamic in your own sale—hopefully for an honest and valuable product, not a fake watch—by laying out options and letting your customer discover the one that piques his interest. For instance, let's say you know your audience is developing a new product for Latin America. Rather than walking in, guns blazing, pitching your Latin American service, you start with some overview of what your company is working on and you mention, in passing, "some big thing in Latin America." Chances are the client will ask you to tell more, and then your pitch begins with the customer having asked for it, rather than you showing up to sell it—a great way to create interest and urgency.

Always Ask for the Order, Never Sell Past the Close

Mike Bloomberg was once asked the most important advice he had ever received. The advice—which, presumably, helped him to become a successful entrepreneur, philanthropist, billionaire, and mayor of New York City—was simply, "First, always ask for the order, and second, when the customer says yes, stop talking."

Every sane human being is afraid of being rejected. As a result, the hardest part of a sale is moving in and asking for commitment on a specific action, whether it is to buy something, sell something, agree to new terms of a partnership, or just commit to a date and agenda for the next discussion. Even really good businesspeople are prone to say, "Well, this has been great; we will follow up," presuming the hard parts can be done by email or other proxy. But you just made your best pitch, the client will never be more enticed by the offer than this minute, and the moment you are most likely to get a commitment is now. So ask for the order. Agree to the product or service, the terms, the date by which it will be shipped, and the people responsible. Say, "It's a deal," and shake hands.

And then, knowing that this is going to get done and how, get the hell out of there, because talking more only adds risk that you say something that unwinds the sale. You don't want this to happen:

> "Thanks, again, Ann. You're really going to be happy with this decision. We had a client buy our other version of this product who is just thrilled."
>
> "Oh, there is another version?"
>
> "Well, yes, but that one is not out of beta test yet; we aren't selling it broadly."
>
> "Oh, well, maybe we should look at that one when it is ready instead of going with this one. I would hate to miss out on the latest and greatest."

Argh! No! You sold past the close and lost the deal! Next time, take the order, say thank you, and run.

Get Team Feedback

The few minutes after the meeting offer your best opportunity to improve your craft. Ask your teammates for feedback on each stage of the sale: prepare, pitch, propose and close. Let them know the specific skills or tactics you are practicing and ask for examples as to how they did. Offer the same to your team and you will find that you can get better with each sales engagement. Again, sales is not some instinct you either have or you don't; it is a set of learnable skills that you can consistently develop and improve.

You are now armed with all the critical sales tools and tactics that I could fit in one chapter of a book. This is such an important skill that I encourage you to incorporate reading a few of the best books on the topic into your Career Roadmap, including the following:

- *Influence*, by Robert Cialdini
- *How to Win Friends and Influence People*, by Dale Carnegie
- *Made to Stick*, by Chip Heath and Dan Heath
- *The Pyramid Principle*, by Barbara Minto
- *How to Make People Like You in 90 Seconds or Less*, by Nicholas Boothman
- *The Language of Trust*, by Michael Maslansky
- *It's Not All about "Me,"* by Robin Dreeke
- *How to Read a Person Like a Book*, by Gerard Nierenberg
- *To Sell Is Human*, by Daniel Pink
- *The Greatest Salesman in the World*, by Og Mandino
- *Getting to Yes*, by Roger Fisher and William Ury
- *The Science of Selling*, by David Hoffeld

This book began with an exploration of the kind of life you want to live and the purpose that will guide you. If yours included "taking advantage of others for my own gain," then I really regret that someone gave you this book. But presuming that you are looking to use your talents to help other people succeed, to improve your community, your company, or your industry, to make the world a little bit better, then you have to take the responsibility of your new selling skills very seriously. Before you start convincing people, make sure you are selling them something that you sincerely believe is in their best interest. Don't become the slick salesperson who proudly claims he can "sell ice to Eskimos," as the old joke goes. Sell quality warm-weather gear to Inuits. People will be warmer, and you'll sleep a lot better knowing that you are using your skills for good.

CHAPTER 11

→ Every Meeting = Awesome

Meetings are an addictive, highly self-indulgent activity that corporations and other large organizations habitually engage in only because they cannot actually masturbate.

—DAVE BARRY

When we acted up in high school, we were made to stay after school and sit quietly in a room for sixty minutes with other perpetrators without being allowed to leave. They used to call this punishment "detention." We do the same thing as adults, but now call it a "meeting."

The average reader of this book will attend sixty-two meetings this month. These meetings are, too often, inefficient, unproductive, and joyless bureaucratic obligations; 90 percent of us will multitask or daydream through a significant portion of them.

But they could be awesome. A meeting led to the successful invasion of Normandy, another to the rescue of the Apollo 13 mission, and yet another to the idea to make an entire movie about a tornado full of sharks.* When a meeting is a focused gathering of the right people aligned around achieving a goal, they can be energizing and hyperproductive.

---

* *Sharknado 3.*

As a meeting owner, or key participant, there are some simple steps you can take to ensure that each meeting is an exceptional use of the talents and time of everyone in the room and leads to impactful decisions and actions. We will focus first on creating action-oriented group meetings, then on making the most of recurring one-on-one meetings, like the regular update you have with your boss. Much of what we explored in the previous chapter will be relevant here, as the goal of internal meetings is often to convince others to support a course of action. Overlap between these two chapters is intentional, and should be helpful to you—once you can deliver productive meetings and effective sales calls, you can achieve just about anything.

Group Meetings

Have you ever walked into a meeting and, after a few minutes of casual indecision, someone says, "So, whose meeting is this?" and, with no response, another says, "Well, while we are here, I suppose we could talk about . . ." A meeting like this, with no clear purpose, is doomed. When this happens to you, you have two choices: spend the next sixty minutes of your life watching your colleagues grope their way through a purposeless meeting, accomplishing nothing, or instantly pick up your phone as if it just rang and excitedly say something like, "She is? And it's a boy?!" and sprint out of the room. The latter is worth considering.

Really well-run meetings, on the other hand, can be one of your most effective tools for achieving your goals at work. When a meeting has a clear and important purpose, defined roles and responsibilities, a crisp and efficient agenda, and the team is held accountable to relevant action items, you can move mountains together. Here are some suggestions for a little extra structure, preparation, and follow-through to make your meetings the most impactful part of your and your teammates' day.

Clear purpose: The TIP method.* Just as you approach each to-do list item by first asking what goal it is intended to achieve (GIST), take the same approach to meetings. For a meeting to be productive, the attendees have to know and buy into the *topic* of the meeting, the *importance* of that topic, and the *purpose* you plan to achieve by discussing it (TIP). "Good to see everyone. The topic of this meeting is reducing the cost of our travel expenses by 10 percent. This is an important topic because our revenues are 10 percent below plan this quarter and we need to offset them with cost reductions. The purpose of this meeting is to agree on specific travel cost reductions and assign an owner to draft a new policy that is expected to deliver the required savings." When you hear that to open a meeting, you can be sure this is going to be a productive session . . . and that, sadly, you are going to be spending your next work trip in a dump of a hotel.

Clear owner or decider: The five Ds. If you are ever trapped in quicksand and ten strangers are standing nearby, there is a decent chance that none of them will take any action to save you—not because they are bad people, but because human beings are mentally weakened by being in a crowd. Psychologists call this phenomenon "diffusion of responsibility," and it has been used to describe all manner of crowd failings, from not calling 911 to help a neighbor to participating in societal-wide war crimes. The right thing to do is known by all involved, but people assume someone else in the crowd has taken that action already, or if they haven't, there must have been a good reason. Diffusion of responsibility happens at work every day: when a researcher sent group emails requesting assistance on an important project, he received half as many helpful responses than when emailing the same people individually. In meetings, this takes the form of one person saying, "You know, someone really should . . ." and, inevitably, no one taking responsibility for a follow-up action.

There is a way to ensure you never again leave a meeting without action: the Five Ds for Getting Sh*t Done in a Group (trademark

---

* We touched on this in the previous chapter, opening our sales meetings strong. The same framework applies to effective internal meetings.

2017), a simple framework that guarantees no one dies in the quick-sand on your watch, and that your meetings and resulting action items always have clear and accountable ownership. Make sure your meeting has each of these five Ds, and you will be well on your way to making things happen.

1. **Directly responsible individual (DRI).** The DRI is the owner of the initiative. She manages the project, calls the meetings, sets the agenda, determines the participants, and presents the recommendations. Assigning a DRI resolves the challenge of diffusion of responsibility, giving the team "one throat to choke" should the job not get done. The DRI announces the TIP at the start of the meeting.*

2. **Data and dissenting opinions.** The need for a DRI is most pronounced in cross-functional initiatives, where a number of people could conceivably be responsible for an outcome. As a result, choosing one owner creates the risk that the best of the collective wisdom of the team is replaced by one person's opinion. To avoid this, a DRI should be told by the group what data points are important to examine in making the decision and whose viewpoints should be considered. If the DRI is recommending a course of action with which others will disagree, she should be prepared to present their views and why she chose a different path.

3. **Decision maker (DM).** Sometimes, the DRI will also be responsible for making the decision; other times, the final decision to take an action is owned by another, like a boss, a board of directors, or a source of financing. The DRI

---

* Contrary to my facetious trademark claims, DRI has been a common phrase and practice at Apple for years.

will be responsible for making a final recommendation, but it is the decision maker who can allocate budget, instruct compliance by other departments, etc.

4. **Deadline.** Often, the work of the DRI is a bottleneck to the actions of others in the organization. It is important that the DRI is responsible for collecting all the right data and viewpoints and presenting the recommended course of action by a certain date, and the DM is accountable for issuing a clear decision by a certain date sometime soon after.

5. **Did it work?** If the course of action were obvious, it probably would have happened already or, at least, would not have needed an elaborate decision-making framework to reach resolution. More likely, the initiative is complex, and its success important to the organization. It is appropriate for the organization to track whether the recommended course of action and the decision were right. The DRI should, as part of her recommendation, include the metrics that will be tracked and reported following the implementation of the recommendation, the targets for those metrics, and how the course of action may change if the targets are not achieved. For instance, "I am recommending that we require all our customers to pay by credit card rather than check to improve our success in collecting the money we are owed. Following this policy change, I will report monthly on our success at achieving 0 percent of customers using checks, fewer than 1 percent loss of customers following the policy switch, and a 50 percent reduction in our total outstanding balances."

A Crisp Agenda Makes It Run Like Clockwork

The DRI for the meeting owes the attendees a clear articulation of how their time is going to be used in this meeting and is responsible for keeping to it. Here are a few tips for making the meeting run like a clock.

- **Publish a time-detailed agenda.** Time is our most valuable resource. Reinforce that by detailing how you are going to spend your minutes together in this meeting. "From 10:05 to 10:15 a.m. Amanda is going to take us through the current travel policies; from 10:15 to 10:30 a.m. Rob is going to share three different travel policy changes under consideration and the impact each will have on costs, along with the supporting analysis. From 10:30 to 10:50 a.m. we will discuss and debate and then each person here will express his or her recommendation. As the DRI, I will take those questions, feedback, and suggestions under consideration in finalizing the recommendation to senior management, who will make the final decision." How hot is that?

- **Get agreement on the agenda.** People will sometimes come to a meeting with their own goals, desires, and axes to grind. If you try to force an agenda on them, they will, soon enough, derail the meeting with unrelated questions and suggestions. You can ferret this out by simply restating the agenda and asking the attendees if they agree with it. If someone requests a deviation from the agenda, you could accommodate it, or gain agreement to cover the topic in a separate meeting. "Does everyone agree with the topic, importance, purpose, and agenda we have set for this meeting? Would anyone like to suggest any changes? Great, then, Sam, you have the floor."

- **Start on time exactly five minutes late.** People suck at being on time, and whether it is because their last meeting ran over, they failed to allocate extra minutes for a bathroom trip, or they needed time to watch a cute cat video, they are probably going to be late to your meeting. A good way to still honor a sharp start time is to always start exactly five minutes after the hour or half hour. You can use those first five minutes for catching up and socializing with your co-workers, which has been scientifically proven to improve productivity.

- **End at twenty-five or fifty-five minutes after the hour.** If your meeting uses the entire hour, it is essentially impossible for people to be on time for their next meeting, continuing the vicious cycle of lateness. Set your agenda to end twenty-five or fifty-five minutes after the hour. (With a few exceptions, if your meeting is longer than fifty-five minutes, you are committing a crime against humanity.)

- **Wrap up early, if you can.** The purpose is not to meet for fifty-five minutes, it is to accomplish a goal. If you have accomplished the goal in forty-five minutes, thank everyone for their time and adjourn the meeting. To be known for making efficient use of people's time builds significant goodwill, and it gives you the appearance of really knowing what you are doing. One proven technique for making meetings go faster is to do a stand-up meeting. A stand-up meeting signals urgency, literally keeps people on their toes, and makes them all slightly uncomfortable, which builds a collective will to move more quickly to resolution. It is also better for your health—sitting is the new smoking.

- **Set ground rules.** People multitasking on their phones or computers are not fully focused on your meeting, so you might want to consider banning internet use from your meetings. Eating in the meeting can be productive, but if you've got a guy who always heats up his smelly leftovers for lunch, you probably want to deal with that. If this is a brainstorm meeting, you may want to set a ground rule that there are no bad ideas, and that everything will be captured on the whiteboard for debate at a subsequent meeting. Setting ground rules that are consistent with your organization's culture and improve the focus of your meeting will help to maximize its success.

- **Get the attendees right.** Part of the Steve Jobs legend was that he would remove anyone from a meeting who was not necessary to achieve its goal, once simply telling a new marketing leader, "I don't think we need you in this meeting, Lorrie. Thanks." Invite the people who are necessary for the successful achievement of the goal and no one else. The more people are in the room, the less likely you are to have productive and honest debate. And having someone without the relevant expertise or authority chiming into the discussion can destroy the meeting's flow. There is no magic number, but I can tell you if there are twelve people in the room, you are not going to get anything decided. And if you know someone who just loves to hear himself talk, don't invite him.

- **Put it in the bike shed.** A British naval historian coined Parkinson's Law of Triviality in 1957 to explain his observation that committees considering important and difficult issues have a strong tendency to digress into trivial discussions, because those issues are less painful to think about and less unpleasant to debate. He used the example of a committee considering a nuclear power plant that kept spending most of its time debating the proper materials to use for the employee bike shed. Software engineers are fond of calling out "bike shedding" when it happens in their meetings. When you see this happening in your meetings, proactively take the issue and put it in the "parking lot," a list of out-of-scope topics that the team can decide to revisit sometime in the future.

- **Publish your meeting details in advance.** Send the agenda by email and include it in the notes of the calendar invite. Include the TIP, meeting owner, and required attendees. If possible, share the materials in advance to increase the likelihood that your participants are prepared and productive. Standardize your meeting invites so that folks know what they are in for when they glance at their calendars. Like this:

Meeting title: Travel Policy Change Decision

Owner/DRI: Mike

Purpose: Reduce travel costs 10 percent. Collect input on potential changes to travel policy to be recommended to senior management (decider).

Agenda:

10:00–10:05 a.m.: Socialize. We'll start at 10:05 a.m. sharp.

10:05–10:15 a.m.: Review current policies—#Sam*

10:15–10:30 a.m.: Review three options and implications— #Rob

10:30–10:50 a.m.: Discuss; recommendations. Facilitated by #Mike.

---

* Using a # before someone's name is a handy way to indicate that they own an action item; it is consistent with our MTD To-Do tracking protocol in chapter 6.

Attendees: Mike, Sam, Rob, Suzie Q, Evangeline, Seattle Mike, and the Hammer*

Ground rules: No internet. No smelly reheated food (Seattle Mike!). #Sam to email presentation 24 hours before meeting; please read in advance.

- **Prewire the meeting.** Achieving the goal of a meeting will often require support from someone in the room who is not yet convinced, often the decision maker. Other times, a meeting topic will risk upsetting someone who will lose resources, authority, or goodwill because of the decision your meeting seeks. Often that person will be on a personal mission to ensure the meeting does not achieve its goals. Meetings featuring one or more undecided or unprepared decision makers and belligerent dissenters can certainly be fun to watch, but they are a terrible way to get things done. You can prewire a meeting for success by engaging with key stakeholders in advance. Talk openly with dissenters in advance to ensure you understand their point of view, share your counterview and rationale, and ensure them that they will have an opportunity to provide their perspective in the meeting. Similarly, give busy decision makers advanced context and prime them for the decision: "Amanda, attached is our presentation today and recommendation that you approve launch of the new project; you will hear some dissent by those who are concerned that the launch will disrupt our sales channel, but you will see in the attached that our three market tests were a resounding success with no disruption. I am at your disposal if you have questions in advance, and look

---

* Seattle Mike is another guy named Mike, but he is from Seattle. The Hammer is just a cool nickname.

forward to exploring further in our Friday 10:00 a.m. meeting."

- **Talk to your doctor about reiteritis.** "I just want to reiterate . . ." is a popular conversation starter among the least useful people in your organization. (We heard you the first time, Jerry.) Don't be afraid to gently interrupt people when they are not adding to the quality of debate in your meeting or helping get closer to achieving the goal. And as a meeting attendee, take the responsibility of saying only what is necessary to achieve the goals of the meeting; if you've made your point, and it has been understood, everyone will appreciate your not repeating yourself.

Follow-Up Actions—Get It Done

The final step in ensuring your meetings achieve their goals is to set clear and accountable follow-up action items to which the stakeholders are committed. Follow the five-D framework where applicable to appoint a directly responsible individual and a decision maker, set a deadline, clarify the data that is needed, and establish the did-it-work metrics that will be tracked going forward. Publish these action items, along with relevant notes and commentary, to all meeting attendees as well as other stakeholders who need to know.

Let's return to our super-dull travel policy meeting as an example, first restating the TIP, agenda, and attendees, then laying out the notes and action items.

- August 27 meeting: Travel Policy Change Decision
- Owner/DRI: Mike
- Purpose: Reduce travel costs 10 percent. Collect input on potential changes to travel policy to be recommended to senior management (decider).

- Agenda:

  10:00–10:05 a.m.: Socialize. We'll start at 10:05 a.m. sharp.

  10:05–10:15 a.m.: Review current policies—#Sam

  10:15–10:30 a.m.: Review three options and implications—#Rob

  10:30–10:50 a.m.: Discuss; round-the-horn recommendation of each attendee. Facilitated by #Mike.

  Attendees: Mike, Sam, Rob, Suzie Q, Evangeline, Seattle Mike. Not in attendance: The Hammer, who had the flu.

- Notes:

  ○ Discussed three options: fewer trips, room sharing, and lower-cost room options.

  ○ Lower-cost room options prioritized. Requiring second-tier hotels would save 10–15 percent of overall travel costs. Team examined four options, all of which were clearly safe and clean. Team recommended this approach. Suzie Q expressed concern that other hotels on the list may not meet requirements, will pull examples and recommend exclusion. Team agreed.

- Action items:

  ○ #Mike is DRI for overall project; Amanda (senior VP) will be decider.

  ○ #Mike to schedule meeting with Amanda to take place in about two weeks. Due: August 29

  ○ #Suzie Q to review second-tier hotel list, recommend any to be excluded from policy due to safety or cleanliness, to be included in recommendation deck. Due: September 3

By bringing this structure and accountability to your meetings, your attendees will know that their time is being used wisely, they will come prepared, and they will contribute usefully and positively to the achievement of your shared goals. Impactful group meetings are one of the most powerful weapons in your get-things-done arsenal and are well worth the time it takes to prepare and follow up effectively.

One-on-One Meetings with Your Boss

The one meeting that likely has the biggest impact on your success at work is also the one you are managing most poorly: the one-on-one meeting with your boss. Ostensibly, its purpose is to "check in" and "manage you," or, in more enlightened organizations, to "help you achieve your goals," though the conversation is, more often than not, disorganized and unpredictable. In most companies, these are intended to be regular meetings, though most bosses are constantly rescheduling or skipping them. The head of an important media business once told me, "I'm not really comfortable telling people what they should do in our weekly meetings"; another time, the founder and CEO of a billion-dollar technology company asked me, "What am I supposed to do in these weekly meetings my executives keep insisting on having with me?" In most organizations, this important opportunity for alignment and collaboration is going to waste.

These meetings are broken for a few basic reasons, which are quite easy to remedy. But first, I have to tell you some uncomfortable truths about your manager, you, and your one-on-ones.

- **Your manager is too busy.** Your manager has at least twice as many emails, twice as many meetings, and twice as many to-do list items as you. He is responsible for his output as well as yours and your peers. He is expected to hit goals, hire well, coach, fire underperformers, communicate well across the organization, share best practices, and deal with his manager, who is, in turn, even busier than he is. If he is managing a team of six, he has over three hundred weekly one-on-one meetings to execute this year. If your most important meeting seems to be the least important thing on his list, try to sympathize: your manager is overwhelmed.

- **Your manager is not a very good manager.** Your manager is also probably not a very good manager. Ninety percent of managers lack many of the critical capabilities needed to manage successfully. And in our fastest-growing industries, a large proportion of the managers are relatively new, given field promotions as the company expands to keep up with industry growth. Most managers receive less than two hours of training a year for this difficult and complex role. It is no surprise that three-quarters of employees report that their boss is the worst part of their job, and half of the people who quit their jobs do so because of their boss—the poor guy probably doesn't know what he is doing!

- **Managing people can be a real pain in the butt.** Even if you are a wonderful coworker and a dream to work with, managing people can be a real headache, so it's likely that you are part of that pain, whether you like it or not. While your manager struggles with this very difficult job for which no one adequately prepared him, there you are, not communicating clearly enough your progress against your goals, interrupting him with routine issues that you should have been able to solve yourself, making excuses, failing to hear and respond to feedback, and then asking why you haven't been promoted yet. And even if you don't do any of these things, you still have to be managed, which is, as we said, a real pain sometimes.

- **Your one-on-one is not very effective (yet).** When your poor overwhelmed manager comes into your one-on-one expecting thirty minutes of catch-up but not a lot of progress—or worse, expects that you will bring him more problems to deal with—he just doesn't look forward to the meeting, which is why it gets canceled, moved, or truncated every week. As the meeting tends to lack a clear agenda, he takes it over with whatever is at the top of his mind, which is likely whatever was the topic of the meeting he is coming from, rather than anchoring the meeting in the thing you both actually care about: achievement of the team's goals.

Don't worry, we are going to fix this. As we have been doing throughout this book, we are simply going to start with your purpose, make a plan, and articulate a simple framework that you can follow every week for mind-blowingly fantastic one-on-ones with your manager. With this new one-on-one agenda organizing your interactions with your boss, the clouds of wasted time will part, the birds of productivity will sing, and the sun will shine gloriously on your career.

Get It Scheduled

Get your boss to commit to this regular time with you every week or every other week. It is a significant commitment, but the TIP of the meeting is compelling: "Our *topic* is a regular, structured one-on-one check-in to ensure I am working on the right things in the right ways to achieve the team's goals; the *importance* is that your regular feedback will maximize my effectiveness and output in achieving our team's goals; the *purpose* of the meeting is to review goals, progress, feedback, and opportunities to do better for which I will be fully accountable." You, the supervisee, will be the DRI for proposing the agenda, doing all the preparation, and capturing the feedback and action items each week.

PART 1, REVIEW THE THINGS YOU OWE YOUR BOSS

Spend the first half of your one-on-one giving your boss insight into how you are progressing against your goals, raising any issues or concerns, and working through roadblocks so that you can successfully do your part to help the team achieve its goals.

1. **Goals! We run this mother (yeah).**[*] A consistent theme of this book is that knowing the goal you want to achieve is essential to success in any activity. It sounds so obvious, and yet millions of Americans will show up at meetings today without articulating a clear and important goal that the meeting is designed to achieve. To make the one-on-one with your manager highly effective, begin by restating your goals for the relevant period of time: "To start, I want to recap my third-quarter goals to ensure I am focused on the right things to help our team succeed this quarter: (1) finalize market analysis for Samsonagra, our new prescrip-

---

[*] Yes, that's another Beyoncé reference. She is so productive.

tion hair growth product coming to market next quarter,* and successfully deliver to senior management; (2) complete full competitor profiles in hair growth category, showing relative benefits of Samsonagra, for sign-off by product development team; (3) create new collateral materials that the sales team will take to market in the fourth quarter with the Samsonagra launch, leveraging market and competitor work; and (4) develop customer "frequently asked questions" document, in partnership with sales leadership, and get legal team approval of all claims and statements in the materials. Before I update you on progress, I want to make sure we agree that I have been focusing on the correct goals." With this, your manager can either confirm that you are focused on the right things or redirect you to different goals, which you can update in real time. This prevents the great career tragedy of you doing an excellent job on something that is no longer on strategy and that your boss no longer cares about.

2. **Progress against your goals.** The biggest concern of most managers is that you will screw something up and make her life harder. But the better your communication, and the more reliable your track record, the less your manager will worry about your delivery. In your one-on-one, offer to show your manager your progress against these goals by bringing along completed work product and data that demonstrate where you stand in relation to your objectives. When you are off pace or at risk of not achieving your goals, say so very clearly, and then indicate how you are working to resolve it. If you believe the goal will be missed, do not surprise your manager; call it out early, and invite input into how you can close the gap. Use consistent data every week to credibly show progress, for

---

* I regret to inform you that this is also not a real product.

instance, "In order for the FAQs to be approved in time for the fourth-quarter launch, I need to have all fifteen pages drafted by September 15. Twelve pages are complete and I can do three in a day. I plan to use this Friday to finish the product, and will be turning it over for approval a week early. I have brought the draft pages along, if you would like to see the work in progress."

3. **Other action items.** Your manager will often give you additional assignments and should not have to lose time or energy worrying whether you will get them done. List your action items and communicate that they are done, when they will be completed, or, if they are not getting done, what could be done and what help you need. "Last week you suggested I read Chip Heath's *Made to Stick*.* I did, and am applying the learnings to the marketing materials by incorporating memorable stories from our clinical trials into the narrative for sales. You also asked me to get to know the new sales trainer, Andy. We are having lunch Friday. Is there anything else on your list that I may have forgotten?"

4. **Issue resolution.** Ideally, you would solve everything yourself, but your manager will, at times, have authority, insights, and experiences that you need to complete your tasks successfully. Your one-on-one is the right place to seek the advice or support that you need; for instance, "I need legal team approval of all claims, but have been unsuccessful in getting a lawyer assigned to work on it with me. If we do not have one by the end of the week, I believe we will miss this goal. Can you help by getting our general counsel to assign someone to work with me on this next week?"

---

* Very good book on marketing and communications, FYI.

PART 2, ADDITIONAL THINGS YOUR BOSS NEEDS FROM YOU

It is important to create time in your one-on-one for your manager to bring you items that you did not cover in your goals, progress, and action items. Putting this in every one-on-one agenda means your boss can put his items aside while you run through yours, knowing they will be covered later in the one-on-one. Your boss's issues will often be related to your goals and progress, and may all be covered in the first part of the agenda. If your manager assigns additional action items in this discussion, be sure to capture them and report progress in part 1 of your next one-on-one agenda. It is fair to expect that you will not have to try very hard to get your boss to use your one-on-one to assign you more work.

PART 3, FEEDBACK

Every time I have looked back on my career, I have noticed that three or four years previous, I was an idiot. I am always embarrassed to think about all the things I know now that I did not know then, the mistakes and blind spots that had been holding me back just a few years earlier. I suppose this is the nature of constantly striving to improve. Unfortunately, presuming this trend continues, in three or four years I will look back and marvel at what a complete idiot I am *right now*. And, at the moment, I don't know what I am an idiot about.

This is terrifying—and why constant feedback is so important: other people see our weaknesses and development needs well before we do. It takes discipline and humility to absorb that feedback and make it useful—when we have been told our whole lives what a smart, wonderful, unique, and perfect child we are, it is hard to subdue that need for praise with an openness to feedback and improvement. It tastes like crap, but it is the fertilizer that grows our abilities and seeds great performance in our future.

The standard corporate structure of annual reviews fails to pro-

vide timely and actionable feedback, as most of the feedback we receive in our annual look-back is outdated. It is also nearly impossible
to process feedback during a review, since we are so consumed with
whether or not the annual review is leading to a promotion. The solution is to use your one-on-one for regular, timely, raw feedback from
your manager.

There are a few methods that should ensure your manager is giving you the feedback you deserve:

1. **Ask for it directly.** Deep down, we all just want to be
   liked, which makes it hard to give someone else feedback.
   Telling another human being, "You seem to like to hear
   yourself talk in meetings," or, "People do not trust your
   conclusions because you do not demonstrate how you are
   using data to make the decision," or, "Please stop wearing
   that ridiculous hat," is uncomfortable for all of us. Make it
   easy on your manager by asking directly for feedback,
   telling your manager how important you believe it is to
   your ability to succeed at work, and making it a weekly
   item on your one-on-one agenda.

2. **Agree on a high standard.** As the kind of person driven
   enough to read twenty-five pages about how to have effective meetings, I suspect you are a high performer on
   your team. This can make it hard for a manager to give
   you feedback, because your work is better than your
   peers'. People like you will often hear, "You're doing
   great, keep it up." This is the Curse of the Good Employee
   and, as nice as that positive feedback feels, it teaches you
   nothing and is worthless to you. If you are in this position, ask your manager to give you feedback against the
   expectations of someone more senior than you. If you are
   an associate director, ask to be compared to a senior director or a vice president. For example:

You: "How did I do in the meeting where we reviewed the fre-
    quently asked questions materials with the senior vice presi-
    dent of sales?"

Boss: "Great. The materials were thorough, you got her to give us
    some really good feedback, and the next steps were clear."

You: "Anything I can do to improve?"

Boss: "No, keep up the great work."

You: "Can I ask you—what would a successful vice president
    with this same assignment have done differently?"

Boss: "What? Well, she would not have needed so much feedback—
    the FAQs would have been just about right on the first draft.
    But you're not expected to . . ."

You: "That's great feedback! How would a vice president have
    gone about making sure the FAQs were right the first time?"

Boss: "Well, if it were me, I would have pulled a bunch of compa-
    rables from other companies, identified the best practices, and
    I would have run this draft by a bunch of sales folks and a
    couple of friends who are customers, too, first."

You: "That is what I will do next time. Thanks for that. I'll always
    make use of feedback like this to do a better job next time."

Inner monologue: "When I am in charge of this place, I am going
    to take good care of you, boss."

3. **Use a safe word.** Understanding that feedback is uncomfortable, it is important to create a structure that forces it
   to happen. There are two sets of phrases that are invaluable to getting clear and actionable feedback.

   "Missing," "meeting," or "exceeding" expectations—As you
   proudly review your progress toward your goals, and
   your boss says, "Okay, thanks for the update," for all you
   know he may be thinking, "Geez, we have been talking
   about this one goal for a month, why is this so hard for
   you?" You can get a clear read from your manager by asking for a direct assessment: is this missing, meeting, or exceeding your expectations? It is almost impossible for an

ambiguous assessment when using those words. When the answer is "missing" expectations, you now have an opportunity to ask how you could do it better, and agree to a plan for you to deliver better results. When it is "meeting," you get to ask how you could have done it better. When "exceeding," you can say, "Great, what further work is important to our team's success that I can take off of your plate?" If the answer is always "exceeding," then you are not taking on hard enough assignments, so ask for them. Employees who take this kind of responsibility for their performance are the ones who get assigned the most important projects, raise their profile in the organization, become indispensable, and are treated accordingly.

"Stop," "start," and "continue"—As important as whether you achieved your goals is how you went about it. Your manager, as a regular observer of your approach, and a more experienced professional, is in a great position to coach you on better behaviors and tactics in your work. But, as we have discussed, doing so requires criticizing you in a way many people would find painful. To force it, ask your manager for feedback couched in the terms "stop," "start," and "continue." It is nearly impossible to tell someone, "I would like you to stop___," or, "Please start ___," without filling in the blank with constructive criticism, or to ask someone, "Continue to ___," without pointing out something that is being done well or is a good sign of progress. For instance:

- Stop emailing me all these small tactical questions. I trust you to make good decisions.

- Stop expressing yourself passive aggressively in meetings; if you disagree, just say so clearly.

- Stop beginning all of your statements with the word "actually." It makes you sound like a tween.

- Start communicating more concisely. It takes you too long to make a point.

- Start illustrating your points with charts and graphs so that we better understand how you came to this conclusion.

- Start dressing for the job you want, not the job you have.

- Continue working on your PowerPoint skills; your decks have improved a lot and are looking super.

- Continue including folks from other departments in your work; you have been doing that regularly and are developing a reputation as a great teammate.

- Continue volunteering to take on more work; you are becoming an extremely valuable member of the team.

4. **Track and report.** Your manager will be motivated to give you feedback when you show progress on the coaching you have already received. Just as you track your goals and open action items, track feedback and report back how you are reacting to it, asking for additional input along the way:

—Feedback August 1: "Stop emailing small tactical questions." I used to send, on average, twelve emails a week to you. Since our discussion, I have been sending four, handling the rest myself. Have you noticed a change, and do you feel I am addressing the issue appropriately?

—Feedback September 15: "Stop checking Facebook at work." I installed a browser add-on that blocks social media sites. I just wanted to assure you this one won't happen again.

The additional benefit to this approach is that it addresses a common problem with managers: if you have a bad habit, anything resembling it is noticed immediately, but the fact that you have remedied the issue goes unnoticed. Take the first example above, sending too many emails. Even if your emails were reduced, the ones you send are still at risk of being viewed through the lens of "This person sends way too many emails." Your manager doesn't stop to count them, she just thinks, "Another email?!" In the second example, your manager noticed you on Facebook a lot, which irritated her and formed a semipermanent mental association between you and the Facebook Incidents. Even if you stop, the absence of the bad habit is less likely to be noticed and remembered. (We notice when people burp; we don't take notice when people do not burp.) Calling out the areas of feedback and your specific actions taken to improve will change your manager's perception and give you the benefit of the doubt going forward.

PART 4, OPEN MIC

The items above are critical to the achievement of your professional goals and to your ability to succeed and grow in your role. When they are being addressed to your manager's and your satisfaction, and when time permits, have an "open mic" period in your session to cover further topics that can be valuable to your longer-term success.

1. **Get your umbrellas out and brainstorm.** Creating an agenda item specifically for brainstorming gives you the liberty to throw out ideas and issues that are not necessarily relevant to your immediate goals, and for which you are not expected to already have an answer. You can raise

observations about the market, technological changes, competitors, team performance and culture, throw out new business ideas, and so on, and get the benefit of the perspective of a more seasoned professional. Tapping your collective creativity can also unlock new ways to address your current goals. Plus, if you enjoy your field of work, these conversations are fun and an effective way to bond with your manager.* "How does this business look in five years?" . . . "What technologies are going to change our business the most?" . . . "Did you see that Zaxacorp just launched their new social anxiety drug solely on social media? Maybe there is something to explore here that could be relevant to our Samsonagra launch." Like the other agenda topics, this one will be most effective if you have done some preparation. For instance, if you want to brainstorm about which large companies are most exposed to changes in technology, and how they will be affected, include the question in your one-on-one agenda, and bring a list of companies with market caps over $100 billion, or something like that.

2. **Career Roadmap and career covenant.** A core principle of this book is that you are the CEO of your own career, setting the purpose and plan that you will execute to achieve the impact you want to have in your life. Your manager is a critical stakeholder in the current stage of your career development: she is generally more experienced than you, has a broader network, directly influences the work you are assigned, decides whether to present you for promotion, and is in a position to provide you with regular coaching. We discussed the career covenant in chapter 4, a relationship between a supervisee and supervisor wherein the supervisee delivers results and helps the

---

* If you don't enjoy your work, go back to chapters 1 and 2!

team succeed, and the supervisor, in turn, provides career coaching, advice, and sponsorship.* Ask for your manager's commitment to provide you with this kind of career support, so long as you are delivering outstanding performance, and use a portion of your one-on-ones, when time permits, to explore career questions, longer-cycle development areas, and so on. You might share your Impact Map and Career Roadmap and seek feedback and advice. You can ask for your manager's support in developing certain skills or experiences critical to your plan, whether through taking courses, attending conferences, sitting in on meetings, being introduced to experts within or outside of the organization, or taking on projects at work. At times, five to ten minutes in a one-on-one will be hugely impactful; at other times, when you and your manager have the opportunity, you might ask for a full hour on this topic, for which you should prepare an agenda, goals, and questions.

Side hustle. Your Career Roadmap will be full of skills and experiences that you need to earn in order to progress toward your career goals, many of which will be outside the scope of your current job and, most likely, things you are not yet qualified to do. In *The Five Patterns of Extraordinary Careers,* Jim Citrin, one of the top CEO recruiters in the world at the time of this writing, describes how successful professionals grow in their careers by solving "the Permission Paradox," or the age-old dilemma that you cannot get the job without the experience, but you cannot get the experience without the job. He covers various solutions for gaining additional responsibilities, such as going to school to earn new credentials,

---

* I know about the career covenant because a star employee once gave me the *Feiner Points of Leadership* book and said, "I would like to have a career covenant with you," which seemed reasonable to me.

getting a strategic mentor, or getting a manager's blessing to try something new. I have found the most success with asking a manager to support low-risk, optional projects that are outside of your current skills and responsibilities and will provide you with the opportunity to learn by doing new things. If your Career Roadmap requires you to become a good business-to-business marketer, ask if you can come in on the weekends to rewrite some outdated sales marketing materials for the team. If you want to learn to be great at sales, ask if you could take on a couple low-quality accounts to practice the craft. If you are developing people leadership skills, suggest you build a mentoring network in your organization for new hires. Good side hustle ideas will often spring from your brainstorms and your Career Roadmap discussions. "Last week we talked about the impact of social media on our industry, and today we identified strategy as a skill I need to refine. What if I took on a side hustle project to propose a social media strategy to you that you might want to implement on our team? I would interview experts, read Guy Kawasaki's new book, and customize a plan for our team's specific needs over weekends for the next eight weeks. Would that be worth your time and mine?"

Open mic will backfire badly if you are using precious minutes with your manager for it while you are in any way missing her expectations. It only works when your goodwill bank with your manager is full: your work is done on time, you are hitting your goals, you are getting along well with your teammates, and you are making good use of your manager's time. Under those circumstances, open mic is invaluable to developing rapport with your manager, flexing your creative muscles, advancing your Career Roadmap, and creating side hustle opportunities.

To tie it all together, here is a one-on-one agenda template that you might introduce to your manager for your next meeting.

1:1 / Aug 15
ME—*Goals, Progress, & Help Needed*—<u>15 Minutes</u>
YOU—*Issues, Troubleshooting, Delegation, etc.*—<u>10 Minutes</u>
OPEN ACTION ITEMS—<u>5 Minutes</u>
FEEDBACK—*Stop-Start-Continue*—<u>10 Minutes</u>
OPEN MIC—<u>20 Minutes (Time Permitting)</u>

This high-impact framework for your one-on-ones with your manager will ensure you are always aligned on goals and performance, receiving valuable feedback, and investing together in your professional development. If you consistently deliver effective one-on-ones with your manager, you are going to have this person's trust, support, and sponsorship throughout your career.

CHAPTER 12

⟶ Stakeholder Management: Heaven Is Other People

If you want to go fast, go alone. If you want to go far, bring others.

—African Proverb

Think of the last time you could not get something done at work. I'll bet the reason was someone else.

More than ever before, work has become cross-functional, with success in most any project dependent on the cooperation of other people or other teams; i.e., stakeholders. Many of the world's leading companies have diminished or eliminated the role of general managers, leaving their various teams (sales, marketing, engineering, product, etc.) to need to work together without a single arbiter of decisions. A few companies are even attempting to remove managers entirely from their organizations, leaving people to self-organize and self-manage.*

Today, someone else's failure to cooperate is not an accepted excuse for missing your goals. Those who succeed in the modern workplace are the ones who know how to effectively communicate and earn the support of others in the organization. Trevor in marketing may be a real pain, but you can't get your job done without him.

We have reviewed in this book foundational tactics to help. For

---

* Leading, in most instances, to complete chaos.

instance, maximizing your personal energy and productivity makes you a more effective contributor, which earns the goodwill of others. Developing a strong network gives you relationships on which to build your collaborative success. Sharpening sales skills helps you to convince others when you are confident that you have the right answer. Hosting effective meetings facilitates good discussions and clear action items. But these skills alone will not ensure cross-functional success. What follows in this chapter will provide you with the tools to be an effective stakeholder manager, one who is collaborative and attuned to others, who can effectively investigate and understand the views of other people, and who can articulate paths to resolution and action. But first, we need to understand why this is so damned hard.

People Are Strange

An entire industry has emerged from the realization that people have different personalities. At some point in your career, you may have been forced to take something like a Myers-Briggs assessment, which told you that you were "ISTJ," a logical, introverted, practical decider who likes clear and actionable outcomes, who operates with detail and rigor, and who is ready to jump to action. Or you might have been "ENFP," an extroverted, open-minded, flexible, and dreamy person who sees the big picture, imagines new possibilities, and is guided by his or her gut. If you are the former, the outcome of this test would have you believe you are likely the finest factory operator to never be invited to a party; the latter, maybe a cool artist, hippie, or graduate of Brown University. And while these simple personality tests are generally disputed by credible scientists, they do serve a useful purpose, reminding us that we are each a unique and beautiful snowflake, inadvertently ruining the meetings of others.

What's more, not only are our personalities fundamentally different, we are each the victim of the behavior of our minds in that exact moment. Think back to our discussions on habits and productivity in part 3, which were based on the foundational understanding that our thoughts are not always rational, nor under our full control (System 1 versus System 2). The same is true for others, but unlike you, faithful reader, they probably don't realize it (share this book, y'all). This truth is well illustrated by the experiment run by psychologist Donald Dutton in the 1970s, in which men traversing a high suspension bridge were propositioned by an attractive woman, and men walking down the street were similarly propositioned by an attractive woman; the men crossing the bridge were more likely to engage, because they mistook the adrenaline created by being in a high place for romantic arousal. We think we know why we are in a certain frame of mind, but we usually do not.

Further, human communication is fantastically inefficient. The neurons in your brain generate a thought, your brain converts it into words, and you speak it to someone else in a language littered with ambiguity, homonym confusion, misattributed pronouns, and vague phrases like "synergy" and "value add." Then the counterparty's neurons have to translate your words back into his own thoughts and context, which are different from yours, because he is an "INTJ" or a libertarian or a suffering Mets fan. Rarely is the thought transferred to someone else's mind with all the original information and intent intact.

This all presumes you can hold someone else's attention long enough for the information even to be heard, which is unlikely, as scientists have estimated the average human attention span to be *eight seconds*. Note, the attention span of goldfish is nine seconds. In fairness, goldfish do not have iPhones.

Beyond the substantial feat of just conveying your thought to someone else in a way he can understand, you now have earned the challenge of getting agreement on that thought from someone whose goals, incentives, abilities, and worldview are different from yours.

Maybe this is what Jean-Paul Sartre meant when he said, "Hell is other people."

However, effective communication and collaboration can be done—and must be done—for you and your teammates to effectively achieve the right outcomes. So let's get it right.

Stop, Collaborate, and Listen

The key to understanding others is to listen to them intently. All the limitations of the human mind and human communication apply not only to other people, but also to you. In fact, it has been my experience that the smartest and most motivated people—who often assume they already understand the issues and are eager to jump to the answer—can at times be the least effective listeners. This is a bad habit that some competent people never shake, to the significant detriment of their careers. Failing to truly hear and appreciate your audience leads to, at best, misunderstanding, and at worst earns you the disdain of people who feel ignored and disrespected by you. However, by committing to the following good habits of active and empathetic listening, you can transform into a good listener, which is the first step to being a good communicator and stakeholder manager.

Put your agenda aside. Chances are, you arrive in most conversations already knowing what you want to say; if not, it does not take you long to come up with something. This thought—your personal agenda—is the number one thing stopping you from actively listening to the other person. Your urge to speak is at times so strong that holding it back manifests physically: you start to fidget, your hands clench, your mouth starts to open every time the other person pauses to take a breath. All the while, you are missing the opportunity to invest in the conversation by truly listening. To remedy this, consciously put aside the thing you want to say until you have had a chance to understand the other person. As a reminder to yourself, exercise the physical trigger of intentionally unclenching your hands and silently exhaling, as if to release the thing that is stopping you from giving the other person the gift of your attention. Only once you have cleared your mind of your own agenda can you effectively hear the other person. If you are concerned you will forget what you wanted to say, write it down on one of your index cards, and put it aside until the appropriate time.

Be happy to be wrong. Putting your agenda aside also gives you the opportunity to learn. Too often, our egos are in the way, making us resistant to seeing the world from another perspective, because it may mean that we were—gasp!—wrong. This need to be right is a handicap that holds many smart people back in their careers, as they waste countless learning opportunities by applying their existing knowledge to impulsively accept or reject what they hear. That is why millions of Republicans watch Fox News and millions of Democrats watch MSNBC, rarely coming to understand how the other side sees the world. If, instead, you approach each conversation with an intellectual curiosity to understand the other person's perspective, and a growth mind-set that assumes you may be about to learn something new, or see it from a unique angle, you will find many better solutions, while improving your own understanding of the topic. If you never change your mind, you will never learn something new.

Empathize and encourage. Once you have given the other person your full attention to understand her point of view, keep asking yourself two questions: what is she saying, and why is she saying it? In most conversations, we are disagreeing over something—what is it, and why? Do we have the same facts and are we interpreting them the same way? What is the other person's agenda and how is it coloring her view? Your colleague from finance may view a proposal in the context of how expensive it is, while your friend from sales sees a chance to improve revenue and beat her quota. As they explain themselves, keep nodding and expressing an appreciation for each perspective, repeating back what you have heard, and encouraging further elaboration. When you can sincerely say something like, "That must be frustrating," or, "Now I think I know why you are so eager to solve this," you have begun to earn the goodwill that is afforded to someone who seeks to understand. And once you have walked through the issue in their shoes as a good thought partner, you have earned the right to start assessing the elements of each person's argument.

Investigate

Beyond just listening patiently, you will need to dig deeper to appreciate what your audience is trying to tell you, and begin to dissect their communication to better comprehend the concern or the proposed solution. A combination of these tactics can take you a long way toward understanding the issues.

Ask why five times. One of the most effective strategies for getting to the root cause of a problem, invented over a hundred years ago by Sakichi Toyoda, the founder of Toyota,* is known as the Five Whys technique. This is a root-cause analysis method that has become a key element of process-improvement practices like Six Sigma and lean manufacturing, which industrial giants like General Electric and Motorola use to make their lightbulb and beeper factories more efficient. It is a simple technique for getting to the core of an issue. For instance, imagine you are told, "I think we need more salespeople. We have lots of leads, but sales are down from last month." Before engaging in the discussion about how many salespeople are needed, you investigate the root cause of the problem, asking first why sales are down:

> Why are sales down? (Why #1)—Because new business activations are lagging.
> Why is that? (Why #2)—The team is making 30 percent fewer new business outreach calls than last month.
> Why are calls down? (Why #3)—They have been struggling to learn the new sales force management tool, which is making them less productive.
> Why haven't they learned the new tool? (Why #4)—Most of them have not had sufficient training on the new tool.
> Why not? (Why #5)—We have only two sales trainers, and

---

* For all his contributions, you would think they would have spelled his name right on the backs of their trucks.

they are working through the sales force as fast as they
can, but it's not enough.

Bingo. The problem isn't that we need more salespeople, it is that
we need more sales trainers. In practice, you will be more conversational than just saying "Why?" repeatedly like a five-year-old who
has been denied more screen time, but you get the idea. I believe this
to be one of the most important techniques in problem solving at all
professional levels.

Disambiguate. A challenge in communication is that we all have
a tendency to speak in generalities, which others can interpret in myriad ways, leading to an instant disagreement. Further, we are prone to
conflate multiple issues when leaping to a single perceived solution. For
instance, imagine this discussion between a marketer and a developer:

Marketer: "We really need to improve our Android app."
Tech lead: "Our Android app is terrific; it has a four-star rating,
    and my team worked really hard on it!"
Marketer: "Well, it doesn't work right."
Tech lead: "It has industry-leading load times and never crashes."
Marketer: "It doesn't matter if it doesn't crash."
Tech lead: "How could it not matter? You want an app that
    crashes?"
Marketer: "I want an app with push notifications!"
Tech lead: "You marketers think the key to everything is more
    features! We are working beyond full capacity right now try-
    ing to ship everyone else's brilliant feature ideas . . ."

At best, these two are about to waste thirty minutes of their lives;
at worst, their failure to communicate effectively is going to feed a
low-grade antipathy for each other that will undermine their ability
to work together in the future.

Does that sound like conversations you have had at work?

Typically in these conversations, we confuse goals, strategy, performance, and priorities in ways that make it difficult to resolve the

issue collaboratively. Adding to the challenge, we use vague observations and adjectives rather than clear data. In our example, one member of the team is articulating how the product is performing to its reliability goals. The other seems to want to discuss a strategic idea, though the goal of that strategic idea is unclear. Let's imagine a more productive version of this discussion:

Marketer: "I have an idea that could improve our Android app."

Tech lead: "Really? Well, you have good instincts—I would love to hear your thoughts."

Marketer: "Thanks! I have been reviewing our performance metrics for the Android app. Reliability is excellent, to tech's credit, but visits per user are below goal. I was wondering if you would be open to some ideas on how to resolve that issue?"

Tech lead: "I have been having the same concern. It's like our users download the app, it works perfectly, but they somehow forget why they liked it enough to download it in the first place."

Marketer: "I was reading an industry report on how push notifications can increase user return rates by 50 percent. We don't have push notifications. If we increased user return rates by 50 percent, we would be exceeding our goal for user visits."

Tech lead: "I would love to dig into that. But I am concerned that we don't have the resources to work on more feature requests."

Marketer: "If we conclude this would not be high impact enough to pursue, I certainly wouldn't want to disrupt your current product roadmap. But if you and I analyze the push notification opportunity and agree it would be high impact, I would be happy to help compare the opportunity to the other things your team has been asked to prioritize and, if appropriate, work with you to advocate for changing the priorities to improve our chances of exceeding our goals."

Tech lead: "That sounds great. You complete me."

Marketer: "And you had me at hello."

Okay, you don't necessarily need the *Jerry Maguire* ending, but you get the point: these are the same people addressing the same topic, but by avoiding generalities and focusing the discussion on precise issues and potential decisions, they are able to collaborate more effectively. You will often find yourself in similar situations. Here is a simple process for disambiguating the ideas being presented by others so that you can develop a helpful mutual understanding of the issue and drive toward a solution.

1. **Goal: What problem are we trying to solve?** The late economist Theodore Levitt once famously said, "People don't want to buy a quarter-inch drill. They want a quarter-inch hole." Just as getting sh★t done demands that we approach our action items by first asking what goal we are trying to achieve (GIST—chapter 8), and effective meetings start with a clear statement of topic, importance, and purpose (TIP—chapter 10), good communication starts with reestablishing the problem we are trying to solve. We are not going to begin a discussion by debating whether we should have push notifications, if we should hire two more people to work in accounting, or if we should buy a new coffeemaker for the cafeteria; we are first going to talk about achieving our goal for app usage, the importance of protecting the company by delivering accurate financials, or the fact that everyone in the company has to leave the office to get a decent coffee. By beginning with the goal, we have the opportunity to first get everyone's buy-in that the issue is important and should be addressed, thus laying the groundwork to then explore the solution that you have in mind, or perhaps identifying a better one together. If you cannot reach agreement on the importance of the goal, then you will have identified a critical misalignment in your organization that likely needs to be escalated to someone more senior to reconcile before there is any chance of agreeing to your solution.

2. **Data: Numbers talk.** To paraphrase one of my dad's favorite adages: numbers talk and bullsh*t walks. Effective professionals learn not to waste time debating whether "things are going really great" or a situation is "a really huge problem," when the data can do that for you. There are numbers, called key performance indicators (KPIs), that directly drive the success of the organization; these often involve critical data points like customer adoption, in-store traffic, average spend per customer, number of key actions taken per customer, primary drivers of cost, organizational productivity statistics, and so on. Your group should have targets for each of these KPIs, or at minimum historical numbers so that you can benchmark current performance against past years. A good professional (that's you) should know these numbers in detail and understand what drives them and how they interoperate. While one KPI, such as total unit sales, may suggest high performance, others, such as price per unit, or productivity per channel, may tell a different story. A firm handle on the numbers would equip you to assess broad statements, like, "Hey, sales are going great," in the context of other insights, like, "But isn't it true that we increased sales staffing by 20 percent, and marketing by 30 percent, and introduced a self-serve channel that now accounts for 5 percent of our revenue, implying that revenue per salesperson is actually down significantly year over year?" The right data helps us to have a more informed conversation and reach the best outcome; without it, we are just trading opinions, a situation that Jim Barksdale, the CEO of internet pioneer Netscape, famously used to call out by saying, "If we have data, let's look at data. If all we have are opinions, let's go with mine."

3. **Potential solutions: "Yes, if."** When stakeholders work together to first understand the problem being addressed,

and take the time necessary to interpret the relevant data, both parties are brought naturally to the point of discussing solutions. Sometimes, the groundwork done in the discussion automatically rules out a solution that otherwise would have been put on the table, by refocusing everyone on more appropriate goals, or by revealing data that points the team in another direction. Other times, it may become clear that you do not share the same goals, or you do not have sufficient data to truly understand the problem and potential solution. In these situations, rather than debate a point without a mutual understanding of the foundational issues, it is best to agree to what additional information is required: you may conclude that ambiguity over goals requires the input of a more senior stakeholder before moving forward, or you may agree on a set of data that needs to be reviewed. More often than not, the time invested in agreeing on goals and understanding the data leads to an energetic exploration of solutions, including whatever solution one party may have had in mind at the beginning of the discussion.

Unfortunately, too often potential solutions are drowned in a downpour of noes before the ideas can germinate. There are endless reasons that something can't work: there is no budget, there is no time, there is no one to focus on it, there is not enough expertise, there are competitors doing it, we tried that before and it didn't work, blah, blah, blah. Somehow, mankind built the pyramids and sent a space probe to Pluto, but it is just impossible to get the legal team to make a small change to your company's terms and conditions? As a general rule, if you are motivated, all of these noes can be overcome, so don't let them stand in the way of a good brainstorm. Every time you feel the urge to say, "No, because . . ." replace it with "Yes, if . . ." Can we offer a much higher level of service to our customers when they call with an issue? *No, it would require more people.* Scratch that. *Yes, if the results justify the investment in more customer service reps.* Can we improve benefits for our employees? *No, it's too expensive.* Scratch that. *Yes, if we can show that it improves retention and productivity enough to offset the higher costs.*

Sometimes you will spend cycles on an idea that is ultimately implausible. But it is worth the effort. Nothing in the world was built by saying no.

4. **Priority: GIST . . . again.** Once you take a "Yes, if" approach, coming up with creative solutions is, in many ways, the easy part. In most organizations, there are more good ideas than there is capacity to pursue them. Just as with managing the limited hours in your own calendar (chapter 7) and your finite capacity to tackle your to-do list (chapter 8), the hard part of anything is prioritizing. Our GIST (goals, impact, speed, timing) model can similarly be applied to team projects. We have already invested in understanding the *goal* that this solution could address. Exploring the data together informs the kind of *impact* this solution could have on our goal. Next, assessing the difficulty of execution, in cash costs or human effort, gives a sense of the *speed* with which this could be done. Finally, its relevance to things happening now informs the *timing*, whether it should be prioritized right away. If the same team is working on three other projects right now with an end-of-quarter deadline, and they would all have a bigger impact for a similar amount of effort, then we would likely all agree that either the great solution we just identified has to wait or more resources need to be brought to bear to tackle it in parallel. Alternatively, if we have just found a higher-leverage fix that will give us more impact on our top goals for equal or less effort, then we may conclude together that it is time to reprioritize.

5. **Follow-up: Use the five Ds again.** In seeking to understand this opportunity better, it is likely that we have come to establish next steps, whether it's to collect more information that needs to be analyzed to make a better decision or because we have agreed to work to prioritize a new initiative. Employing the five Ds we discussed last chapter will ensure follow-up by designating a directly responsible individual, a decision maker, and a deadline. And that sh*t will get done.

Explain What You Are Doing, and Why

This chapter has so far focused on the daily back-and-forth elements of stakeholder management: listening, debating, and finding common ground. Another key element to stakeholder management is clearly and consistently articulating your work in the context of your goals. Many professionals struggle with this. Here are a few tools to help you do it well.

Plant your strategy tree. Repeating the wisdom of Henry Ford, nothing is particularly hard if you break it down into small jobs. Achieving your goal relies on the successful execution of a series of initiatives that, in the aggregate, yield the result you desire. It is important that others understand how your many small jobs, requests for resources, and so on tie back to those goals. A simple tool can help you effectively think through and communicate your plan: the strategy tree. The strategy tree divides your top-level goal into smaller goals, initiatives, and action items whose achievement would, in the aggregate, result in success.

To illustrate, let's say we are working on improving children's literacy in the United States. Imagine that our mission is to put a book in the hands of every child in America, and one of our key goals is to launch our new $1.5 million children's literacy project. Let's break this down and turn it into action.

Strategy Tree (Children's Literacy Project Example)

OBJECTIVE: *Raise $1.5 million to support the children's literacy project* (top-level goal)*

FROM WHAT SOURCES? *(second-level goals, which sum to the top-level goal):*

1. Raise $500,000 from large corporate sponsors

2. Raise $900,000 from government

3. Raise $100,000 from social media campaign

HOW DO WE ACHIEVE EACH OF THESE?
(third-level goals, which sum to each second-level goal):

1. Raise $500,000 from large corporate sponsors:

   - Five new corporate sponsors

   - Average contribution of $100,000 each

2. Raise $900,000 from government:

   - Two successful state or city support grants

   - $450,000 contribution each

3. Raise $100,000 from social media campaign:

   - One thousand donations

   - $100 each

---

* Whatever you are doing, always, always, always start with the goal you are trying to achieve.

Once you branch the strategy tree to a sufficient level of detail, you have to validate that each of the subgoals makes sense. For instance, here is a quick verification of the assumptions in the second-level goals above.

Raise $500,000 from large corporate sponsors

1. Five new corporate sponsors—*We have fifty solid leads from our board of directors and have a track record of closing 10 percent of strong leads over the past few years. This is achievable.*

2. Average contribution of $100,000 each—*Our average corporate contribution since 2009 has been $100,000; we expect this trend to hold. We will seek more, but are budgeting a continuation of our historical performance.*

Then, once you are comfortable that the assumptions are sound, you lay out the initiatives that will lead to achieving each.

Raise $500,000 from large corporate sponsors

1. Five new corporate sponsors

   - *Hire full-time development person*

   - *Begin calling on five high-potential corporate donors a week for ten weeks*

   - *Close 10 percent of prospects*

Finally, once you have these more detailed initiatives, lay out the action items that need to be completed to help achieve them, the due dates, and the directly responsible individual for each.

Raise $500,000 from large corporate sponsors

1. Five new corporate sponsors

   - Hire full-time development person

   ☐ Write job description—August 1—#Anthony
   ☐ Contract with executive recruiter—August 7—#Anthony
   ☐ Establish interview guide—August 14—#Anthony
   ☐ Secure two board members to assist in interviews—
      August 14—#Anthony

By starting with your top-level goal, breaking it down to validated subgoals and key initiatives, and then converting these to action items, you can be sure that you and your teammates are spending time on the right actions to achieve your important goals. Once the strategy tree is complete, these action items should be given the GIST treatment and put into MTD or your productivity tool of choice for prioritization and execution (see chapter 8).

Funnel it. A complementary tool to the strategy tree is the funnel. At times a sales funnel, marketing funnel, purchasing funnel, or blueberry muffin funnel (which is only really relevant in the muffin industry), the funnel starts with a large addressable opportunity set and then narrows it down through successive conversion steps. I know, that sounds technical—let's use an example.

Say you run a small bakery that sells blueberry muffins (and there

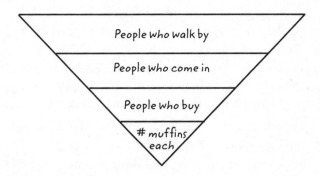

you thought that last muffin reference was arbitrary!). You want to sell more muffins. What is the best way to do it? You can start by assessing the steps in a basic funnel. How many people walk by your shop in a week? How many walk in the door? How many buy a muffin? How many muffins does each person buy? These numbers shape your funnel.

Improving any one of these metrics will improve your total muffin sales, and a careful analysis of each step will likely tell you where your best opportunity for improvement lies. For instance, let's say you are in a neighborhood where very few people walk by (funnel level 1). It's hard to sell muffins if the top of your funnel has few potential customers. Maybe you need to move the shop, or sell your muffins through resellers in better neighborhoods. Let's say plenty of people walk by, but few people walk in (funnel level 2). Maybe you need a better sign and call-to-action, more attractive storefront, or better-smelling muffins to draw them in. If many people walk in but they don't buy (funnel level 3), the layout of the shop may be turning people away, the muffins may not look appetizing, or you may be charging too much. If people who buy are purchasing only one muffin (funnel level 4), you have an opportunity to improve upsell at the register or push special offers like buy two, get one free. Observing the funnels of other shops in your neighborhood and other muffin shops in other neighborhoods would tell you where your funnel is underperforming and where you have opportunities to improve.

If you actually run a bakery, then this example should be a huge help to you. If, strangely, you work in some other industry, you should know that this tool also works for you. If you are in telesales, then your sales funnel goes something like this: total customers on call list (level 1), customers called per day (level 2), customers who answer per day (level 3), customers who buy (level 4), how much they each buy (level 5). You can improve your sales performance by focusing on whichever of those levels offers the most upside, perhaps increasing the percentage of customers who buy through an improved pitch that creates more urgency to act (see "Purpose and Close" in chapter 10). If you are marketing something to people via email, then your marketing funnel goes like this: emails sent (level 1), emails received (level 2), emails opened (level 3), email links clicked (level 4), clicks to purchases (level 5). You may find that too few of your received emails are being opened and conclude that you need a more enticing offer in your subject line.

Send the Golden Email. You were hired because something needed to be done, and people are depending on your performance. If those people have any experience in business, then they are accustomed to being told, "Oh, everything is just super," even when everything is not just super. As a result, they will often assume the worst about your performance, overreact to small data points, and cause you all kinds of distraction when you least need it. To succeed, you need to manage your stakeholders well. A simple email, sent weekly, biweekly, or monthly, articulating the information everyone needs to know, that is factual and clear and holds you accountable to your commitments, can build the goodwill and trust you need from your colleagues to succeed in your role.

The Golden Email directly states for your stakeholders the following five things (while indirectly stating that you, my friend, are a baller):

1. **Goals**—Again, always start with your goals. You never want to get to the end of a successful quarter and then have someone suggest that you were not successful because he or she did not agree with the goal. Repeat your goals every chance you get, and anchor every presentation and progress report with those goals. For example:

    Second-quarter goal: "Our goal is to sell one hundred cars from the lot this quarter for $1,000,000. To achieve this, we need five hundred visits to the lot, a 20 percent close rate, and a $10,000 average price per car sold."

2. **KPI pacing**—Your key performance indicators should also be well understood by your stakeholders and should, if they are hit, presage the accomplishment of your top-

level goals. You can offer more clarity on why you chose your KPIs by linking your Golden Email to your strategy tree or funnel. KPIs should not be removed or changed during the quarter, as that would be like moving a goalpost during the game, though you might choose to add other KPIs that have arisen as relevant during the reporting period to offer added transparency.

Your Golden Email should show the expected performance against those KPIs as of this day in the month or quarter—for instance, if your KPI is to sell ninety things, and we are thirty days into the quarter, then the expected pacing right now is thirty. Your actual performance, divided by the expected performance, will tell your audience your current percent-to-goal pacing. If your business is seasonally affected in some way—for instance, sales are always highest in the last month of the quarter—then you can apply a seasonally adjusted pacing and performance as well. See the chart for an example.

More often than not, the numbers will be good, and receipt of this email will serve to inform your colleagues that all is fine. Other times, the numbers will be behind pace. You should never try to obscure these numbers—when stakeholders find out from other sources that you are behind pace, your credibility and trust will suffer. You also now have the opportunity to explain why this is happening, what you plan to do about it, and invite feedback and added support.

3. **What you did**—Here you share what you have done, at a high level, since the last communication to influence the KPIs:

   "This month we rolled out enhanced sales training for the floor reps to improve close rate, which has come up 5 percent since our last communication. Thanks to Gina's team for all the support."

Second-quarter KPI	Straight-line expected pacing (as of May 15)*	Seasonally adjusted expected pacing†	Actual performance	Percent-to-goal pacing†
Visits to dealership: 500	250	200	160	80 percent
Close rate: 20 percent	20 percent	20 percent	20 percent	100 percent
Cars sold: 100	50	40	32	80 percent
Average price: $10,000	$10,000	$10,000	$9,000	90 percent
Total sales: $1,000,000	$500,000	$400,000	$288,000	72 percent

"We increased sub-$9,000 inventory by 10 percent to accommodate unusually high demand for lower-cost models. This has benefited close rate, but not average dollars per sale."

4. **What you're doing**—Here you acknowledge any and all brutal truths and lay out a plan to address them:

"Our number one issue this quarter is an unusually low number of visits to the dealership, pacing at a seasonally adjusted 80 percent to goal. This week we are rolling out a

---

* Divide the number of days that have passed in the quarter by 90, then multiply that number by the KPI to get your straight-line expected pacing.

† You can apply the seasonally adjusted pacing by dividing past years' performance as of this date by performance for the quarter to give you a seasonal adjustment ratio. Multiply that number by your KPI for the seasonally expected pacing.

‡ Divide Actual Performance by seasonally adjusted expected pacing. If this number is 100 percent or higher, you are on target; if below 100 percent, you have a problem.

digital and print advertising campaign in the market to drive an expected 40 percent increase in visits. If this initiative achieves the expected impact, we will achieve our visits goal.

"Our second issue is weaker sales for higher-price vehicles. Our new marketing campaign is focused on our SUV, truck, and luxury sedan inventory, which average a 50 percent higher price point. We have limited experience with the impact of this marketing tactic and will be tracking the data closely in the next two weeks to assess whether this campaign will successfully return us to the proper pace for the quarter. The marketing campaign is within our budget for the quarter. I acknowledge that we should have launched this sooner, and will apply this lesson in future quarters."

5. **What you need**—At times, it is proper to inform all stakeholders of something you need to be successful; other times your one-on-one with your manager or another venue is more appropriate. When it makes sense, you can include your request for help here:

"There is sizable risk to this quarter, given the slow start. I would like to add a sales incentive spiff for the team to motivate harder work and more hours. This would take us 2 percent above the sales compensation budget for the quarter. I believe it is the right thing to do, and will be circling up with management and finance for feedback and, if appropriate, support."

And that's it. Once you are in a rhythm, preparing your Golden Email will take you a half hour or less, and it will be symbiotic with your thinking and planning for the week. Stakeholders will know where your progress stands, what you are doing to improve it, and how they can help. Its successful execution will also free up time in your manager one-on-one that is used for reporting on performance and key activities, giving you more time to spend on coaching, feedback, and brainstorming.

By practicing the tactics discussed in this chapter to be a better listener, collaborator, and communicator, you will be in a better position to earn the trust and goodwill of your teammates and managers, conditions necessary to achieve your goals and to earn more responsibility in the future. Establishing these habits will take some System 2 effort, but will be well worth the work.

Next, we will turn our attention to how you handle all this work, and the pressure that goes along with it, as you make your way toward your life's calling.

PART 5

Presence: Enjoy the Journey

The path to an extraordinary career and life is incredibly rewarding, but it is hard. This life comes with many challenges that create the risk of unhealthy levels of stress, dissatisfaction, and even unhappiness. In this section, we will explore proven techniques for preventing and curing stress and enjoying every single day of your ambitious journey.

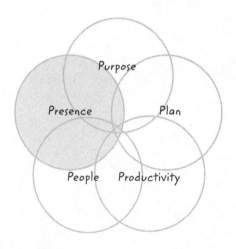

CHAPTER 13

→ Don't Worry, Be Happy

Like Pac told me, the best time would be when I was coming up.

—Biggie Smalls, *Notorious*

This is stressful.

I have to finish this chapter and then do a full edit before this book is due to the publisher in three weeks. *Three weeks.* (In case it wasn't already obvious to you, I have never written a book before.)

Not to mention, work was a grind today, with ten intense hours of meetings and countless difficult decisions. An additional month's worth of work has been written on the index cards in my pocket, and this voice in my head kept asking me if I am sure I am any good at my job.

I'll bet you have felt like this, too. Maybe today.

You have chosen to trade the well-trodden, leisurely path for a more aspirational and ambitious one. You have signed up for hard work, deep thinking, striving for big goals, refusing to give up . . . and it will test you. Some days will exhaust your strength and break your confidence.

As Teddy Roosevelt once said, "Far and away the best prize that life offers is the chance to work hard at work worth doing."

Teddy Roosevelt failed to mention that some days it still kind of sucks.

But it doesn't have to, at least not for very long. The point of The Career Manifesto is not a life of suffering as a slave to your ambition. The reason you set a purpose and a plan to pursue great things is because of the deep joy and sense of fulfillment you can create for others and for yourself.

With the right habits, we can stay positive and enjoy ourselves. Thanks to the booming field of positive psychology, we know better than ever before the thoughts and actions that can shape our view of the world, our attitude toward others, and our own sense of satisfaction and happiness.

According to renowned happiness researcher Shawn Achor, 90 percent of our happiness can be attributed not to what we have, or to what we achieve, but to how we view the world. Our sense of happiness is not some uncontrollable force that the universe exerts on us. It is the way our brain processes the things that happen to us. Depending on how we choose to think and act, our brain releases concoctions of the chemicals that scientists have come to understand make us happy: dopamine, which controls the brain's reward and pleasure centers and gives us motivation and payoff for achieving goals; serotonin, which regulates mood and other critical functions; endorphins, which alleviate pain and anxiety and are released by exercise, laughter, and, according to one study, chocolate; and oxytocin, which creates feelings of contentment and attachment to a loved one. That is a gross oversimplification of an incredibly complex branch of science and medicine, but it helps to illustrate an important point: we feel exhilarated or depressed not because something has happened, but because we have provided our brain a signal that it is time to release one chemical or another.

Now, there are real catastrophes in life that are hard for anyone to handle: things like serious health scares or the loss of a loved one. I am unqualified to help you with those, and what follows is not a recipe for dealing with tragedy. The focus here is on the day-to-day stresses that often take over our lives, which can be addressed by controlling the way our brains process them. We can thrive in the face of stress by honoring the proven habits that help us interpret the world in positive ways, by executing strategies for dealing with challenging and stressful situations, and by committing to choices that have been proven to correlate to a happy life. Let's take a look.

Prewire Your Positive Psychology

There are a few basic things you can do to increase your overall positivity, happiness, and resilience.

Sleep. We already explored the profound impact sleep has on your productivity. In case you were not already convinced to get to bed on time, also consider the significant effect it has on your positivity. Sleep deprivation inhibits the hippocampus, the part of the brain responsible for positive memories, much more than the amygdala, which processes negative memories. Demonstrating this, Dr. Matthew Walker at the University of California, Berkeley, conducted an experiment on sleep-deprived college students in which they were asked to memorize a list of words, some with happy associations, like "sunshine," others with negative connotations, like "cancer." The sleep-deprived students were able to remember 81 percent of the negative words, but only 31 percent of the positive words. This is why when you are tired, you can be a real Debbie Downer.

Exercise. Oh, this again, too? Yes. Exercise has been proven to alleviate depression and anxiety. Mice who are bullied by an aggressive mouse (probably a mouse from "corporate") show significant negative psychological effects if they do not exercise, and zero ill effects if they do exercise. Exercise triggers serotonin and endorphins, improving one's mood. As famous runner Monte Davis once said, "It's hard to run and feel sorry for yourself at the same time."

Smile. If asked to diagram the cause-and-effect relationships between external stimuli and our facial responses, most people would naturally suggest it goes like this:

{something good happens} ☞ {it makes us happy} ☞ {we smile}

or

{something bad happens} ☞ {it makes us unhappy} ☞ {we frown}

Turns out, that assessment is, in many ways, backward. In a landmark experiment in 1988, renowned psychological researcher Fritz Strack asked participants in a study to report on the enjoyment they received from watching a cartoon. Some were asked to also hold a pencil in their teeth during the experiment, which forced them to artificially reproduce a smile. Those people reported enjoying the cartoons more than those not forced to smile. Another experiment, seeking to prove the converse, asked participants to assess unpleasant photographs, with some of the participants holding two golf tees together in their brow, simulating a sad face. When asked to rate the photos, those frowning over the golf tees reported the images to be more unpleasant. Smiling *makes* you happy. Frowning *makes* you sad.

Researchers (and the more popular Starbucks baristas) have also proven that smiling causes others to smile back at you, creating a virtuous cycle of smiling and an inclination to positivity. People caused to smile or frown during a test of creative thinking proved to be more creative and less creative, respectively. There is also research suggesting that the larger your smile, the longer you will live. So, to set yourself up for positive thinking, better social interactions, and more success, say cheese.

Express gratitude. Feeling, and expressing, gratitude is one way to put your stresses in context and find a happier equilibrium in life. In a 2003 experiment, subjects who were asked to keep a journal for three weeks on things for which they were grateful reported more happiness, a more positive and optimistic outlook on life, better sleep, and more exercise, and they were more likely to have done something good for another person during the study.

One way to practice gratitude is to take two minutes each day to jot down a few things that you appreciate. There are apps that make it very easy: the Five Minute Journal is an elegant app that allows you to record three items of gratitude and three goals each day, plus a photo; vJournal is a simple journaling app that automatically syncs to Evernote. More simply, you can also just think about one or two things for which you are thankful when you hit the sack or first wake up in the morning. "I have so many emails to deal with," "I am out of shampoo," and "I very specifically said no mayonnaise on this sandwich!" seem a lot less horrible when you remind yourself, "I have a promising career on which to build," "I have kind of nice hair," and "I live in a first-world country where people bring me sandwiches in exchange for a small percentage of my daily earnings."

Sleep, exercise, smiling, and expressing gratitude are simple practices that help you to have a positive and optimistic outlook and build up your emotional resilience to the inevitable challenges and minor disappointments that life will bring you. They are good habits with an extremely high return on investment. When you are most busy and stressed out, and you feel like you don't have enough time to practice these essential behaviors, remember what Gandhi said when his handlers told him he was too busy to meditate for a full hour a day: "Well, if that's the case, then I need to set aside two hours a day to meditate."

Strategies for Responding to Stress

Unmanaged stress can literally kill you.

Stress can cause your body to experience fight-or-flight responses, including escalated levels of adrenaline and cortisol. The eventual desensitization to cortisol caused by chronic stress limits the body's ability to regulate inflammation, creating arterial plaque that leads to stroke and heart disease. Stress further causes chromosomal irregularities, with effects ranging from gray hair to malignant tumors. High levels of stress also make you unfocused, unproductive, bad at prioritizing, forgetful, and just generally kind of pissy.

The good news is that your stress can be harnassed so that it not only has no negative health effects, but actually improves your performance and productivity. It all depends on how you choose to manage stress when it comes. The good energy and positivity habits above will prepare you with added strength to deal with stress, and the following tactics will help you convert stressful situations into productive ones.

Interpret stress as a performance enhancer. Have you ever noticed that when things are easy at work, like the week after a big deadline has passed, you get a lot less done? Without the pressure of a big deliverable, your focus and drive seem to wane. This is why seasoned managers honor the old adage "If you want something done, give it to a busy person." As much as extreme, unmitigated stress can harm our performance, having a bit of urgency actually makes us more productive.

Researchers set out to prove this by giving rats intermittent stress by restraining them. Two weeks later, those rats had more nerve cells in the hippocampus and better mental performance than rats who did not have any stress. This point is articulated by the Yerkes-Dodson law, which states that performance increases with arousal, but only to a point, after which the stress makes you less effective. Which is to say, if you don't let stress overwhelm you, it actually makes you better at your job.

This counterintuitive relationship between stress and good outcomes has also been observed in mortality rates. Health psychologist Kelly McGonigal has demonstrated that people who experience a lot of stress in the previous year have a 43 percent increased risk of dying. But among people who reported that they believed stress to be a positive thing, a performance enhancer, those people had no increase in their risk of death.

Having a constructive relationship with stress helps you stay in the optimal range on the Yerkes-Dodson curve, keeps you healthy, and is a lot more enjoyable than freaking out all the time. So when the stress comes, note it for what it is, remind yourself that it will actually improve your performance if harnessed, and deploy some of the tactics that follow as needed.

Live to fight another day. Think of anything that has been stressing you out: a quickly approaching deadline, a tough boss, a troubled relationship, a professional goal in jeopardy. Why is it stressful? It is probably not because of the work you need to do to try to improve the outcome—between school and your profession, you've likely done more than ten thousand hours of hard work by now. Presumably, then, it is the outcome itself you are stressing over. It is the voice that says, "What if I miss the deadline? What if I don't achieve the goal? What if I fail?" You're a winner, and the thought of losing makes you sick to your stomach. As Tony Robbins once said, "Stress is the type A person's word for fear."

To some degree, that stress is a good thing. The drive to succeed gets you out of bed earlier and pushes you harder than a person who lacks that motivation. But as you focus too much on the outcome, that performance-enhancing stress starts to become uncontrolled anxiety; you sleep poorly, you get distracted easily, you start prioritizing badly, and the cycle of stress gets worse. When that level of obsession starts to kick in, a little perspective can help. For example, let's say you are responsible for delivering an important analysis by a certain deadline for your boss. Imagine that deadline as a circle, like this:

One of two things is going to happen: either you are going to hit the deadline successfully or you are going to miss the deadline. If you hit the deadline, everything worked out just fine in retrospect, and it's good that you stepped up your game to get it done, but there was no reason for you to be so wracked with angst. As usual, you made it work. But if you missed the deadline—uh-oh! Imagine hitting the deadline as a light circle, indicating the good outcome, and missing it as a dark circle, the bad outcome. Like this:

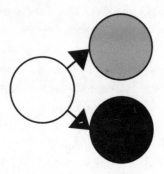

The fear of that dark circle is what is giving you an ulcer. Let's pretend it happened—you missed the deadline. Bad news. But, let's acknowledge, it probably did not kill you, so this is not the end of the line for you. What happens next? Either you do something to make it okay, like get a deadline extension, make it up to your boss on the next project, or come to some other arrangement . . . or you don't. If you make it okay, things are fine, and there's nothing to worry about. You get to the next light circle. All is good. But what if you fail to recover?

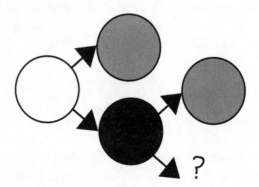

Let's just play this out. You missed the deadline, and then you don't make it up to your boss, and your boss comes to hate you. After a while you are fired (next dark circle). Now, one of two things can happen next: you can rather quickly get another job, and recommence your path to success following that anomalous failure, or you don't get another good job so quickly. Now you are unemployed for a few months, and two things can happen: this can become an opportunity for you to start an exciting new chapter of your life, or you never recover, ending a promising career living on the street, or in your parents' guest room, never again tasting the success that once came so frequently to your life.

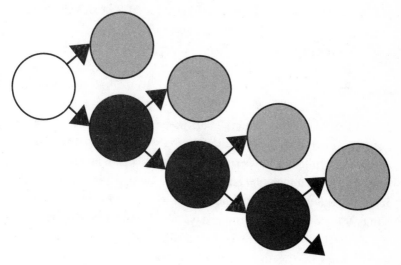

I am having a hard time imagining you missing a deadline next week and winding up in your parents' basement. The further down the chain you go, the more unlikely the bad outcome sounds. And yet the big dark circle in front of us—the risk of missing the deadline—can drive us to the point of anxiety that makes us unhappy, unproductive, and unhealthy. We forget that even if we fail, the most likely outcome to follow that is success. If you applied a probability to each step of this chain, I suspect you would find the likelihood of even an unpleasant outcome to be less than 1 percent. Which is to say, you are stressing yourself needlessly and making yourself preemptively miserable over a less-than-1-percent chance of future unhappiness. As Mark

Twain said, "I've had a lot of worries in my life, most of which never happened."

And what if the terrifying unlikely thing down the chain actually comes to pass? In an oft-referenced 1978 study, researchers tested the impact of truly extreme outcomes on individual happiness by interviewing victims of spinal cord injuries and winners of the lottery. In the study, the paraplegic people reported being only marginally less happy than the people who won the lottery. Apparently, even when one of the worst or best things imaginable actually happens, we adjust to our new reality and the new light and dark circles ahead.

So set big goals, work hard, and stop being so afraid that you will fail. You probably won't. And if you do fail, you'll probably recover brilliantly. And in the infinitesimally small likelihood that you don't recover, you'll still be fine.

Think like an optimist. There's a famous comedian who has a great bit in which he rails against people who complain over airline delays and cell phone coverage, explaining that people should try instead to appreciate how incredible it is that we can fly through the air and that "the sh*ttiest cell phone in the world is a miracle." He has a point. More often than not, our days are ruined by bad meetings or flight delays, not dysentery or kidnapping. Failing to appreciate the many things that we have, while obsessing over life's minor disappointments, is a proven recipe for stress and unhappiness.

Dr. Martin Seligman, one of the pioneers of positive psychology, performed a now-famous series of experiments in the 1960s in which a poor group of dogs were subjected to unpleasant electrical shocks. Some dogs could stop the shock by pressing their heads against a panel; others couldn't. The dogs were then moved to another experiment where avoiding the electrical shock required jumping over a barrier. Those who were able to stop the shock in the first experiment rather quickly learned to avoid the shock in the second experiment. Those who could not stop the shock in the first instance generally did not even try to escape the shock in the second instance, and began exhibiting symptoms of depression and social anxiety. Dr. Seligman termed this sad state "learned helplessness." Most importantly, he found that when the experiments were rearranged so that the dogs could first learn to avoid shocks, then put in a situation where they couldn't, they never stopped trying. Learning up front that the shock could be avoided gave them the optimism they needed to not develop learned helplessness in the future.

Seligman has spent his career professing the advantages of an optimistic mind-set over a pessimistic mind-set on our success and well-being, and showing that the way we talk to ourselves about the things that happen determines whether we will be an optimist or a pessimist. He has shown that people who view negative outcomes as the result of permanent conditions, i.e., "I'm always bad at presentations," or, "You never call me back," are more susceptible to helplessness and depression than those who associate bad outcomes with temporary conditions, like, "I wasn't very good at today's presentation," or, "You haven't called me back lately." Similarly, those who view positive outcomes as the result of permanent conditions ("I'm usually pretty lucky") rather than temporary ones ("I guess I just got lucky this time") are more likely to remain positive. How we assign credit or blame has a similar effect: attributing success to internal factors ("I earned that promotion") versus external ones ("My boss decided to give me a promotion") produces positivity; attributing failures to internal factors ("I am incapable of being loved") versus external ones ("He wasn't ready to love me back") makes us pessimistic.

The benefits of the optimistic mind-set are significant. According to Shawn Achor, a positive brain is 31 percent more productive, while positive people perform 37 percent better at sales and positive doctors are 19 percent faster and more accurate in making the correct diagnosis. Optimists have been shown to recover more quickly from a setback, while pessimists become helpless.

All of which is another way to say that you decide whether you will be happy. Will you view a hectic week at the office as a burden, or as the privilege of exciting and challenging work? Will you view being stuck in a boring meeting as a maddening frustration, or as a rare opportunity to relax and clear your head? Will you be stressed out the next time it feels like the weight of the world is on your shoulders and everyone takes you for granted, or will you appreciate that you matter to other people?

You can start applying these lessons tomorrow morning when the first person inquires about your day. You can choose to engage in the ever-popular Exchange of Sorrows:

"How's work?"
"Busy, you?"
"So busy. Brutal."
"Thank goodness tomorrow's Friday."

Or you can set the tone of positivity for you and everyone around you:

"How's work?"
"Awesome. Big project due tomorrow on a tight deadline. It's exciting and I'm learning a ton. How about you?"
"Oh. I have some pretty good stuff going on, too."
"You deserve it. I can see why they count on you."

I guarantee you that the latter two people are about to spend the next hour having a different—and much more positive—relationship with the things bringing them stress.

Life Choices to De-stress and Be Happy

There are a number of choices you can make in your life that have been proven to bring you greater overall satisfaction.

Be a "satisficer" and be happy with your choices. Trillions of dollars in commercial product development and mass marketing have conspired to convince us that tiny feature enhancements and small differences among the things we buy will make us happy. In a nation with thousands of varieties of running sneakers and unlimited micro-brew beer alternatives, it is rarely questioned that more is more. It turns out, that is not true.

First, abundant choice has a tendency to stop us from making a choice at all. Columbia University psychologist Sheena Iyengar offered to sell people a delicious jam in two experiments: one in which participants could choose one of six jams, another in which they could choose one of twenty-four. When offered four times as many jams, people were ten times less likely to make a choice at all. Somehow, people initially interested in jam saw more jam and thought, "Ugh, I can't even," and went home jamless. That's crazy. Now apply that thinking to a generation of people who have what appears to be an unlimited number of romantic options through Tinder or Match or some other dating app, but can't seem to find the right person. Aziz Ansari captured this phenomenon in his book *Modern Romance*, putting the jam experiment in the context of online dating: "Don't you see what's happening to us? There's just too much jam out there. If you're on a date with a certain jam, you can't even focus, 'cause as soon as you go to the bathroom, three other jams have texted you. You go online, you see more jam there."

Our brains use happiness as a tool for regulating us—once we achieve happiness from a new event, our brain incorporates that new reality and resets our level of happiness. The new car that promised irrevocable social status and endless 320-horsepower arousal becomes just another thing we own. The promotion at work that motivated countless late nights quickly becomes just another step toward what we really want, which is the next promotion. The date with a charming person competes with the promise of a date with someone else.

Psychologist Dan Gilbert proved this in an experiment with college students who were invited to take a free photography course. Half were told that they could keep one of the photos they developed; the other half were told that they could keep one and if they changed their minds and wanted a different one, they could come back and swap them out. The latter group, which was given more choice and a free option to upgrade later, subsequently reported being less happy with their choice than those who'd had to make a permanent decision. Those who could swap photos did not psychologically commit to their choice, as they continued to wonder if they'd made a mistake. Those who could not change benefited from the mind's natural tendency to adapt to its circumstances.

Another psychologist, Barry Schwartz, developed a test to determine if someone is a "maximizer," someone who pains over decisions, trying to make the perfect choice, or a "satisficer," who finds an item that meets his requirements and stops looking. If you would be happy with whatever is the most popular forty-two-inch high-definition TV, you are probably a satisficer; if you pain over consumer reviews and technical specs on refresh rates and contrast ratios, then you're a maximizer. Dr. Schwartz found that maximizers have a fear of regretting their choices, blame themselves for bad decisions, and are more likely to be pessimistic and depressed. Satisficers live more happily with their decisions and spend less time being bored to death by *Consumer Reports* and online user reviews.

So, quick, should you get the new iPhone in black or rose gold? You have five seconds to decide . . . four . . . three . . . two . . . one. Great news: if you tell yourself you made a pretty good choice, then the color you just picked will be the one your brain ultimately convinces you that you like better. Or say a new job opportunity has materialized. Should you pursue it? Go on a long run to clear your head, and pretend you have no job at the moment and have been offered your current job and the new one. Which most closely aligns with your values? Which better meets the critical elements of your Career Plan? Whichever you choose, that's probably the right job for you.

As much as I hate to contribute to the use of a made-up word that sounds like a hashtag, you really will be happier when you satisfice.

Live in the moment. Work used to end. Twenty or so years ago, one would put in a good day at the office, log off the computer, which was about as portable as a small oven, and not see it again until the following business day. Phones were tethered to the wall, and email was only for hard-core nerds. Sure, people might bring home some papers, but they didn't buzz every two minutes if you tried to ignore them. Now your entire job, social life, and all the content in the world sits in the phone in your pocket, incessantly beckoning, offering something better. You see groups of people in a restaurant checking in on social media rather than talking to their actual human companions at dinner. Parents ignore their kid at the ice cream shop while checking an email or sports score. Twenty percent of people check their phone during sex. Come on, people!

It is not just technology that interrupts us. In 47 percent of our waking moments, our minds are wandering, thinking about something else. Yet presence of mind is what makes everything from time with a friend to a mouthful of your favorite food actually enjoyable. We spend nearly half of our lives failing to notice the thing we are doing, and thinking about something else instead. I hate to sound like a slogan on a pothead's T-shirt, but it's time to remember how to live in the moment.

Research has shown the significant benefits of mindfulness, the mental state achieved by focusing one's awareness on the present moment. One way to become more mindful and, therefore, less stressed and happier is to meditate. People who practice daily meditation (which is an extreme implementation of mindfulness practice) have been found to have an improved immune system, lower blood pressure, enhanced mental function associated with self-awareness and compassion, and lower stress.

If you are a personal trainer type, you can find a meditation coach. Or there are numerous apps that can help guide you through simple meditation exercises, including Headspace, 10% Happier, Calm, and Omvana. Considering its culpability in distracting you from the joys of your life, helping you become more mindful is the least your iPhone could do.

There are other ways to achieve similar benefits. You can engross yourself in life's pleasures without distraction. If you like to cook, turn off the TV or radio in the background and instead take careful notice of the smells and the sensations while you do it. When you shower, rather than think about the stresses of the day, notice how nice it feels to be doused in clean, warm water. When you exercise, pay careful attention to how your body feels. When your mind starts to wander (every eight seconds, on average, as mentioned in chapter 12), just bring it back to the present moment. Notice your breath. Feel the ground under your feet, or the chair under your butt. Turn your phone off once in a while. It's nice.

The sad alternative reminds me of a quote that was floating around the internet a few years ago that had been attributed to famous author John Green: "One day, you're seventeen and planning for someday. And then quietly, and without you ever really noticing, someday is today. And then someday is yesterday. And this is your life." I really internalized that as a reminder to appreciate each moment, rather than always thinking ahead to what comes next. Then I learned the actual source of the quote is the closing soliloquy of the hit teen high school drama *One Tree Hill*, but it was too late; the quote had already made an impression on me.

Maintain strong (analog) relationships. The greatest predictor of happiness is the strength of your personal relationships. In studies, people who have a loving companion are significantly happier than people who do not. Friends are worth more than money: having more true friends has a similar impact on subjective well-being as being 50 percent wealthier. Having a best friend at work is one of the biggest predictors of whether you will like your job. And people with friends live longer, enjoying a significantly better survival rate than people who do not.

These relationships are grown and developed by spending time together, face-to-face. Research shows that in-person communication makes us much happier—we even laugh 50 percent more frequently when we can see a friend's face versus speaking on the phone or communicating digitally. One needs only think back to a recent get-together with a good friend to know, instinctively, that this is true.

Contrast this with how we feel when we engage in social media. Whereas the average person reports that there are only four people on whom she could truly depend in a personal emergency, the average

Facebook user has 338 online "friends." Checking in on these Facebook friends tends to make people less happy the more they do it, according to numerous studies. The finding is not surprising: our online acquaintances spend significant effort curating perfect online lives, selectively sharing their work promotions, romantic vacation sunsets, and perfect skinny selfies (chin up, turn, elbow out, fish lips!), while conveniently leaving out their career setbacks, relationship anxieties, and just-woke-up headshots. As a result, researchers find that using social media causes us to significantly overestimate the positive experiences others are having and underestimate the number of negative ones they have, leading to envy and even a higher risk of depression.

One solution, of course, is to stop using social media, though in many circles that risks turning you into some kind of digital hermit. You could unfriend everyone who would not visit you in the hospital on a moment's notice, but you might also want to change your privacy settings, if you do not want people to know you only have four Facebook friends. A better option may be to utilize the sharing and following settings on Facebook to interact with people only in ways that optimize your happiness: you can (1) unfollow, without unfriending, people who are not good friends or whose Facebook posts do not bring you happiness (a particularly useful feature during elections), or (2) use the option to categorize your true friends by selecting "Close Friends" on their profile page, or alternatively to categorize your acquaintances by selecting "Acquaintance," and then selectively sharing each Facebook post with only "Close Friends" or "Friends, Except Acquaintances." These changes are visible only to you, which means you can make your Facebook experience less time-consuming and more enjoyable, without having anyone accuse you of unfriending them.

With the time and mental energy you save, you could invest instead in the activities that improve your state of mind, like seeing your good friends, getting a solid night's sleep, working your Career Plan, or, perhaps the most impactful option, doing something for someone else.

Perform nonrandom acts of kindness. This book begins with the premise that each of us wants to lead a life that has a positive impact on others, and for those who are ambitious, to make that impact as big as possible. At times, working the plan to achieve that impact can feel hard and thankless. The good news is that the things you do to positively affect others have been scientifically proven to make you happier over the course of your life. Nearly every form of kindness leads to improved life satisfaction, such as:

Daily acts of kindness—Researchers in Great Britain had some participants in a study practice daily acts of charity for ten days, then surveyed all participants to assess their life satisfaction. Those who performed good deeds reported significantly higher life satisfaction than those who did not. Carrying a package for someone, planting a tree, giving away an old coat, or surprising a friend with a coffee takes very little time or money, and yet has an outsized impact on your happiness and that of others.

Giving time—One in four Americans will volunteer this year through an organization, and two-thirds will go out of their way to help a neighbor. There are many good reasons to join them. A systematic review of forty different studies on well-being found that people who volunteer have lower levels of depression, increased life satisfaction, and a 22 percent lower mortality rate. A professor of sociology at the University of Wisconsin proved that teens who volunteer earn better grades, stay out of trouble, and form better social habits into adulthood. Volunteering appears to release oxytocin and strengthen the immune system, while also offering the benefit of increased socialization and fitness-inducing activity. As discussed earlier in this chapter, stress can increase the likelihood of death—however, researchers found that people who had high levels of stress who also volunteered to help others had no increase in their mortality rates, suggesting that helping others is a very effective way to also help yourself in times of high pressure and anxiety.

Giving money—Science has proven what wise people have always told us: it is better to give than receive. Researchers have found that people who spend money on others report higher levels of personal happiness than people who spend money on themselves. When we give to charity, the part of the brain responsible for primal feelings of reward is activated, developing a "helper's high" in the same region of the brain that processes desires for food and sex. You can make a donation to a worthy cause in under a minute, and likely enjoy the feeling of having done something good the rest of the day.

From the Career Manifesto to the Happiness Manifesto

The risk of this book, and the risk any ambitious person faces, is that we focus so much on the goals we hope to achieve that we confuse attainment of those goals with happiness. When happiness is always believed to be something on the horizon, something that requires suffering to attain, then we have ensured our own misery. That can be exacerbated by the constant feeling of unfinished business, work that hasn't been done, or Career Plan actions that haven't been executed. The stress mounts, and it can be hard to find joy when we have so many things to do in order to achieve our goals and therefore our happiness.

You deserve a better life than that.

You should set big goals and strive to achieve them, because a life of purpose is a more useful and fulfilling life. You should make proactive and productive use of your time, because driving impact feels so much better in the long run than watching TV. You should hustle, because you are talented and there is work to do. But you shouldn't suffer. Apply the tactics in this chapter: sleep, exercise, express gratitude, smile, manage stress strategically, be with the people you love, and do good for others. It will help you rise above the day-to-day challenges and enjoy the journey.

And in the darker moments, when you are obsessing over outcomes and living in fear of failure, try to remember this: if someone came to you today and offered you all the success at the end of your

Career Plan, everything you desire, in a nice neat package, and all you had to exchange was your own arms and legs, or the health of a loved one, or a cherished relationship with a sibling or parent or significant other, would you make the trade? Of course not. Which means you value the things you already have more than all the things you are pursuing. You already have boundless happiness, if you just permit yourself to enjoy it.

Thank you for reading this book. Go forth and do amazing things. I believe in you, and the world needs you.

NOTES

CHAPTER 1

8 **deeply ingrained habits:** Charles Duhigg, *The Power of Habit: Why We Do What We Do in Life and Business* (New York: Random House, 2012).

CHAPTER 2

12 **small food rewards:** "Operant conditioning," modified May 25, 2017, https://en.wikipedia.org/wiki/Operant_conditioning.

17 **more likely to follow through:** Nancy L. Anderson, "5 Ways to Make Your New Year's Resolutions Stick," *Forbes*, January 3, 2013, https://www.forbes.com/sites/financialfinesse/2013/01/03/5-ways-to-make-your-new-years-resolutions-stick/#55d1d2041ebd. Dr. Gail Matthews, of Dominican University in California, did a study on goal-setting with 267 participants. She found that, on average, you are 33 percent more likely to achieve your goals just by writing them down.

CHAPTER 3

30 **economic output by industry:** Richard Henderson, "Industry Employment and Output Projections to 2022," *Monthly Labor Review*, U.S. Bureau of Labor Statistics, December 2013, https://doi.org/10.21916/mlr.2013.39.

37 **$75,000 a year:** Belinda Luscombe, "Do We Need $75,000 a Year to Be Happy?" *Time*, September 6, 2010, http://content.time.com/time/magazine/article/0,9171,2019628,00.html.

37 **McAllen, Texas:** "Cost of Living: How Far Will My Salary Go in Another City?" CNN Money, December 2015, http://money.cnn.com/calculator/pf/cost-of-living/.

37 **everyone from Ben Franklin:** "Money has never made man happy, nor will it, there is nothing in its nature to produce happiness—the more of it one has the more one wants." —Ben Franklin. S. Austin Allibone, ed., *Prose Quotations from Socrates to Macaulay* (Philadelphia: J. B. Lippincott & Co., 1880); Bartleby.com, 2011, http://www.bartleby.com/349/authors/77.html.

CHAPTER 5

59 **System 1 and System 2:** Daniel Kahneman, *Thinking, Fast and Slow* (New York: Farrar, Straus and Giroux, 2011).

59 **hard to control:** Jonathan Haidt, *The Happiness Hypothesis: Finding Modern Truth in Ancient Wisdom* (New York: Basic Books, 2005).

60 **the "future self.":** Her great TED Talk here: https://www.ted.com/talks/kelly_mcgonigal_how_to_make_stress_your_friend.

60 **eschewing the cookie:** Roy F. Baumeister, *Willpower: Rediscovering the Greatest Human Strength* (New York: Penguin Press, 2011).

60 **"decision fatigue.":** John Tierney, "Do You Suffer from Decision Fatigue?" *New York Times*, August 17, 2011, http://www.nytimes.com/2011/08/21/magazine/do-you-suffer-from-decision-fatigue.html.

61 **they are habits:** Charles Duhigg, interview on Daniel H. Pink's blog, March 2012, accessed May 29, 2017, http://www.danpink.com/2012/03/the-power-of-habits-and-the-power-to-change-them/.

62 **caffeine is fantastic:** Neal D. Freedman, PhD, et al., "Association of Coffee Drinking with Total and Cause-Specific Mortality," *New England Journal of Medicine*, May 17, 2012, doi:10.1056/NEJMoa1112010. Jean-Louis Santini, "More and More Medical Experts Are Backing the Major Health Benefits of Coffee," *Business Insider*, April 2, 2015, http://read.bi/2rzvdgN.

68 **on your desk:** Sue Shellenbarger, "The Battle of the Office Candy Jar," *Wall Street Journal*, April 12, 2011, http://www.wsj.com/articles/SB10001424052748703841904576256982872752032.

69 **"What gets measured gets managed.":** Often attributed to Peter Drucker. Read all his books!

70 **long-term-oriented choice:** David Desteno, "A Feeling of Control: How America Can Finally Learn to Deal with Its Impulses," *Pacific Standard*, September 15, 2014, https://psmag.com/social-justice/feeling-control-america-can-finally-learn-deal-impulses-self-regulation-89456.

70 **happier and more productive:** Laszlo Bock, "Two Minutes to Make You Happier at Work, in Life . . . and Over the Holidays," LinkedIn, November 24, 2014, https://www.linkedin.com/pulse/20141124163631-24454816-two-minutes-to -make-you-happier-at-work-in-life-and-over-the-holidays.

CHAPTER 6

71 **97.2 percent of Americans:** "More Than 97% of Americans Guilty of Unhealthy Lifestyle, Study Says," *Health*, March 23, 2016, http://www.health.com /mind-body/less-than-3-percent-of-americans-live-a-healthy-lifestyle.

71 **decade or more:** Antonio Pasolini, "U.S. Study Quantifies the Effects of Exercise on Life Expectancy," *New Atlas*, November 19, 2012, http://newatlas .com/physical-activity-live-longer/24972/.

72 **drunk nine-year-old:** Jill Duffy, "Why Six Hours of Sleep is as Bad as None at All," *Fast Company*, March 7, 2016, https://www.fastcompany.com/3057465 /why-six-hours-of-sleep-is-as-bad-as-none-at-all.

73 **quality of your sleep:** "Scary Ways Technology Affects Your Sleep," Sleep .org, accessed May 29, 2017, https://sleep.org/articles/ways-technology-affects -sleep/.

74 **removes one brick:** William C. Dement, *The Promise of Sleep: A Pioneer in Sleep Medicine Explains the Vital Connection Between Health, Happiness, and a Good Night's Sleep* (New York: Delacorte Press, 1999).

75 **time to start:** Aaron E. Carroll, "More Consensus on Coffee's Effect on Health Than You Might Think," *New York Times*, May 11, 2015, https://www.nytimes .com/2015/05/12/upshot/more-consensus-on-coffees-benefits-than-you -might-think.html?_r=1. The health benefits of coffee include protecting against Type 2 diabetes, Parkinson's disease, liver disease, liver cancer, and promoting a healthy heart.

75 **Hitting the snooze button:** Maria Konnikova, "Snoozers Are, In Fact, Losers," *New Yorker*, December 10, 2013, http://www.newyorker.com/tech/elements /snoozers-are-in-fact-losers.

75 **in the future:** Vivan Giang, "The Surprising and Powerful Links Between Posture and Mood," *Fast Company*, January 30, 2015, https://www.fastcompany.com /3041688/body-week/the-surprising-and-powerful-links-between-posture -and-mood.

75 **alpha primates and powerful human leaders:** Amy Cuddy, "Your Body Language Shapes Who You Are," TED Talk, October 2012, https://www.ted .com/talks/amy_cuddy_your_body_language_shapes_who_you_are/transcript ?language=en.

76   **live happier, healthier lives:** Shawn Achor, *The Happiness Advantage: The Seven Principles of Positive Psychology That Fuel Success and Performance at Work* (New York: Crown Business, 2010).

76   **brain cells for you:** Melissa Dahl, "How Neuroscientists Explain the Mind-Clearing Magic of Running," *New York*, April 21, 2016, http://nymag.com /scienceofus/2016/04/how-neuroscientists-explain-the-mind-clearing-magic -of-running.html.

77   **did not exercise:** Pasolini, "Effects of Exercise on Life Expectancy."

77   **hours to your life:** Carey Goldberg, "Every Minute of Exercise Could Lengthen Your Life Seven Minutes," CommonHealth blog, March 15, 2013, http://commonhealth.wbur.org/2013/03/minutes-exercise-longer-life.

77   **in the evening:** Harini Suresh, "How Different Workout Styles Affect Your Mood, Schedule and Energy," Jawbone blog, October 22, 2015, https://jawbone .com/blog/how-different-workout-styles-affect-your-mood-schedule-and -energy/.

77   **moderate-intensity exercise:** Len Kravitz, PhD, "Vigorous Versus Moderate-Intensity Exercise," *IDEA Fitness Journal*, 2006, https://www.unm.edu/~lkravitz /Article%20folder/VigorModerateEx.html.

77   **Strength training:** "American Heart Association Recommendations for Physical Activity in Adults," American Heart Association, modified July 22, 2016, http://www.heart.org/HEARTORG/HealthyLiving/PhysicalActivity/Fitness Basics/American-Heart-Association-Recommendations-for-Physical-Activity -in-Adults_UCM_307976_Article.jsp#.Vv-jm6QrI2w.

78   **you have eaten:** Christa Miller, "How Long Does It Take Your Brain to Register That the Stomach is Full?" Livestrong.com blog, modified August 16, 2013, http://www.livestrong.com/article/480254-how-long-does-it-take-your -brain-to-register-that-the-stomach-is-full/.

CHAPTER 7

82   **revenue growth and profit growth:** Kelly Askew and Patrick Daoust, "Fueling Growth Through Zero-based Budgeting: How Winners Know Where to Place Big Bets," Accenture, 2016, https://www.accenture.com/t20160802T041253 __w___/us-en/_acnmedia/PDF-15/Accenture-Strategy-Smart-Budgeting-Zero -Based-Budgeting-V2.pdf.

85   **You can spend two hours:** See chart: http://static1.businessinsider.com/image /5627c31f9dd7cc1b008c3a7c-1200/slide.jpg.

86   **phone for entertainment:** Ibid.

86 **21.8 minutes:** Gretchen Reynolds, "Get Up. Get Out. Don't Sit," *New York Times*, October 17, 2012, https://well.blogs.nytimes.com/2012/10/17/get-up -get-out-dont-sit/.

CHAPTER 8

98 **quick keys in Gmail:** Go to the gear icon in the upper right of Gmail, select settings, and choose the option next to "Keyboard Shortcuts" to turn them on. Anytime thereafter, simply type a question mark when navigating to see the list of quick keys. Or check out this handsome infographic: https://visual.ly/community /infographic/how/minimalistic-gmail-cheat-sheet.

99 **they are thinking:** Quick primer on microexpressions here: http://www.npr .org/2013/05/10/182861380/microexpressions-more-than-meets-the-eye. For further study, check out *Spy the Lie* by Philip Houston and *People Watching* by Desmond Morris.

100 **you left off:** Shamsi T. Iqbal and Eric Horvitz, "Disruption and Recovery of Computing Tasks: Field Study, Analysis, and Directions," via Eric Horvitz's website, http://research.microsoft.com/en-us/um/people/horvitz/chi_2007_iqbal _horvitz.pdf. Brian Dumaine, "The Kings of Concentration," *Inc.*, May 2014, http://www.inc.com/magazine/201405/brian-dumaine/how-leaders-focus -with-distractions.html.

101 **eighty-eight business emails per day:** "Email Statistics Report 2015–2019," The Radicati Group, Inc., March 2015, http://www.radicati.com/wp/wp -content/uploads/2015/02/Email-Statistics-Report-2015-2019-Executive -Summary.pdf.

101 **times per day:** Matt Rosoff, "People Either Check Email All the Time, Or Barely at All," *Business Insider*, August 17, 2015, http://www.businessinsider.com /how-often-do-people-check-their-email-2015-8.

101 **daydreaming through them:** Corey Wainwright, "You're Going to Waste 31 Hours in Meetings This Month," HubSpot blog, June 12, 2014, http://blog .hubspot.com/marketing/time-wasted-meetings-data.

107 **checking business and personal email:** Patricia Reaney, "U.S. Workers Spend 6.3 Hours a Day Checking Email: Survey," *Huffington Post*, updated May 13, 2016, http://www.huffingtonpost.com/entry/check-work-email-hours -survey_us_55ddd168e4b0a40aa3ace672.

113 **eight hours of lost productivity:** Rachel Emma Silverman, "The Productivity-Crushing Power of 'Reply to All,'" *Wall Street Journal*, December 28, 2012, http://on.wsj.com/Vfts0V.

119 **1.5 hours a day:** Lisa Belkin, "Time Wasted? Perhaps It's Well Spent," *New York Times*, May 31, 2007, http://www.nytimes.com/2007/05/31/fashion/31work.html?smprod=nytcore-iphone&smid=nytcore-iphone-share.

120 **two weeks late:** Jeanne Sahadi, "Nearly 8 Out of 10 U.S. Taxpayers Get Refunds," CNN Money, January 14, 2015, http://money.cnn.com/2015/01/13/pf/taxes/taxpayer-refunds/.

121 **retrieval of memory, and focuses attention:** "Norepinephrine," modified May 19, 2017, https://en.wikipedia.org/wiki/Norepinephrine.

121 **release of this powerful chemical:** Dumaine, "The Kings of Concentration."

121 **"switching between them very rapidly.":** Jon Hamilton, "Think You're Multitasking? Think Again," NPR blog, October 2, 2008, http://www.npr.org/templates/story/story.php?storyId=95256794.

122 **return to the original task:** Iqbal and Horvitz, "Disruption and Recovery of Computing Tasks."

122 **irrelevant information:** Dumaine, "The Kings of Concentration."

122 **4.4-second interruption:** Erik M. Altmann, Gregory J. Trafton, and David Z. Hambrick, "Momentary interruptions can derail the train of thought," *Journal of Experimental Psychology: General* 143(1):215–226, February 2014, http://dx.doi.org/10.1037/a0030986.

CHAPTER 9

131 **(what you actually say):** Institute of Judicial Studies handout, http://bit.ly/1zT2b7R.

136 **English language:** "Most common words in English," modified February 2, 2017, https://en.wikipedia.org/wiki/Most_common_words_in_English.

CHAPTER 10

154 **do not like:** Robert Cialdini, *Influence: The Psychology of Persuasion* (New York: HarperBusiness, 2006).

154 **ten-second video:** Maria Konnikova, "On the Face of It: The Psychology of Electability," *New Yorker*, November 18, 2013, http://www.newyorker.com/tech/elements/on-the-face-of-it-the-psychology-of-electability.

169 **"please try again.":** Cialdini, *Influence*.

173 **"stop talking.":** "The best advice I ever got," *Fortune*, modified April 30, 2008, http://archive.fortune.com/galleries/2008/fortune/0804/gallery.bestadvice.fortune/.

CHAPTER 11

176   **portion of them:** Wainwright, "Meetings."

178   **same people individually:** Greg Barron and Eldad Yechiam, "Private E-mail Requests and the Diffusion of Responsibility," *Computers in Human Behavior* 18(5):507–520, September 2002, https://www.researchgate.net/publication /222533703_Private_ e-mail_requests_and_the_diffusion_of_responsibility.

182   **improve productivity:** Jennifer Robison, "Workplace Socializing Is Productive," *Gallup Business Journal*, November 13, 2008, http://www.gallup.com /businessjournal/111766/news-flash-workplace-socializing-productive.aspx.

182   **new smoking:** James A. Levine, M.D., PhD, "What Are the Risks of Sitting Too Much?" Mayo Clinic blog, September 4, 2015, http://www.mayoclinic.org /healthy-lifestyle/adult-health/expert-answers/sitting/faq-20058005.

183   **"Thanks":** Drake Baer, "3 Ways Steve Jobs Made Meetings Insanely Productive—and Often Terrifying," *Business Insider*, August 28, 2015, http://www .businessinsider.com/steve-jobs-meeting-techniques-2015-8.

189   **manage successfully:** Randall Beck and Jim Harter, "Why Great Managers Are So Rare," *Gallup Business Journal*, March 25, 2014, http://www.gallup.com /businessjournal/167975/why-great-managers-rare.aspx.

189   **complex role:** "The Bottom Line-Necessity of Training Your Managers," *HR Professionals*, http://hrprofessionalsmagazine.com/train-your-managers/.

189   **part of their job:** Maeghan Ouimet, "The Real Productivity-Killer: Jerks," *Inc.*, November 5, 2012, http://www.inc.com/maeghan-ouimet/real-cost-bad -bosses.html.

189   **because of their boss:** Benjamin Snyder, "Half of Us Have Quit Our Job Because of a Bad Boss," *Fortune*, April 2, 2015, http://fortune.com/2015/04/02 /quit-reasons/.

CHAPTER 12

205   **credible scientists:** Kate Bratskeir, "The Myers-Briggs Personality Test Doesn't Actually Mean Anything," *Huffington Post*, February 10, 2016, http:// www.huffingtonpost.com/entry/myers-briggs-personality-test-is-moot_us _56bb69abe4b0c3c5504f9b36.

206   **nine seconds:** Leon Watson, "Humans Have Shorter Attention Span Than Goldfish, Thanks to Smartphones," *Telegraph*, May 15, 2015, http://www.telegraph .co.uk/science/2016/03/12/humans-have-shorter-attention-span-than-goldfish -thanks-to-smart/.

CHAPTER 13

230 **achieving goals:** "Dopamine," modified May 20, 2017, https://en.wikipedia.org/wiki/Dopamine.

230 **critical functions:** Colette Bouchez, "Serotonin: 9 Questions and Answers," WebMD, modified October 12, 2011, http://www.webmd.com/depression/features/serotonin#1.

230 **chocolate:** Linda Ciampa, "Researchers Say Chocolate Triggers Feel-Good Chemicals," CNN, February 14, 1996, http://edition.cnn.com/HEALTH/indepth.food/sweets/chocolate.cravings/.

230 **loved one:** Donatella Marazziti, Bernardo Dell'Osso, Stefano Baroni, Francesco Mungai, et al., "A Relationship Between Oxytocin and Anxiety of Romantic Attachment," *Clinical Practice and Epidemiology in Mental Health* 2(28), October 11, 2006, doi:10:1186/1745-0179-2-28.

231 **positive words:** Highlighted in *NutureShock: New Thinking About Children*, by Po Bronson and Ashley Merryman.

231 **do exercise:** Kirsten Weir, "The Exercise Effect," *Monitor on Psychology*, December 2011, http://www:apa:org/monitor/2011/12/exercise:aspx.

232 **forced to smile:** Fritz Strack, Leonard L. Martin, and Sabine Stepper, "Inhibiting and Facilitating Conditions of the Human Smile: A Nonobtrusive Test of the Facial Feedback Hypothesis," *Journal of Personality and Social Psychology* 54(5), May 1988, 768–777, http://dx:doi:org/10:1037/0022-3514:54:5:768.

232 **more unpleasant:** Randy J. Larsen, Margaret Kasimatis, and Kurt Frey, "Facilitating the Furrowed Brow: An Unobtrusive Test of the Facial Feedback Hypothesis Applied to Unpleasant Affect," *Cognition and Emotion*, February 28, 1990, http://www.tandfonline.com/doi/abs/10:1080/02699939208409689.

232 **back at you:** Association for Psychological Science, "People Anticipate Others' Genuine Smiles, But Not Polite Smiles," *ScienceDaily*, June 12, 2013, www.sciencedaily.com/releases/2013/06/130612133321.htm.

232 **creative, respectively:** Enrique G. Fernández-Abascal and María D. Martín Díaz, "Affective Induction and Creative Thinking," *Creativity Research Journal* 25 (2013):213–221, published online May 17, 2013, http://dx.doi.org/10.1080/10400419.2013.783759.

232 **you will live:** Erik Hayden, "Smile to Live Longer?" *Pacific Standard*, March 11, 2010, https://psmag.com/smile-to-live-longer-f8c186b52dcd#.pianqyfzr.

232 **during the study:** Robert A. Emmons and Michael E. McCullough, "Counting Blessings Versus Burdens: An Experimental Investigation of Gratitude and

Subjective Well-Being in Daily Life," *Journal of Personality and Social Psychology* 84(2):377–389, February 2003, doi:10:1037/0022-3514:84:2:377.

233 **heart disease:** Timo Heidt, Hendrik B. Sager, Gabriel Courties, Partha Dutta, et al., "Chronic Variable Stress Activates Hematopoietic Stem Cells," *Nature Medicine* 20, June 22, 2014, http://www.nature.com/nm/journal/v20/n7/full/nm.3589.html.

233 **malignant tumors:** Duke University Medical Center, "At Last, a Reason Why Stress Causes DNA Damage," *ScienceDaily*, August 22, 2011, www.sciencedaily.com/releases/2011/08/110821141135.htm.

233 **kind of pissy:** "Stress Symptoms: Effects on Your Body and Behavior," Mayo Clinic blog, August 28, 2016, http://www.mayoclinic.org/healthy-lifestyle/stress-management/in-depth/stress-symptoms/art-20050987.

234 **any stress:** Robert Sanders, "Researchers Find Out Why Some Stress Is Good for You," *Berkeley News*, April 16, 2013, http://news.berkeley.edu/2013/04/16/researchers-find-out-why-some-stress-is-good-for-you/.

234 **less effective:** Francesca Gino, "Are You Too Stressed to Be Productive? Or Not Stressed Enough?" *Harvard Business Review*, April 14, 2016, https://hbr.org/2016/04/are-you-too-stressed-to-be-productive-or-not-stressed-enough.

238 **won the lottery:** Philip Brickman, Dan Coates, and Ronnie Janoff-Bulman, "Lottery Winners and Accident Victims: Is Happiness Relative?" *Journal of Personality and Social Psychology* 36(8):917–927, August 1978, http://dx.doi.org/10.1037/0022-3514.36.8.917.

239 **in the future:** Maria Konnikova, "Trying to Cure Depression, But Inspiring Torture," *New Yorker*, January 14, 2015, http://www.newyorker.com/science/maria-konnikova/theory-psychology-justified-torture.

239 **makes us pessimistic:** "Learned Optimism," modified September 1, 2016, https://en.wikipedia.org/wiki/Learned_optimism.

239 **correct diagnosis:** Beth Kuhel, "To Increase Productivity: Work Less, Get Happy," *Huffington Post*, modified April 11, 2015, http://www.huffingtonpost.com/beth-kuhel/to-increase-productivity-_b_6639482.html.

241 **more jam there:** Aziz Ansari and Eric Klinenberg, "How to Make Online Dating Work," *New York Times*, June 13, 2015, http://www.nytimes.com/2015/06/14/opinion/sunday/how-to-make-online-dating-work.html?_r=0.

241 **level of happiness:** Jon Gertner, "The Futile Pursuit of Happiness," *New York Times Magazine*, September 7, 2003, http://mobile.nytimes.com/2003/09/07/magazine/the-futile-pursuit-of-happiness.html.

242 **its circumstances:** Dan Gilbert, "The Surprising Science of Happiness," TED

Talk, September 2006, https://www.ted.com/talks/dan_gilbert_asks_why_are
_we_happy/transcript?language=en.

242 **stops looking:** The term was coined by the late psychologist Herbert Simon—
read more about him here: http://www.economist.com/node/13350892.

242 **pessimistic and depressed:** Barry Schwartz, "The Tyranny of Choice," *Scientific American*, April 2004, http://www.swarthmore.edu/SocSci/bschwar1/Sci
.Amer.pdf.

243 **during sex:** Emily Payne, "Study: 20% of Young People Text During Sex," *Bost-Inno*, July 15, 2013, http://bostinno.streetwise.co/2013/07/15/study-20-of-young
-people-text-during-sex/.

243 **something else:** Steve Bradt, "Wandering Mind Not a Happy Mind," *Harvard Gazette*, November 11, 2010, http://news.harvard.edu/gazette/story/2010/11
/wandering-mind-not-a-happy-mind/.

243 **lower stress:** "How Science Sold Me on Meditation, with Dan Harris," Big Think blog, http://bigthink.com/think-tank/how-science-sold-me-on-medita
tion-with-dan-harris; Dan Harris's book *10% Happier* is a great read on this topic.

244 **significantly happier:** Anahad O'Connor, "The Secrets to a Happy Life, From a Harvard Study," *New York Times*, March 23, 2016, https://well.blogs.nytimes.com
/2016/03/23/the-secrets-to-a-happy-life-from-a-harvard-study/?mcubz=1&_r=1.

244 **50 percent wealthier:** John F. Helliwell and Haifang Huang, "Comparing the Happiness Effects of Real and On-Line Friends," *PLoS ONE* 8(9), September 3, 2013, https://doi.org/10.1371/journal.pone.0072754.

244 **like your job:** Alice LaPlante, "If Money Doesn't Make You Happy, Consider Time," Insights by Stanford Business blog, April 1, 2011, http://www.gsb.stan
ford.edu/insights/if-money-doesnt-make-you-happy-consider-time.

244 **survival rate:** Julianne Holt-Lunstad, Timothy B. Smith, and J. Bradley Layton, "Social Relationships and Mortality Risk: A Meta-analytic Review," *PLoS Medicine* 7(7), July 27, 2010, https://doi.org/10.1371/journal.pmed.1000316.

244 **communicating digitally:** Jenny Hope, "Why Facebook Friends Don't Count: People Are Happier and Laugh 50% More When Talking Face-to-Face," *Daily Mail*, April 9, 2013, http://www.dailymail.co.uk/health/article-2306546/Why
-Facebook-friends-dont-count-People-happier-laugh-50-talking-face-face.html.

244 **personal emergency:** R. I. M. Dunbar, "Do Online Social Media Cut Through the Constraints That Limit the Size of Offline Social Networks?" *Royal Society Open Science* 2, January 20, 2016, doi:10.1098/rsos.150292.

245 **online "friends.":** Aaron Smith, "6 New Facts About Facebook," *Pew Research Center*, February 3, 2014, http://pewresearch.org/fact-tank/2014/02/03/6
-new-facts-about-facebook/.

245 **numerous studies:** Ethan Kross, Philippe Verduyn, Emre Demiralp, Jiyoung Park, et al., "Facebook Use Predicts Declines in Subjective Well-Being in Young Adults," *PLoS ONE* 8(8), August 14, 2013, https://doi.org/10.1371/journal.pone.0069841.

245 **risk of depression:** John M. Grohol, Psy.D., "The Psychology of Facebook Depression: Avoid Social Comparisons & Envy," Psych Central blog, April 9, 2015, http://psychcentral.com/blog/archives/2015/04/09/the-psychology-of-facebook-depression-avoid-social-comparisons-envy/. Libby Copeland, "The Anti-Social Network," *Slate*, January 26, 2011, http://www.slate.com/articles/double_x/doublex/2011/01/the_antisocial_network.single.html.

246 **who did not:** Kathryn E. Buchanan and Anat Bardi, "Acts of Kindness and Acts of Novelty Affect Life Satisfaction," *Journal of Social Psychology* 150(3), August 8, 2010, http://dx.doi.org/10.1080/00224540903365554.

246 **help a neighbor:** "New Report: 1 in 4 Americans Volunteer; Two-Thirds Help Neighbors," Corporation for National and Community Service, December 15, 2014, http://www.nationalservice.gov/newsroom/press-releases/2014/new-report-1-4-americans-volunteer-two-thirds-help-neighbors.

246 **22 percent lower mortality rate:** "Go On, Volunteer—It Could Be Good for You!" University of Exeter, August 23, 2013, https://www.exeter.ac.uk/news/featurednews/title_315358_en.html.

246 **strengthen the immune system:** Jane Allyn Piliavin and Erica Siegl, "Health and Well-Being Consequences of Formal Volunteering," *Oxford Handbook of Prosocial Behavior*, published online July 2014, doi:10.1093/oxfordhb/9780195399813.013.024.

246 **in their mortality rates:** MJ Poulin, SL Brown, AJ Dillard, and DM Smith, "Giving to others and the association between stress and mortality," *American Journal of Public Health*, September 2013, doi:10.2105/AJPH.2012.300876.

247 **spend money on themselves:** Elizabeth W. Dunn, Daniel T. Gilbert, and Timothy D. Wilson, "If Money Doesn't Make You Happy Then You Probably Aren't Spending It Right," *Journal of Consumer Psychology* 21(2), April 2011, https://doi.org/10.1016/j.jcps.2011.02.002.

247 **food and sex:** James Randerson, "The Path to Happiness: It Is Better to Give Than Receive," *Guardian*, March 20, 2008, https://www.theguardian.com/science/2008/mar/21/medicalresearch.usa.

ACKNOWLEDGMENTS

To write a book while working full-time requires the sacrifice of countless weekend days. When you are a dad and a husband, those weekends are not yours alone. I want to thank my amazing wife, Kemp, and our kids, O and G, for their inspiration and their loving support. Writing a first book also requires a completely unjustified belief in yourself; the confidence and discipline that I was able to muster for this project are gifts that my parents gave to me. Thank you, Mom and Dad, for everything. Absolutely everything.

When I started this book, I tried to imitate a real writer; the results were inauthentic and dull. My brother, Chris, who is a real writer, and also the man who knows me best, intervened. He read my first draft, informed me it was terrible, and convinced me to find my own voice and begin again. His feedback throughout this process has been invaluable.

Most good things start with some good luck or kindness. This book received both. My friend Adam Rosante made me admit I had a book I wanted to write and then made me meet his agent, Joy Tutela, who was willing to invest her time in someone long on passion and short on experience. Jeanette Shaw, my original editor at TarcherPerigee, was the first to believe in our project, and senior editor Stephanie Bowen adopted it and loved it like her own.

I want to thank my friends who have provided ideas, feedback, and support. The first to get behind *The Career Manifesto*: Tim Armstrong, Peter Brown, John Saroff, Jesse Haines, Matt Derella, and Jeff Sharp. Dear friends who were quick with advice and support when I needed it, and quicker to keep me humble, whether I liked it or not: Todd Mahoney, Joe Carlon, Jordan Matusow, Anthony Napolitano, Keric Kenny, John Santiago, and Andrew Bennett, who is very cheap. Finally, I want to thank Justin Bieber and Sting, who have always been so cool to me.*

I can share the wisdom in this book thanks to my trusted mentors, friends, and colleagues from XO Group, VPUSA, Google, NBC Universal, Walker Digital, McKinsey, and YPO Gotham who have challenged me through their own stellar examples for the last decade and a half; you all know who you are. Thank you.

I am a proud product of the South Brunswick, New Jersey, public school system. I want to thank all of the teachers who have touched my life, none more than Joe Dougherty, who taught me how to lead, and Harry Schultz, who taught me how to write.

Profits from this book will go to Literacy Partners, a New York City–based nonprofit that fights every day for our less fortunate neighbors, providing free family literacy and support services. Please consider Literacy Partners as part of your charitable giving: www .literacypartners.org.

---

* I'm just kidding, I've never met Justin Bieber or Sting.

INDEX

Note: Page numbers in *italics* refer to illustrations.

"achieve–by" framework, 95–96, 104

Achor, Shawn, 230, 239

action, taking, 8–10

adrenaline, 233

agents and principals, 33

alarms and snooze buttons, 75

alumni network, 144

ambitions, 4, 49–50

American Heart Association (AHA),
77

amygdala, 231

Ansari, Aziz, 241

anxiety, 231, 238

articles, reading, 109

associative memory, 134

attention spans, 206

authorities, leveraging, 168–69

automating tasks, 98

Barksdale, Jim, 213

behavioral change, 6–8

benchmarks, 213

Bloomberg, Mike, 173

body language

    of customers, 163–64

    and networking, 131–32

bonus projects, 48–49

Boomerang app, 118

brain

    evolution of, 58, 94

    and happiness, 241–42

    and neurological basis of emotions,
        230

    and sleep deprivation, 231

    and task management, 94

    two systems of (*see* Systems 1 and 2 of
        human brain)

Build Your Dream Network (Hoey), 128

calendar and schedule

    audits of, 84–85

    fixed hours in, 82, *83*, 83–84, 89

    and goal setting, 95

    as operating system, 88–90

    proactively allocating, 87–91

    and spontaneity, 90

    zero-basing your, 82–86, *83*

Calm app, 243

career choices, 27–40

    and choosing a job function, 31–33

    and choosing an industry, 29–30

    and Eulogy exercise, 39–40

    and money considerations, 36–38

    and size/stage of companies, 33–36

career covenants with managers, 48–49,
        49n, 200–201, 201n

"Career Manifesto" (original document),
    x–xi
Career Roadmap, 41–53
    and being a giver, 49–50
    and career covenants with managers,
        48–49
    and changing jobs, 50–51
    committing to an unusual path in,
        46–47
    as to-do list for career, 44–46
    and goal setting, 95
    and good habits, 64
    keeping the big picture in mind, 52
    periodic review of, 94
    role of research in, 47–48
    skills/experience building in, 48–49,
        201–2
    soliciting feedback in, 201
    and time management, 51–52
    your responsibility for, 49n
Carnegie, Dale, 70, 133, 134
changing jobs, 50–51
charity, acts of, 246–47
choices, abundance of, 240–42
Citrin, Jim, 201
Cocktail Party Test, 30
communications
    components of, 130–31
    disambiguating, 210–16
    effective listening, 207
    and eliminating filler words,
        160
    encouraging, 208
    and Five Whys technique, 209–10
    good grammar in, 161–62
    inefficiency of, 206
    and learning opportunities, 207–8
    in-person, 244

    practicing, 162–63
    precision in, 161
    and punctuating down, 160–61
    and setting agendas aside, 207–8
companies
    fastest-growing, 30
    size/stage of, 33–36
compensation, 36–38
confidence, instilling, 159–63
Confucius, 79n
connections, making, 143–45
context switching, 99–100
conversations
    cowardice in, 137–40
    initiating and ending, 132–33
    talking about ourselves in, 136–37
    See also communications
cortisol, 75, 233
Covey, Stephen, 39, 96n
creativity, 19
crowds, leveraging in sales, 169
Cuddy, Amy, 75
customers
    building rapport with, 154
    decision making authority of, 152
    and instilling confidence, 159–63
    and reading the room, 163–64
    studying needs of, 149–50
    understanding goals and motivations
        of, 150–52

Daily Tracker app, 69
data, 213
Davis, Monte, 231
deadlines, 100, 235–37
decision making
    and decision fatigue, 60

and satisficers/maximizers, 242
See also career choices
delegated tasks, tracking, 104–5
Dement, William, 74
depression
and exercise, 231
and learned helplessness, 238
and optimistic/pessimistic mind-sets, 239
and satisficers/maximizers, 242
and social media, 245
and volunteering, 246
Dewey, John, 12
diffusion of responsibility, 178
disambiguating communications, 210–16
discomfort, necessity of, 6
distractions
eliminating, 85–86
and habit formation, 122
and stress, 235
dopamine, 12, 230
Duhigg, Charles, 61–62
Dutton, Donald, 206

eating habits, 67–69, 78–80
The Effective Executive (Drucker), 45
ego depletion, 60
electronics, personal, 73. *See also* phones
email management, 107–19
and archive/search functions, 116–17
of articles emailed to you, 109, 115
automated responses, 98
batch processing, 108
and Boomerang app, 118
canned responses, 112n
of junk emails, 108, 110–11

of project-related emails, 109, 114–15
and quick-key functions, 117
of quick-win emails, 109, 113–14
and "reply all" function, 112–13
and threaded emails, 117–18
and triage approach to in-box, 118–19
of waste-of-time emails, 108–9, 111–13
embodied cognition, 75
emotional intelligence (EQ), 7
emotions, positive, 69–70
empathy, 208
endorphins, 230, 231
Eulogy exercise, 39–40
and goal setting, 40, 51
and habits, 65–66
Evernote, 102, 103–4
Execution (Bossidy and Charan), 45
exercise, 76–78, 231
expectations, missing/meeting/exceeding, 196–97
experience required for positions
gaining, with side hustles, 48–49, 201–2
and Permission Paradox, 201
experts, leveraging, 168–69
eye contact, 132

Facebook, 5, 245
failure, 67, 237, 238
feedback from managers, 194–99
Feiner, Michael, 48
The Feiner Points of Leadership (Feiner), 48, 201n
fight-or-flight responses, 233
filler words, eliminating, 160
Financial Management (Brigham and Ehrhardt), 45

fitness, 63–64, 76–78

Five Ds productivity framework, 178–80, 216

Five Minute Journal app, 233

Five More Hours to Live, 81–91
  and calendar audits, 84–85
  and distraction elimination, 85–86
  and fixed hours, 82, *83*, 83–84, 89
  and outsourcing, 85
  and proactively allocating your calendar, 87–88, *88*
  and zero-basing your calendar, 82–86, *83*

The Five Patterns of Extraordinary Careers (Citrin), 201

Five Whys technique, 209–10

focusing, 120–23

Foer, Joshua, 135

Ford, Henry, 14, 44, 216

Fortune, 30

Franklin, Ben, 95

friendship, cultivating, 145–46, 244–45

funnels, *219*, 219–21, 222

Gandhi, Mohandas, 233

Getting to Yes (Fisher and Ury), 174

Gilbert, Dan, 241–42

GIST (Goals, Impact, Speed, Timing), 94–100
  applying, 103–7, 119–20
  and disambiguating ideas, 215
  goals, 94–96, 119
  impact, 96–99, 119
  speed, 99–100, 119–20
  timing, 100, 119

givers/takers, 49–50

Gladwell, Malcolm, 90n

goals, 94–96
  and action items, 218–19
  and communicating with stakeholders, 221
  and disambiguating ideas, 212
  focusing on correct, 192
  in GIST framework, 94–96, 119
  and happiness, 247
  missing, 204
  reviewing progress with, 191–93
  and strategy trees, 216–19

Golden Email, 221–25, *223*

grammar and effective communication, 161–62

gratitude, exercising
  benefits of, 70
  and morning routine, 76
  and overall well-being, 232

The Greatest Salesman in the World (Mandino), 174

Green, John, 244

greeting people, 132

growth mind-set, 208

habits, 57–70
  creating meaningful, 65–66
  erasing/replacing, 62
  forming new, 8
  gratitude as, 70
  habit loop, 61–62
  and "if–then" formulas, 64–65
  importance of, 61–70
  and peer pressure, 66–67
  and positive emotions, 69–70
  and setbacks, 70

and Systems 1 and 2 of human brain, 58–60, 62, 67–69
and tactics for resisting temptation, 67–69
tracking progress with, 69
and willpower, 60, 61, 62, 64, 66
Haidt, Jonathan, 59
handshakes, 132, 132n
happiness, 230, 240–47
The Happiness Hypothesis (Haidt), 59
Happiness Matrix, 17–24, *21–22, 23*
and choosing an industry, 29–30, 32
and money considerations, 38
periodic review of, 94
and planning your career, 29
and size/stage of companies, 36
"hara hachi bu," 79n
hard things, doing, 3–10
hashtag system in task management, 103, 104–5, 107, 184n
headhunters, 144
Headspace app, 243
Hello Sense device, 75
helping others, 130, 141–47, 246–47
hippocampus, 231, 234
Hoey, J. Kelly, 128
How to Make People Like You in 90 Seconds or Less (Boothman), 133, 174
How to Read a Person Like a Book (Nierenberg), 164
How to Win Friends and Influence People (Carnegie), 70, 133, 134, 174
hydration, 76

"if–then" formulas, 64–65
immune system, 246

impact
assessing, 13–17, 40
in GIST framework, 96–99, 119
Impact Map, 29–30, 94, 201
Inc., 30
index cards for capturing tasks, 101, 103–4
industry, choosing an, 29–30
industry insiders, 144
inflammation, 233
Influence (Cialdini), 174
interruptions, blocking, 122
introversion, 7, 132
investigating problems, 209–16
and disambiguating ideas, 210–16
and Five Whys technique, 209–10
iPods, 18–19
It's Not All about "Me" (Dreeke), 133, 174
Iyengar, Sheena, 241

jobs
changing, 50–51
job functions, 31–33
Jobs, Steve, 183

Kahneman, Daniel, 59, 154
key performance indicators (KPIs), 213, 221–22
kindness, acts of, 246–47
knowledge sharing, 141–43

The Language of Trust (Maslansky), 174
learned helplessness, 238–39

learning
  leverage afforded by, 98–99
  opportunities for, 207–8
leverage
  cultivating, 97–99
  in sales, 168–69
Levitt, Theodore, 212
listening, effective, 207

Made to Stick (Heath and Heath), 174,
    193, 193n
managers
  career covenants with, 48–49, 49n,
    200–201, 201n
  and Career Roadmap, 201
  decreasing role of, 204
  goals review with, 191–93
  and management challenges, 205–6
  management skills of, 189
  meetings with, 188–203
  soliciting feedback from, 194–99
  truths about, 188–90
  See also stakeholder management
maximizers and satisficers, 242
McCarthy, Jerome, 159n
McGonigal, Kelly, 60, 234
meditation, 243
meetings, 176–203
  agendas for, 181–86
  attendees at, 183, 184
  capturing notes/tasks in, 103
  establishing the purpose of, 178
  Five Ds productivity framework for,
    178–80, 186
  follow-up actions from, 186–88
  goals review in, 191–93
  ground rules for, 183
  for groups, 177–88
  length of, 182
  one-one-one with your boss, 188–
    203, *203*
  "open mic" option in, 199–203
  prewiring for success, 185–86
  soliciting feedback in, 194–99
  standing in, 182
  TIP (topic-importance-purpose)
    method used in, 155, 178, 184,
    191
  trivial discussions in, 183–84
  See also sales meetings and skills
Mehrabian, Albert, 131
melatonin, 73
Microsoft To-Do (MTD) app
  about, 102–3
  and email management, 114–15, 119
  and GIST framework, 119–20
  practical application of, 104–7
Miller, Earl, 121
mindfulness, 243–44
Minto, Barbara, 157n
missing/meeting/exceeding
    expectations, 196–97
Modern Romance (Ansari), 241
money considerations, 36–38
Moonwalking with Einstein (Foer), 135
morning routines, 74–76, 77
motivation, 235
multitasking, 121–22, 183
Musk, Elon, 29
Myers-Briggs assessment, 205
MyFitnessPal app, 78

names, remembering, 133–35
napping, 74

networking, 127–47, *129*
  advancing from familiar to intimate
      network, 130, 136–40
  advancing from intimate to
      meaningful network, 130, 141–47
  advancing from unfamiliar to familiar
      network, 130, 131–35
  and helping others, 130, 141–47
  and making connections, 143–45
  poorly executed, 127–28
  value of, 98
norepinephrine, 121
nutrition, 67–69, 78–80

Ogilvy, David, 137
Omvana app, 243
"open mic" option in meetings, 199–203
operant conditioning, 12
opportunities, creating, 43
optimism, 238–40
organization, value of, 98
organizational chart test, 32
Outliers (Gladwell), 90n
outsourcing, value of, 85
oxytocin, 230, 246

Parkinson's Law of Triviality, 183–84
peer pressure, 66–67
performance
  ability of stress to enhance, 234–35
  benchmarking, 213
  and communicating with
      stakeholders, 222
Permission Paradox, 201
personalities, differences in, 205
pessimism, 239, 242

Petty, Richard, 75
phones
  in meetings, 183
  and presence, 244
  and sleep quality, 73
  taking notes on, 101
Pocket app, 115
positive psychology, 230
positivity, cultivating, 231–33
posture, strong, 75–76, 159–60
The Power of Habit (Duhigg), 61–62
presence, 227, 243–44
pride, personal, 70
principals and agents, 33
problem solving, 20
productivity, 55–123
  ability of stress to enhance, 234–35
  cultivating a system for (*see* habits)
  and to-do lists, 92–94
  and email (*see* email management)
  and focusing, 120–23
  and hashtags in task management,
      103, 104–5, 107, 184n
  and leverage, 97–99
  and mental/physical endurance (*see*
      stamina)
  and positive mind-set, 239
  and task capture/organization system,
      101–7
  and time management (*see* Five More
      Hours to Live)
  See also GIST (Goals, Impact, Speed,
      Timing)
projects for skill development, 48–49
punctuating down, 160–61
purpose, 11–24
  and Happiness Matrix, 17–24, *21–22, 23*
  human desire for, 12

purpose (*cont.*)
  and Impact Map, 13–17
  and morning routine, 76
The Pyramid Principle (Minto), 157n, 174

reading
  allocating time for, 87, 87n
  in bed, 73
  and sharing articles and books, 142–43
recruiters, 144
reduction strategy for leveraging time,
      97–98
relationships, importance of maintaining,
      244–45
resolutions, 67
responsibility, diffusion of, 178
Rilke, Ranier Maria, 70
Robbins, Tony, 235
Roosevelt, Theodore, 229
Runkeeper app, 78

Saint-Exupéry, Antoine de, 97–98
salaries, 36–38
sales meetings and skills, 148–75
  and adapting the pitch, 166
  asking probing questions in, 165–66
  and building rapport, 154
  and closing the deal, 166–73
  and instilling confidence, 159–63
  and listening skills, 164–65
  and opening strong, 155–57
  and positive mind-set, 239
  and practicing the pitch, 162–63
  and preparing for presentations, 149–
      54
  and reading the room, 163–64

role coordination in, 152–54
  and selling past the close, 173
  and skill building, 202
  and team feedback, 174
  and telling your story, 157–59
  value of, 148
Sartre, Jean-Paul, 206
satisficers and maximizers, 242
schedule. *See* calendar and schedule
Schwartz, Barry, 241
The Science of Selling (Hoffeld), 174
self-assessment, 5–6
self-doubt, 32–33
self employment, 51
Seligman, Martin, 238–39
serotonin, 230, 231
setbacks, 70
The Seven Habits of Highly Effective People
      (Covey), 39, 96n
short vs. longterm benefits, 69–70
side hustles, 48–49, 201–2
skills
  acquisition of new, 6–8, 98–99
  creating a checklist for, 45–46 (*see also*
      Career Roadmap)
  using bonus projects to develop, 48–
      49, 201–2
Skinner, B. F., 12
sleep
  and alarms/snooze buttons, 75
  and creating new habits, 66
  and emotional well being, 231, 233
  importance of, 72–76, 89–90
  and stress, 235
smiling, 231–32
snooze buttons, 75
social media
  curation of, 5, 245

and distraction elimination, 85–86
emotional toll of, 244–45
and helping others, 142–43
solutions, potential ("yes, if" approach),
    213–15
speed and productivity, 99–100, 119–20
spontaneity, 90
stakeholder management, 204–25
    and communicating effectively, 207–8
    and disambiguation in ideas, 210–16
    and Five Whys technique, 209–10
    and funnels, *219*, 219–21, 222
    and the Golden Email, 221–25, *223*
    and management challenges, 205–6
    and strategy trees, 216–19, 222
stamina, 71–80
    and exercise, 76–78
    and morning routine, 74–76, 77
    and nutrition, 78–80
    and sleep, 72–74
start-ups, 33–36
"*Stop,*" "*start,*" and "*continue*" framework,
    197–98
Strack, Fritz, 232
strategy trees, 216–19, 222
strength training, 77–78
stress
    and fear of negative outcomes, 235–38
    optimism as counter to, 238–40
    as performance enhancer, 234–35
    strategies for responding to, 233–40
    and volunteering, 246
success
    external/internal factors attributed to,
        239
    path to, 3
Systems 1 and 2 of human brain, 59–60
    and focusing, 120–21

and good habits, 67–69
and management challenges, 206
and task management, 94

task capture/organization system, 101–7
television viewing, 86
temptation, resisting, 60, 67–69
10% Happier app, 243
ten-thousand-hour rule, 90–91, 90n
testosterone, 75
time management, 81–91
    and calendar audits, 84–85
    and distraction elimination, 85–86
    and Eulogy exercise, 51–52
    and fixed hours, 82, *83*, 83–84, 89
    and outsourcing, 85
    and proactively allocating your
        calendar, 87–88, *88*
    and zero-basing your calendar, 82–86,
        83
timing and productivity, 100, 119
TIP (topic-importance-purpose) method
    in group meetings, 178, 184
    in meetings with your boss, 191
    in sales meetings, 155
to-do lists, 92–94
    and email, 108
    and goal setting, 95
To Sell Is Human (Pink), 174
Toyoda, Sakichi, 209
trade magazine journalists, 144
truth, telling yourself, 5–6
Twain, Mark, 237–38

urgency, creating sense of, 169–72
US Bureau of Labor Statistics, 30

visualization techniques, 134, 135
volunteering, 246

Walker, Matthew, 231
water, drinking, 76
why, asking, 209–10
willpower
    and creating new habits, 64, 66
    depletion of, 60, 66
    and nutrition, 79

and power of habits, 61, 62
and Systems 1 and 2 of human brain,
    62, 64
Wunderlist app, 102–3

Yerkes-Dodson law, 234
"yes, if" approach, 213–15

Zuckerberg, Mark, 14

ABOUT THE AUTHOR

Photo by Preston Schlebusch

MIKE STEIB is president and CEO of XO Group Inc (NYSE: XOXO). Mike and the team help millions of couples navigate and enjoy life's biggest moments together through industry-leading products that include The Knot, The Bump, The Nest, and Gigmasters. In his career, Mike has helped to launch or scale more than a dozen innovative businesses, generating more than one billion dollars in new revenue across digital marketplaces, media, ad tech, mobile, video, local, and commerce. He also serves on the board of Fortune 500 financial services company Ally Financial (NYSE: ALLY), and is cochairman of the Board of Literacy Partners, a nonprofit that has provided free family support services to thousands of New Yorkers for over forty years. From 2011 to 2013, Mike served as CEO of Vente-Privee USA, an e-commerce venture backed by American Express. Prior to that, he spent four and a half years at Google helping to build Google's mobile and video advertising businesses. Before Google, Mike was the General Manager of Strategic Ventures at NBC Universal, where he received the GE Imagination Breakthrough award.

He has been recognized as one of Crain's New York 40 Under 40 professionals, TV Week's "Twelve to Watch," and has received CEO World Award, Stevie International Business Award, and Folio 100 recognition. He has appeared on NBC's *Today* show, CNBC, Bloomberg TV, and Fox Business, as well as in the *New York Times*, *Wall Street Journal*, *Fortune*, *Entrepreneur*, TechCrunch, *Fast Company*, *New York Post*, *Business Insider*, *AdAge*, *AdWeek*, *Newsday*, and others.

Mike received a BA in economics and a BA in international relations from the University of Pennsylvania and is a named inventor of three digital media patents. He is married to Kemp Steib, CFO of The Second Shift, a marketplace for highly skilled professional female talent seeking flexible employment options. They live in New York with their family.